DESIGN DIRECTORY Scandinavia

Functionalist steambath.
1951: Antti **NURMESNIEMI** tidies up the sauna.

Horseshoe Stools for Palace Hotel in Helsinki

Bernd Polster

DESIGNDIRECTORY Scandinavia

Charm of a 100-year-old.
On the occasion of its anniversary **ORREFORS** presents a mixture of Pop and Swedish design.

Vase *Ira* by Jan Johansson, 1998

About This Directory 6

Beauty for All 9

Paola Antonelli

Gallery 12

Scandinavian Design Classics

Decades 49

History of Scandinavian Design

The Next Modern Phase: 82

Four Essays on the New Nordic Design

Directory 97

From Aalto to Zero

Guide 361

Scandinavian Design Addresses

Index 367

Designers, Companies, Concepts

About this Directory

Design is a "Scandinavian model." As part of the public welfare programs in the Scandinavian countries, the need for "more beautiful things" was for the first time made a basic right. Since then, good design has become commonplace, and an energetic, new generation of designers is making sure that it will stay that way. Thus it is all the more surprising that for some time now there has been no comprehensive book on the market describing Scandinavian design. This lexicon is intended to remedy the situation and to help readers gain an understanding of the multifaceted Scandinavian design culture. To this end the material is presented in an uncomplicated structure and with a wealth of illustrations that visually reveal the cosmos of designs. In terms of content, the focus will be on furniture and product design, two strong facets of Scandinavian design, but fashion and commercial arts will also be discussed. In addition, important styles and schools of design will be explained and—a first for a handbook such as this—companies will be described in detail. This lexicon is supplemented by an annotated index in which numerous additional key words have been included. Names and terms printed in bold face in the text are included in the index.

Authors

Paola Antonelli is a curator in the Department of Architecture and Design at the Museum of Modern Art. She has written numerous articles in magazines, among them *Abitare, Domus,* and *Nest.* Exhibitions for the MOMA include *Mutant Materials in Contemporary Design.* She lives in New York.

Ulf Beckman is editor-in-chief of the Swedish magazine *Form*, which has been in print for almost one hundred years. He discusses connections between design and mechanisms of desire.

Peter Butenschøn is director of Norsk Form, Norway's top design committee. He stresses the ethical responsibility of his trade.

Bodil Busk Laursen is director of Det Danske Kunstindustrimuseum in Copenhagen. He wants to give young Danish designers a warm welcome.

Anne Stenros is director of Design Forum Finland. She sees no contradiction between tradition and a trend for internationalization.

Bernd Polster has written numerous books on cultural and industrial history, most recently *Highway: Der endlose amerikanische Traum* (*Highway: The Endless American Dream*). He has also authored television and radio features and since 1996 has worked in project development for HOWARD Buch Produktion. He lives in Bonn.

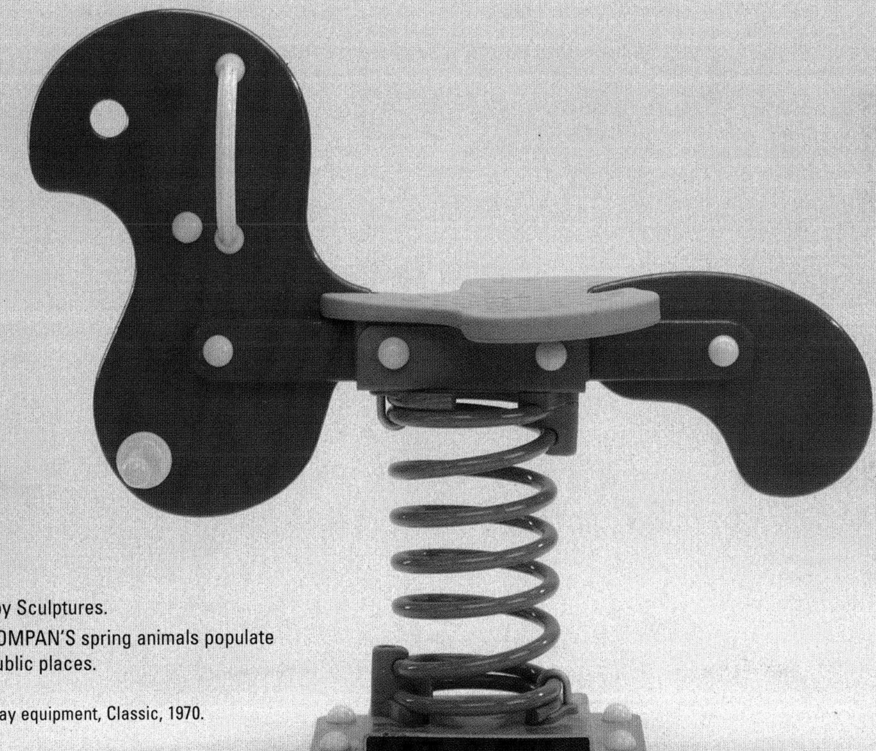

Toy Sculptures.
KOMPAN'S spring animals populate public places.

Play equipment, Classic, 1970.

Beauty for All:

The Message of Simplicity and the Culture of Materials

"All people want well-designed things for their homes. Because they use them every day throughout their whole life, people expect things to be as useful and as beautiful as possible. At this time there is no one who designs better household goods than the Scandinavians," wrote Leslie Cheek, Jr., of the Art Museum in Richmond, Virginia, in the 1950s. He was director of the successful traveling exhibition *Design in Scandinavia.* With their focus on affordable modernism for the home, the Scandinavians taught the world the significance of good design. What they exported together with their design was their own original lifestyle.

Despite their very different cultures and traditional materials, Denmark, Finland, Norway, and Sweden have, each in its own way, devoted itself to a great goal that has so far remained their only common denominator: the endeavor to enhance quality of life through appropriate and affordable technology. The democratic Scandinavian approach, a historical peculiarity that has developed over decades of political and financial independence, drew the designers' attention automatically to the objects of everyday life and to the home as the focal point of society. This special outlook on the world became the universally comprehensible idiom of Scandinavian design and won international success among critics as well as among the public.

Prior to the 1950s, the work of famous artists, commercial artists, and architects, for example, **Alvar Aalto** and **Tapio Wirkkala**, turned with passionate energy such materials as wood and glass into vehicles for their new organic, minimalist message, in the process helping design gain fame. In addition, internal economic conditions—a relatively small unified market and a more or less uniform distribution of wealth—helped Scandinavian design, remarkably compelling and functional and flourishing in the 1950s, to become even more

Fine finish for an exhibition. Plywood leaf by Tapio Wirkkala, 1951 successful. Direct communication between manufacturers and consumers made possible demand-driven manufacturing and marketing of the goods. In the early 1950s many manufacturers willingly took up the movement of designers toward abstraction, organicity, and technified poetry while also working on improving mass production through technology. To mention just one example, Danish furniture manufacturers began to replace solid wood with plywood and to develop new methods of processing it. In addition, parts of chairs and tables were simply made of steel which resulted in greater formal simplicity. True to their motto "more beauty for everyday life," Swedish silver manufacturers worked on unifying mass production and high quality. Thus they guided stainless steel toward its new role as silverware for the populace. A coincidental combination of very different endeavors created a completely new culture of materials that was open to technological innovation. To this day designers are exploring the limits of this new tradition that developed in the 1950s.

Since then, Denmark, Finland, Norway, and Sweden have produced a greater number of design icons than any other region. From **Lego** to **Arabia** to the chairs of **Arne Jacobsen**, Scandinavia invented minimalism and turned it into an affordable, useful, and desirable style. All over Europe and the United States, clothing by **Marimekko**, watches by **Georg Jensen**, and the mysterious and expensive **Bang & Olufsen** stereo systems still make extremely clear cultural and economic statements. Designs for the real world, such as the work of the Norwegian social critic **Peter Opsvik** and the Swedish **Ergonomi** Design Group, as well as the minimalist marketing approach of mass-produced items by Ikea are the other obviously democratic side of the coin and probably even more influential globally.

The democratic tradition continues to this day after new flexible forms such as system and information design appeared on the scene, and new materials and elements such as fiberglass and computer chips competed with traditional materials such as wood and glass for visual supremacy. Scandinavia is still exemplary for its democratic approach to modern social technology; for example, it has the best telecommunications network in the world, and the devices supplementing that network—such as the famous cell phones—still win design prizes for their efficiency and their unsurpassed Scandinavian look. At just this time many young designers and artists in Finland and elsewhere have decided to break with tradition and are responsible for some of the most angular designs in the world. Nonetheless, the reserved but powerful influence of the Scandinavian design of the 1950s continues to affect the contemporary minimalism that has been internationally rediscovered. This new religion, spread globally by the Dutch, Japanese, and British, owes its soul in part to the cult of simplicity the Scandinavians have preached for forty years.

Paola Antonelli
Museum of Modern Art, New York

One cylinder.
Minimalist **MAGNUSSEN** gives a cool form to keeping hot.

Thermos jug for **STELTON**, 1975

Soft wave
For the hospital PAIMIO **Alvar AALTO** gives wood a humane shape.

Easy chair *Paimio*, 1931 for ARTEK

Ships that carry significance.
The artist **Bertel VALLIEN** pours myths into glass.

Crossboat for KOSTA BODA, 1985

In praise of butterflies.
NANNA DITZEL gave chairs wings of plywood.

Chair *Butterfly* for **FREDERICIA**, 1990

16

Piling up of a heap.
Blocks that build a world.

LEGO Blocks, 1958

A piece of furniture by **Poul KJAERHOLM** is as cool as a piece of music by John Coltrane.

Easy chair *PK22* and Table *PK61* for **FRITZ HANSEN.**

Time digits.

The graphic artist **Bjorn DAHLSTRÖM** developed his own unique typography of furniture.

Easy chair *BD* 1 for **CBI**, 1994.

Scenes of a Marriage.

Carl and **Karin LARSSON** furnished the Swedish family idyll.

Watercolor. *When the Children Have Gone to Bed*, 1897.

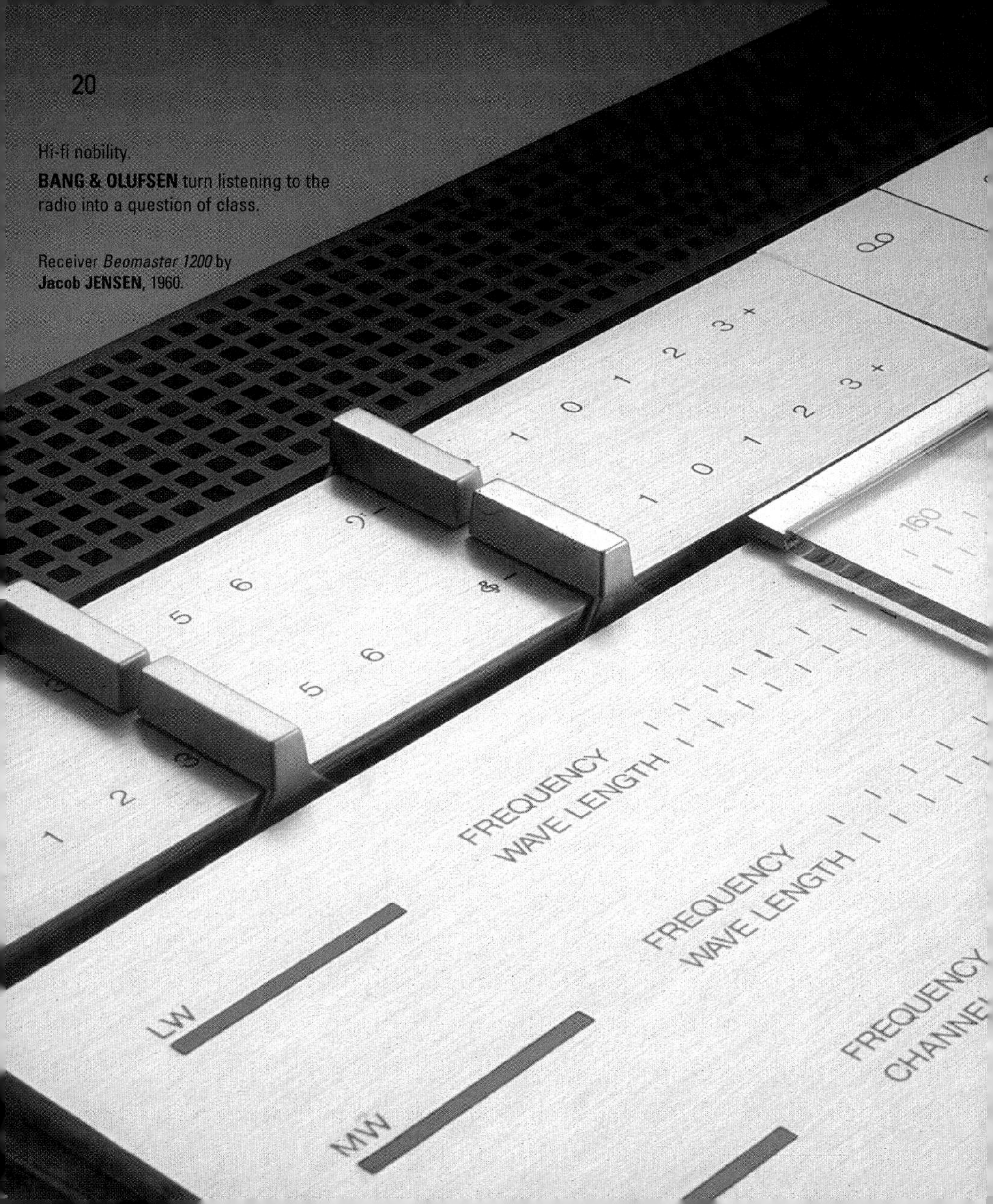

Hi-fi nobility.

BANG & OLUFSEN turn listening to the radio into a question of class.

Receiver *Beomaster 1200* by **Jacob JENSEN**, 1960.

MONO
LW

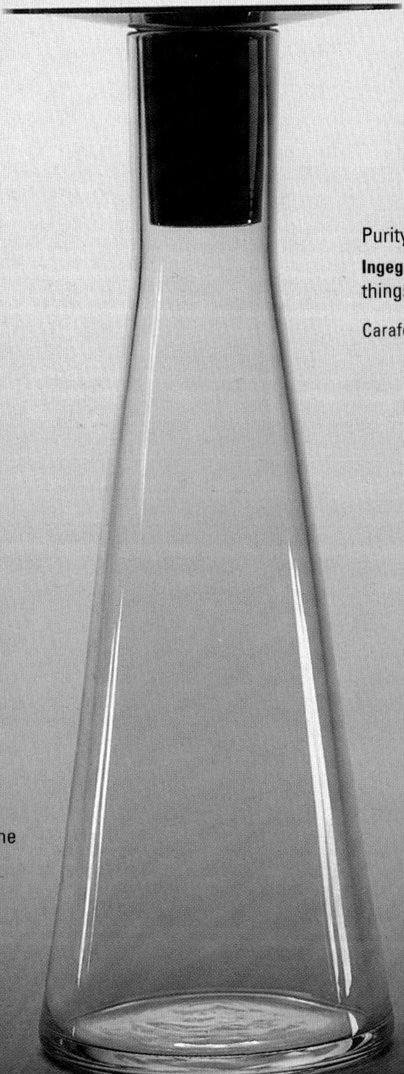

Purity Regulation.

Ingegerd RÅMAN makes sure things are clear.

Carafe *Samuraj* for **SKRUF**, 1989.

Globally intimate.

In 1963 **Eero AARNIO** constructed the space capsule for the home.

Easy chair *Ball* for **ASKO**.

Star pupil.

Fujiwo ISHIMOTO expands the Finnish theory of color.

Fabric *Maisema* for **MARIMEKKO**, 1982

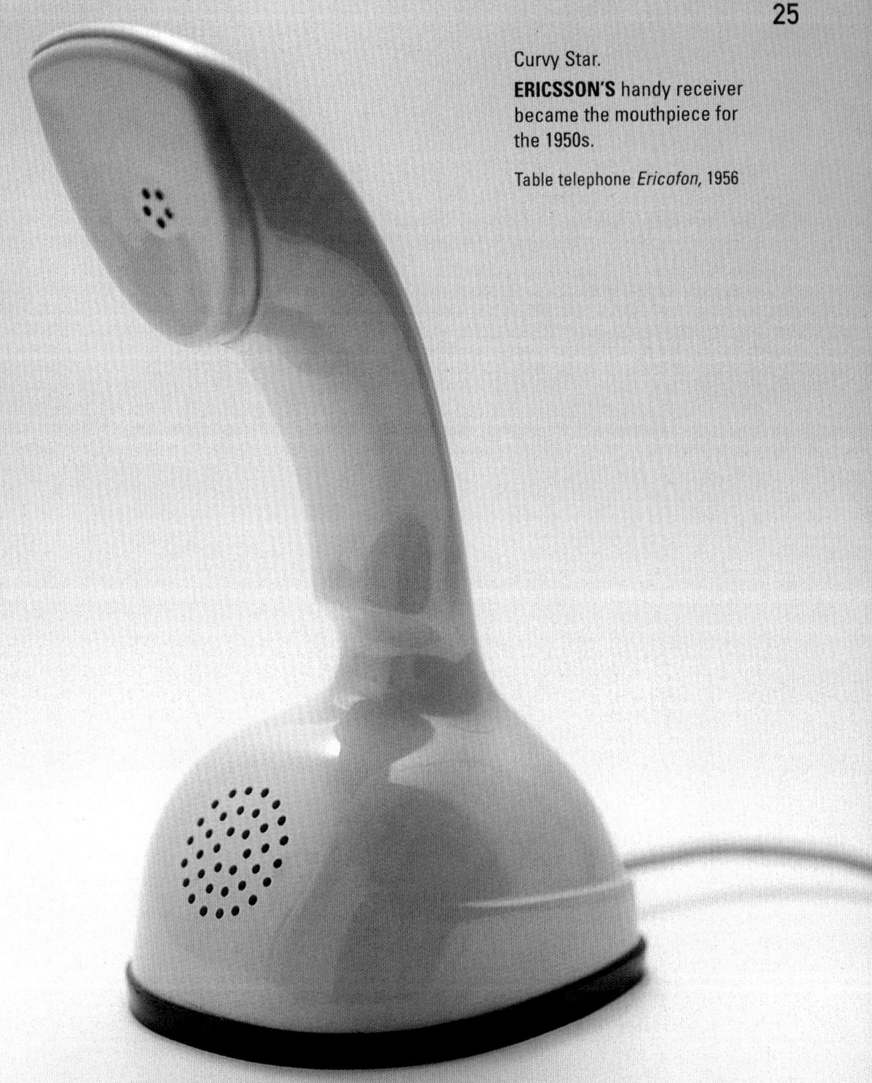

Curvy Star.
ERICSSON'S handy receiver became the mouthpiece for the 1950s.

Table telephone *Ericofon*, 1956

Anti-dazzle.
Poul HENNINGSEN was the first to tame the beam of the lightbulb.

PH-Table lamp for
LOUIS POULSEN, 1933

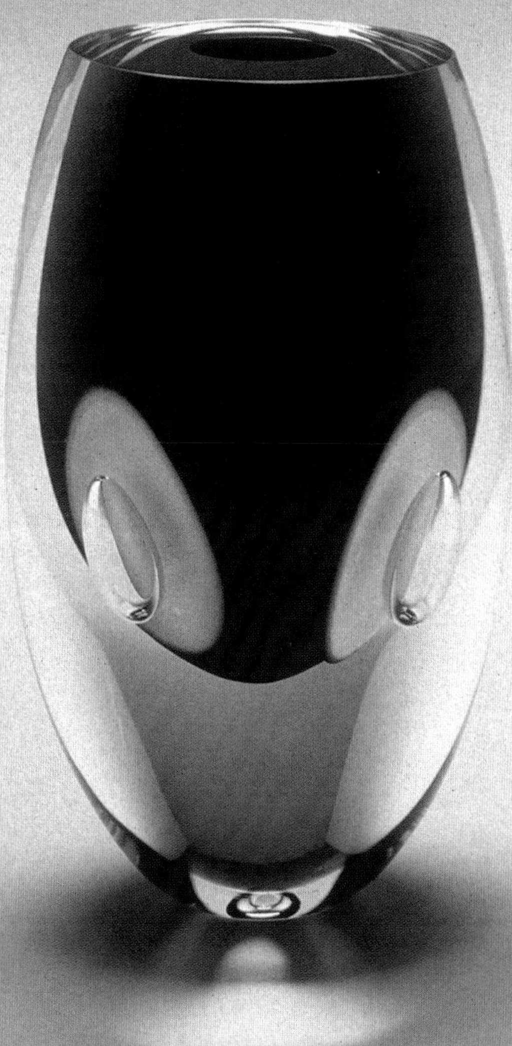

The flowerless one.
Timo SARPANEVA'S glass beauties stand alone.

Vase *Anubis* for IITALA, 1984

The glass.

1955: Reductionist **Kaj FRANCK** launches series production with this prototype.

Pressed glass tumbler for **NUUTAJÄRVI**

Form piecework.
One million "ants" come off the assembly line.

Chair *Myren* by **Arne JACOBSEN** for **FRITZ HANSEN**, 1961

Going one's own way.
Knud HOLSCHER's "tactilograms" guide the blind to their goal.

Pictoform, 1997

Metalayers.
Niels HVASS gives shape to found objects.

Willow-Chair, 1994

Plastic cosmos.
Inside the hull of a ship visitors could immerse themselves in **Verner PANTON'S** world.

Visiona 2 for Bayer, 1970

34

Archetypal figure.
Pia TÖRNELL places cult symbols underneath a candle.

Candlestick *Arcus* for **RÖRSTRAND**, 1995

Finnish show effect.
Vuokko NURMESNIEMI
parades Op-art.

Dress Hood, 1966

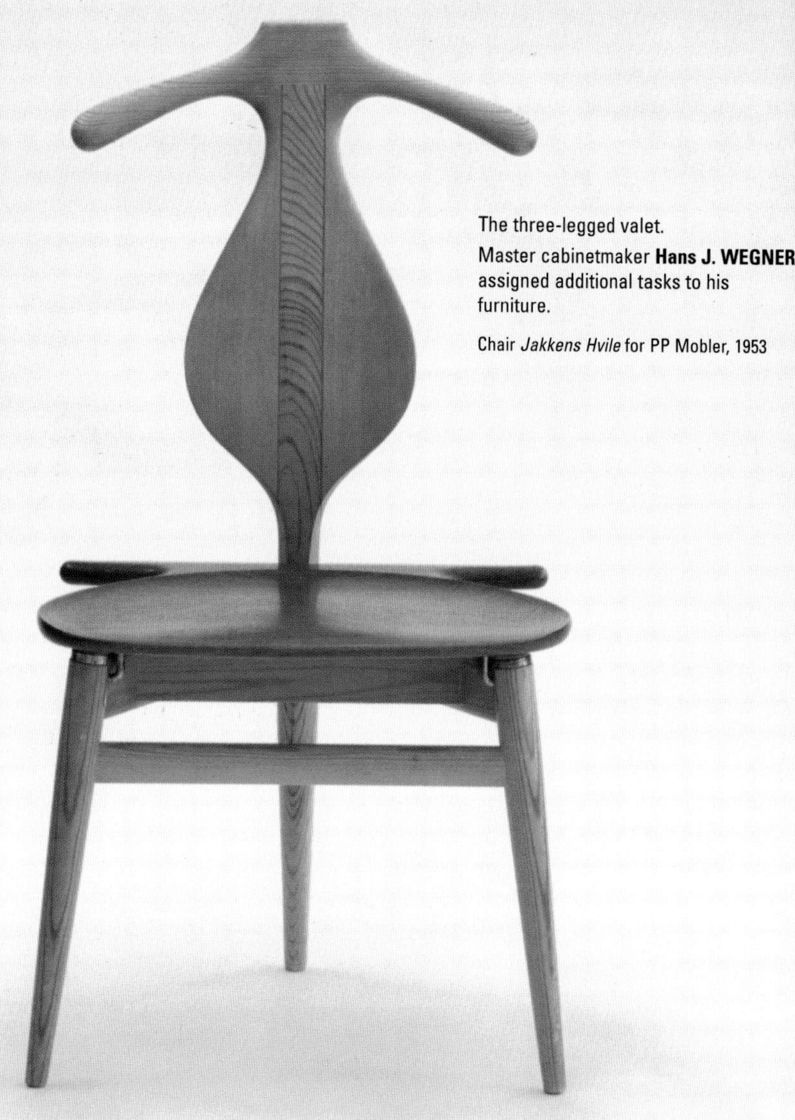

The three-legged valet.
Master cabinetmaker **Hans J. WEGNER** assigned additional tasks to his furniture.

Chair *Jakkens Hvile* for PP Mobler, 1953

Shin supporter.
STOKKE'S rocking chair turns ergonomics into an everyday experience.

Chair *Variable* by **Peter OPSVIK**, 1980

Electric field.

In Finland an energy industry giant puts up designer towers.

by **Antti NURMESNIEMI** for IVO, 1995

Swedish primitive.
With **Thomas SANDELL'S** seat chest
IKEA opens up the design scene.

Bureau on casters from the *PS* series, 1995

Brilliant appearance.

Henning KOPPEL'S fish-serving bowl became a prototype for silver without curlicues.

For **GEORG JENSEN**, 1954

A talented friend of the family.
This kitchenwonder appeared in 1940.

Food processor *Assistent* by and for
ELECTROLUX

Profane altar with seat.

Mats THESELIUS offers an invitation to a private exhibition.

Bengt & Elisabeth's Dream Herb Rack, 1992

Drawn freehand.

Alvar AALTO proves that the intuitive line can be reproduced technically.

Vase Savoy for **IITTALA**, 1936

Solid.

Design archaeologist **Grethe MEYER** draws on the Scandinavian wealth of forms.

Clay bowls for **ROYAL COPENHAGEN**, 1967

Model of success.

Sixten SASON compresses the camera.

Prototype for **HASSELBLAD**, 1947

46

Artful handle.
Finnish scissors make themselves useful all over the world.

Model *Classic* by **FISKARS**, 1967

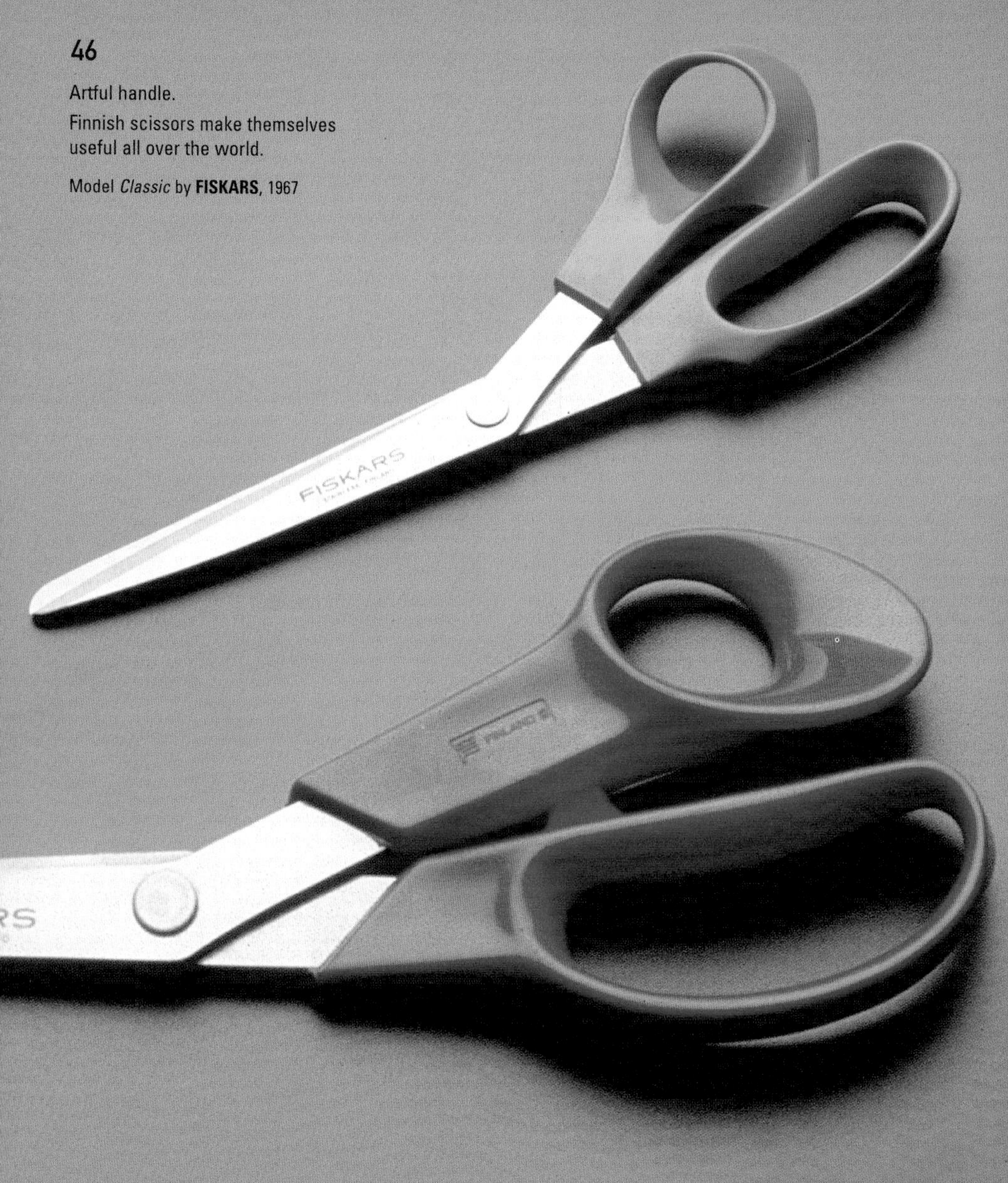

Toeing the line.

SAAB'S flattering bodywork continues to exist after two decades.

Saab *93* by Sixten **SASON**, 1956

Furniture for ascetics.
CLAESSON KOIVISTO RUNE
practices restraint.

Telephone table by Mårten Claesson, 1997

Page 49

Glasses *Bölgeblick* by Aino Aalto for Iittala, 1932

Decades:

History of Scandinavian Design from 1845 to today

1890-1939

Dragons, Artists, Modernists:

Before Skandinavian Design

"Scandinavia is put into museums to teach us living beauty," rejoiced an American daily newspaper. In January 1954 the exhibition *Design in Scandinavia* began its tour of no less than twenty-three museums in the United States and Canada. Its first stop was the Art Museum of Richmond, Virginia. Under the patronage of the American president, the show turned into a triumphal procession. At its penultimate stop alone—in the Conti Museum in Los Angeles—100,000 visitors went to see the well-designed furniture, vases, tableware, and cutlery. These products from the north of Europe managed a leap into American museums and subsequently into American department stores.

Half a century earlier the world had for the first time taken notice of a Scandinavian decor. In 1899 the book *Ett hem* (*At Home*) was published with watercolors by **Carl Larsson**. The Swedish artist presented family scenes and idyllic motifs from his house in rural Dalarna (illustration p. 18). The book became a worldwide best-seller. In the accompanying text Larsson wrote he wanted "to serve as a model for many to furnish their home in a pleasant way." Heavy, mass-produced period furniture was in great demand at that time, in Scandinavia as much as elsewhere. In contrast, the rooms of Larsson's house seemed unusually empty. The few pieces of furniture all had different origins and included simple rustic furniture as well as homemade designs by his wife, **Karin Larsson**. Larsson's house was the exact opposite of the bourgeois desire for ostentation. The Larssons subscribed

"For everything loose and movable that makes a house into a home for living beings."

August Strindberg

Page 50

Bruno Mathsson's house in Värnamo, 1930s

From left to right:

Akseli Gallen-Kallela in Karelia, 1906.

Bottles by Kosta Boda, 18th century.

Tapestry *Liekki* by Akseli Gallen-Kallela, around 1900.

Ice container *Hejrestellet* by Pietro Krohn for Bing Grøndahl, 1888.

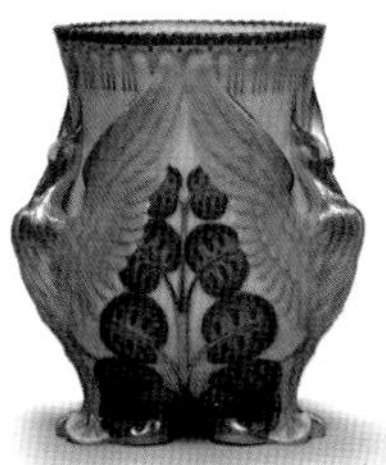

1726 Founding of **Rörstrand**, 1755 (Royal Danish Porcelain Factory)

1809 Sweden loses Finland to Russia; in 1814 Denmark loses Norway to Sweden

1835 Publication of the Finnish epic *Kalevala*

1845 Founding of Svenska Slöjdföreningen in Stockholm

1873 Founding of **Arabia**

1876 Museum for Applied Arts in Oslo

1883 First ceramic works by **Thorvald Bindesbøll**

1888 Exhibition for Industry and Art in Copenhagen, 1897 in Stockholm

1893 The journals *The Studio* and *Jugend* (*Youth*) (1896) appear

1897 Publication of **Carl Larsson's** book *Ett hem* (*At Home*)

1898 The artist **Gunnar Wennerberg** working at Kosta

1900 *World's Fair* in Paris

to the journal *The Studio*, the voice of the English arts and crafts movement, which advocated simplicity and craftsmanship and was well received by artist circles in Scandinavia. The Larsson's rural home was a Swedish version of these ideas, a case of practical design reform in the country, the delicate pen-and-ink drawings of which were to carve themselves into the public's mind.

In 1997 the Victoria and Albert Museum in London presented a Larsson retrospective and named the artistic couple "creators of the Swedish style." The exhibition was sponsored by **Ikea**, a multinational furniture company that regards its product line as the informal continuation of this style. The Larssons were avant-gardists on a kind of bohemian island. They eliminated the false pomp of their time and established a simpler, airy design paradigm. However, this paradigm already contained an inner conflict that runs through all of Scandinavian design. For though their approach was avant-garde and international, it was also introverted and petit bourgeois; in short, it was simultaneously rational and romantic.

Up until the late nineteenth century all Scandinavian countries lived mainly on agriculture. In the villages poverty was standard. Industrialization got under way only slowly and was at first limited to isolated enclaves. Nevertheless, the spread of steam power and smoke was accompanied by social crises and led to unemployment and housing shortages. Tens of thousands emigrated from Sweden to America. When a trade show opened

in Stockholm in 1897, visitors were amazed at the new world of sawmills, spinning machines, and railroads. Incidentally, Larsson's *Ett hem* (*At Home*), the antithesis to the machine age, premiered during the same show.

For centuries proximity in Scandinavia also meant a struggle for predominance. As late as 1905, when Norway attained its independence, war almost broke out. The imperial era of Sweden and Denmark was definitely at an end and so was Finland and Norway's status as provinces. This phase of redefinition—accompanied by the end-of-the-century mood, discontentment with civilization, and rapturous patriotism—led artists and intellectuals to look to the pre-industrial age for orientation. This gave rise to the **national-romantic** movement, which was accompanied, as in the rest of Europe, by the myth of past greatness. That was the time when a number of historical museums were established, such as Skansen near Stockholm, the first open-air museum in the world, and the Ateneum in Helsinki—Finland's first museum—which was affiliated with a school for commercial arts that was to become the cradle of Finnish design.

The movement created its own organizations, such as the very active Suomen Taideteollisuusyhdistys (Finnish Industrial Arts Association) and the Föreningen Svensk Hemslöjd (Society for Swedish Homeworkers), which documented traditional craft techniques from all over the country. To this day Scandinavian design evokes visions of handwoven fabrics, earth colors, and

"I like the idea that my home travels from generation to generation."

Carl Larsson

From left to right:

Iris Room

Iris Dinner Service by Alfred Finch, Finnish pavilion, both at the World's Fair in Paris, 1900

Scissors and Knife

Fiskars, around 1900

Rocking Chair by Karin Larsson, 1906

Watercolor *Mother's and Daughter's Room* by Carl Larsson, 1897

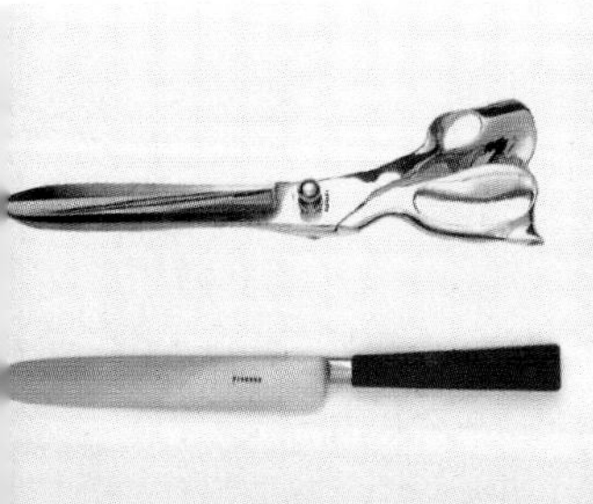

1904 Opening of Georg Jensen's shop in Copenhagen

1905 Norway attains independence

1907 Founding of Landsforeningen Dansk Kunsthåndvaerk and the German Craft Association

1910 Founding of the Finnish society Ornamo

1911 Cubist exhibition in Paris

1912 Olympic Games in Stockholm

1914 Denmark, Norway, and Sweden maintain neutrality in the First World War; *Baltic Exhibition* in Malmö (end of Art Nouveau); exhibition of workers' furniture in Stockholm; publication of Danish journal *Skønvirke*

1916 The artists **Simon Gate** and **Edvard Hald** at **Orrefors**

1917 *Hemutställningen* in Stockholm; Finland attains independence

1918 Finnish civil war

robust wooden furniture. Thanks to the primacy of industrial arts, natural materials and household objects pushed their way into the limelight. There they became the main ingredients of Scandinavia's attractive culture of pleasant, comfortable living, whose atmosphere of warmth was the natural response to an extreme climate. This prompted the design critic Ulf Hård af Segerstad to call Scandinavian design "winter design."

Country life and virgin landscapes, such as in the Swedish Dalarna and the **Finnish Karelia**, became sanctuaries for sore city souls as well as a canvas for the projection of national yearnings. The painter, Axel Gallén, who gave himself the Finnish name **Akseli Gallen-Kallela** and lived for periods in the isolation of the wild, became the protagonist of Karelianism. This grand master and cosmopolitan artist, who also distinguished himself as a furniture and textile designer, brought international know-how into his country in the persons of the Swedish-Italian painter **Louis Sparre** and the English-Belgian potter **Alfred Finch**. These two founded the **Iris** factory in 1897; though it was only short-lived, it was to revolutionize Finland's art industry.

It was thus no accident that Finland—still a Russian province at that time—created a stir at the Paris World's Fair in 1900. Other Scandinavians were very much talked about there, for example, the Norwegian **Gerhard Munthe** with his Scandinavian textiles and the Swedish porcelain factory **Rörstrand**. The main attraction, however, was the Finnish

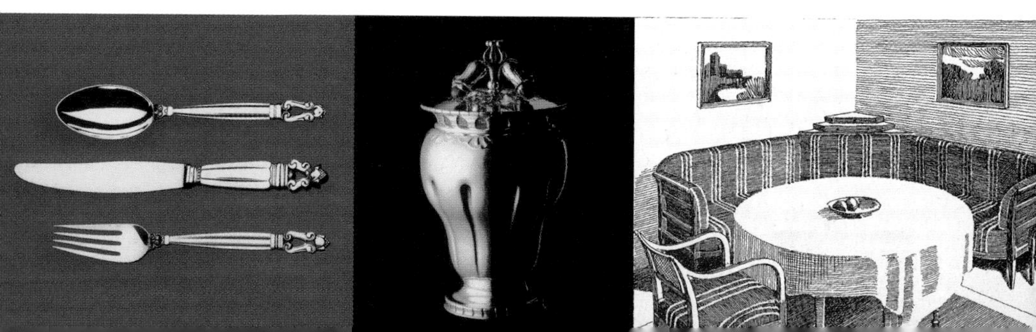

pavilion, universally celebrated as a synthesis of the arts. The plans for this temple of national-romanticism had been contributed by **Eliel Saarinen**. The pavilion's furnishings were contributed by Finch, Sparre, and Gallen-Kallela, and the latter's wall hanging, *Liekki* (*Flame*), is considered a key work. Suddenly Scandinavia, geographically and culturally peripheral, had become the focus of attention and a fashionable topic in Europe's cultural circles. As *The Studio* commented prophetically, "A powerful new art movement is emerging in these remote countries."

Scandinavia's early design history was accompanied by the nations' quest for self-definition, and thus design questions came to be matters of general awareness and took on an unusually great significance. In Scandinavia individual objects can attain enormous popularity, and designers are idolized as top athletes are elsewhere. The national aspect of design took on different forms in different countries; Denmark with its port and trade city Copenhagen developed a predilection for the exotic. The amusement park Tivoli and the porcelain manufacturers reveled in orientalism. The interest in Japanese and Chinese glazes was to give **Royal Copenhagen** an important technological advantage. Already in those early days the Danish art industry maintained experimentation studios in which artists were given free reign to work. Later this exemplary system was adopted by the other Scandinavian countries. Around 1900 Danish design was

"People work better, feel better, and are happier when they have everyday objects of beautiful colors and shapes around them in their homes, regardless of how modest these objects may be."

Ellen Key

From left to right:

Silver cutlery by Johan Rohde for Georg Jensen, 1915

Goblet by George Jensen, 1915

Corner seating arrangement by Kaare Klint, 1913

Scissors by Georg Jensen, 1915

Vase *Valkyrior* by Simon Gate for Orrefors, 1917

Dinner service *Liljeblå* by Wilhelm Kåge for Gustavsberg, 1917

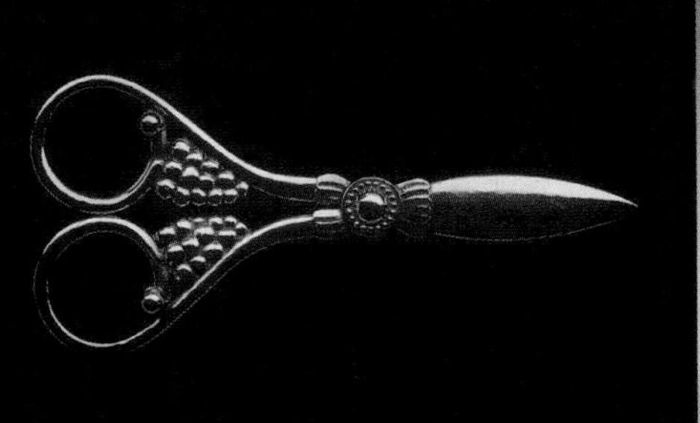

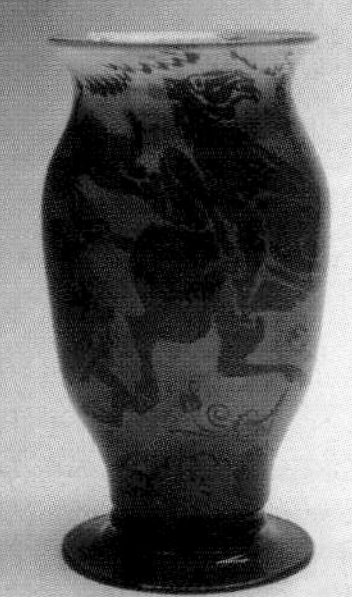

1919 Publication of **Gregor Paulsson's** book *Vackrare vardagsvara* (*More Beautiful Things for Everyday Use*); founding of the Bauhaus

1921 Universal suffrage in Sweden

1924 Founding of furniture school in Copenhagen by **Kaare Klint**

1925 *Exposition des Arts Décoratifs* in Paris; prizes for Orrefors

1926 *PH* Lamps; publication of *Kritisk Revy*

1927 First exhibition and furniture competition of the cabinetmakers' guild of Copenhagen; wood experiments by Alvar Aalto; exhibition *Swedish Contemporary Decorative* Arts in New York; Weissenhof housing development in Stuttgart

beginning to be shaped by strong personalities such as the silversmith **Georg Jensen** and **Thorvald Bindesbøll**, an independent spirit who anticipated free abstraction in his ceramics.

The national-romantic movement's flood of emotions soon began to evaporate. Commercial arts remained a hotly debated topic; however, their economic significance was minimal because the population could not afford the products. At the beginning of the century Sweden was considered the poorhouse of Europe because of its disastrous housing conditions. In 1899 a book with the programmatic title *Skönhet för alla* (Beauty for All) appeared, calling for a proletarian design reform. The author, **Ellen Key**, found comrades-in-arms in the Svenska Slöjdföreningen (today Svensk Form), the oldest industrial arts association of the world, whose drawing school, the Konstfackskola (now a state school), still trains new generations of Swedish designers.

Svenska Slöjdföreningen adopted the program of its German namesake, the German Craft Association, which called for an up-to-date aesthetics suitable for machine production. Following its example, an agency was established in Sweden to set up contacts with manufacturers. The director of the association, **Gregor Paulsson**, eventually authored a book entitled *Vackrare vardagsvara* (*More Beautiful Things for Everyday Use*), which became the battle cry of the design reformers and was never completely silenced. The Stockholm *Hemutställningen* (Home

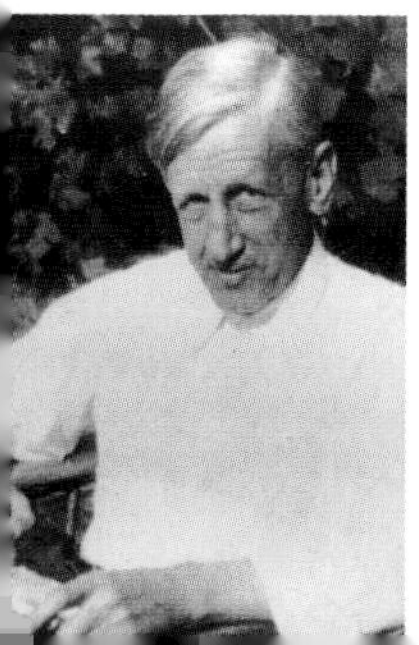

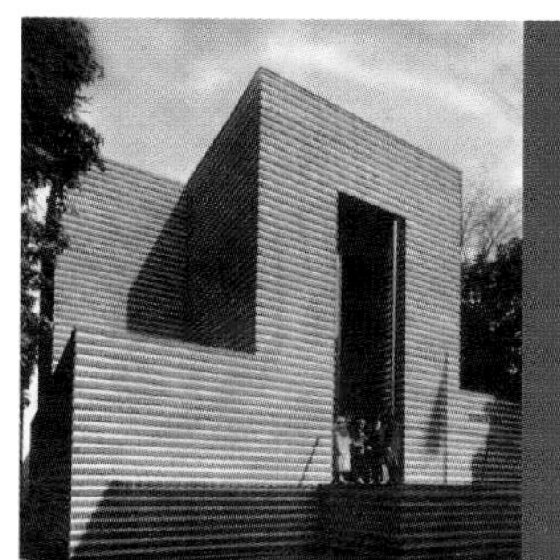

Show) in 1917 was an attempt to turn the theory into practice. Young, promising designers, such as **Gunnar Asplund** and **Carl Malmsten** participated. What they had in common was, above all, their efforts to maintain simplicity. But the concepts underlying their simplicity differed widely, ranging from the return to rustic designs to the influences of the new German design and, especially in Denmark and Sweden, to a widespread preference for classicist forms. For example, **Wilhelm Kåge's** much praised dinner service *Liljeblå* (or *Workers' Dinnerware*) with its folksy decor appears rather undecided between these different trends.

In Sweden the rural bourgeois style of the epoch of King Gustav remained the substratum of all art movements until far into the twentieth century. This subdued and almost sparse historicism made Sweden famous overnight at the 1925 Paris Art Deco exhibition. Certificates and medals poured in, not for beautiful things for everyday use but for extravagant luxury items. Precious crystal glass by **Orrefors**, stylistically at home somewhere between Botticelli and Matisse, received the most accolades because of its virtuosity and craftsmanship. A critic called it "Swedish grace." Ironically, this was also a success for the Svenska Slöjdföreningen, which had referred the artists **Simon Gate** and **Edvard Hald** to Orrefors.

Scandinavian design has continued to be characterized by moderate-classical proportions. The Danish artist **Johan Rhode** exemplified this preference and perseverance, both in positive

"Lighting is like driving a car. The conditions must be right."
Poul Henningsen

From left to right:

Kaare Klint

Chair by Kaare Klint for the Faaborg Museum, 1914

Danish pavilion at the 1925 *Exposition des Arts Décoratifs* in Paris

Flatware *Dansk Standard* by Einar Cohr, 1929

Light diagram by Poul Henningsen, 1920s

Armchair by Gunnar Asplund, 1925

Poul Henningsen

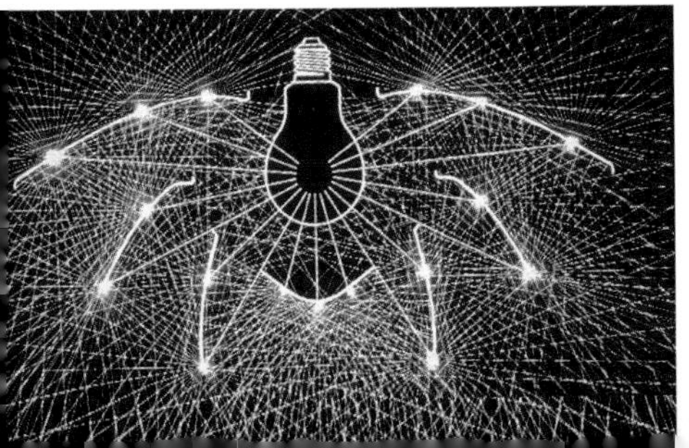

1928 **Nora Gulbrandsen** hired as artistic director at **Porsgrund**

1929 Social democratic government in Denmark, also in Sweden in 1932, in Norway 1935, and in Finland1937; beginning of world economic crisis

1930 *Stockholmsutstälningen* by **Gunnar Asplund** and Gregor Paulsson; March of the Rightists on Helsinki

1931 Easy chair *Paimio* by **Alvar Aalto**; Gallery Den Permanente founded in Copenhagen by **Kaj Bojesen**; Bakelite-telephone by **Jean Heiberg**; Vase *Pearlfisher* by **Vicke Lindstrand** for **Orrefors**

and in negative directions. Like his fellow countryman **Poul Henningsen**, Rhode exhibited in Paris. Rhode and Henningsen personify the contrast between skilled craftsmanship on the highest level and emerging industrial design. Henningsen, co-editor of the left-leaning cultural journal *Kritisk Revy*, the mouthpiece of the aesthetic opposition, reproached his opponents by pointing out that "all modern tasks are still unsolved" because there is "no proper water glass." Poul Henningsen won a gold medal in Paris for his new lamps, which were later marketed under his initials. These ingenious reflection machines became Denmark's most important product design prior to World War II, and they are an early as well as rare example of Scandinavia's break from its pre-industrial legacy.

In 1924 the architect **Kaare Klint** offered a class for cabinetmakers at the Royal Academy in Copenhagen that developed into a training ground for a cadre of new designers. With his meticulous form analyses, the systematist Klint founded a specifically Danish school of furniture functionalism, conservative and innovative at the same time. His *Safari Chair*, an adaptation from colonial times, was the first chair in Europe that was shipped in pieces. Another institution founded in Copenhagen in those days was the annual exhibition of the cabinetmakers' guild, a successful attempt to hold its own in the competition against the furniture industry. This forum and Klint's strict rule served as catalysts in the development of Danish furniture design.

The event that was to divide public opinion and cleave the history of Scandinavian design into "before and after," occurred in the summer of 1930 in Stockholm: Sweden's largest trade show until then. Inspired by the Weissenhof housing development in Stuttgart, Germany, the architect Gunnar Asplund designed an impressive panorama of white pavilions in bold constructivist shapes. Compared to the radically modern architecture of the *Stockholm Exhibition* (and judging by the five million visitors), the objects exhibited were by international standards relatively moderate. Nevertheless the show was felt by lay public and experts alike to be unbearably progressive, a drastic demonstration of functionalist Bauhaus ideals and thus clearly "un-Swedish." Traditionalists like Carl Malmsten did not even participate in the exhibition.

The worldwide economic crisis and the rise of fascism subdued the optimism and belief in the future as well as the desire to experiment but sharpened the social awareness of the public. After the election of social democratic governments—1929 in Denmark and in all of the other Scandinavian countries by the end of the 1930s—social conditions began to change slowly. While a largely conservative consensus prevailed in the well-to-do and aesthetically formative strata of society—for example, in Finland an alliance of critics and institutions took a stand against any kind of modernism—progress also had its advocates. For example, **Artek** in Helsinki, Svenska Slöjdföreningen, and **Kay**

"In modern society, the father could be a stonemason, the mother a professor, and the daughter a film star. The modern dwelling must be built for all of these needs."

Alvar Aalto

From left to right:

Kay Bojesen

Toy monkey by Kay Bojesen, 1930

Pavilion at the *Stockholm Exhibition*, 1930

Kurt Ekholm and Kaj Franck at Arabia, 1930s

Dinner service *Sinivalko* by Kurt Ekholm, 1936

Chair by Bruno Mathsson, 1932

Bojeson's gallery Den Permanente in Copenhagen. And progress also had a symbol of its own, namely, tubular steel furniture. In the early 1930s daring companies included such cool utilitarian designs in their product line. The notorious Poul Henningsen introduced his extensive collection *Stålmobel*, as did Gunnar Asplund, **Arne Jacobsen**, and the early **Alvar Aalto**.

Functionalist ideas also infiltrated the art industry. Aino Aalto's glass series *Bölgeblick* is one of the first utility glass series with a modern design that was suitable for mass production. Prohibition was repealed in Finland in the beginning of the 1930s, which led to greater demand for drinking glasses. At about that time the Norwegian artist **Nora Gulbrandsen** designed a series of simple, geometric china for **Porsgrund.**

Companies such as **Hadeland** and **Gustavsberg** also revamped their product line thoroughly. **Wilhelm Kåge's** dinner service *Praktika* (designed in 1933 for Gustavsberg) was designed specifically for everyday use, allowed space-saving storage in a cabinet, and was multifunctional, with the bowls, for example, also serving as lids. At **Arabia Kurt Ekholm** pursued a similarly functional line. He also set up studios for artists whose presence in the factory came to be normal and expected; this creative principle was then copied throughout Scandinavia and became one of the foundations of the variety of Scandinavian design. Modern design was as yet represented only here and there by lone individuals. One of them was **Bruno Mathsson**; in

1932 Per Albin Hansson elected prime minister of Sweden; program *Volkshem*; artist studios at Arabia; **Eliel Saarinen** director of the Cranbrook Academy, Bloomfield Hills, Michigan; glasses *Bölgeblick* by **Aino Aalto**

1933 *Safari-chair* by Kaare Klint; show of Alvar Aalto's work in London

1934 Chair Eva by **Bruno Mathsson**

1935 Founding of **Artek**

1936 Vase *Savoy* by Alvar Aalto

1937 "Swedish Modern" by **Josef Frank** for **Svenskt Tenn** at the *World's Fair*, Paris

1939 World's Fair, New York, Scandinavian pavilions draw a lot of attention; beginning of World War II

the Swedish province he single-handedly introduced a new idiom into furniture design, namely the curved dynamic line. Across the Baltic Alvar Aalto managed the same accomplishment at about the same time. Mathsson and Aalto also were technical innovators, forcing wood into completely new shapes. Their rejection of the strict Bauhaus geometry went hand in hand with the return to the natural, readily available material.

The new nonangular design drew on many sources. Aalto looked for inspiration in modern art. The label under which the new design became popular was "Swedish Modern" and referred to the decor created by the Austrian **Josef Frank** that had first gained international attention at the Paris World's Fair in 1937. The polyglot Frank, designer-in-chief at **Svenskt Tenn**, drew on historical models, for example, on the Biedermeier style. Two years later, at the New York World's Fair, the Scandinavians were already playing major roles, particularly Alvar Aalto who turned the Finnish pavilion into a "Symphony in Wood." Despite their widely differing backgrounds, Frank and Aalto agreed in the concept of "free-style furnishing" accompanied by a fundamental humanism. Josef Frank also shone again with the room in which he demonstrated the canon of modern design principles: lightness, pieces of furniture that can be "mixed and matched," and bare walls. A trend had been born; the *Architectural Review* commented in 1938: "Swedish Modern sells well in America."

"Away with all universal styles. Away with all leveling down in the art industry. What we need is variety."

Josef Frank

From left to right:

Alvar Aalto

Mahogany chair by Josef Frank for Svenskt Tenn, 1947

Gas station by Arne Jacobsen, 1938

Wood experiments by Alvar Aalto, 1932

Edvard Hald and Simon Gate at Orrefors, 1930s

Brandy decanter by Aino Aalto for Iittala, ca. 1935

Chairs for a movie theater by Arne Jacobsen for the Bellevue Theater, 1935

1940-1969

Most Beautiful Things in the World: The Success Scandinavian Design

Like Norway, Denmark was occupied by German troops in 1940. The borders were closed, travel was prohibited, and goods were rationed. Nevertheless that time of hardship was one of the most fruitful ones for Danish design. The country was isolated, but as a result "we developed in all areas a specifically Danish design," remembers **Finn Juhl**, who made vital contributions to that development with his furniture designs. In 1939 Juhl surprised the guild of cabinetmakers with a sofa that had ears and looked like a sculpture by Hans Arp. Juhl's use of organic forms—for which his preferred material was later teak—was an open rebellion against the rules of the Klint School but fit into the trend and of the time. In the early 1950s it became a worldwide success under the label "Danish Modern."

Borge Mogensen's work is typical of the situation of that era characterized by general shortage as well as by idealism and resourcefulness. In the early 1940s the young cabinetmaker took over the furniture department of the consumer cooperative Forende Danske Brugsforeniger (FDB). There he had the chance to apply **Kaare Klint's** functionalism for the first time on a large scale. By 1950 he had developed numerous series of useful furniture for people with a small amount of space and tight budgets. The furniture industry followed his groundbreaking example when manufacturers realized that the investment in a qualified designer could pay off handsomely. This turned out to be a trendsetting development in the Danish furniture industry,

"A pot by Henning Koppel is like a good picture by Henri Matisse."
Henrik Sten Mller

Page 62

Bar in the Royal Hotel in Copenhagen by Arne Jacobsen, c. 1960.

From left to right:

Paper lamp by Kaare Klint for Le Klint, c. 1945

Sofa by Finn Juhl, 1939

Borge Mogensen

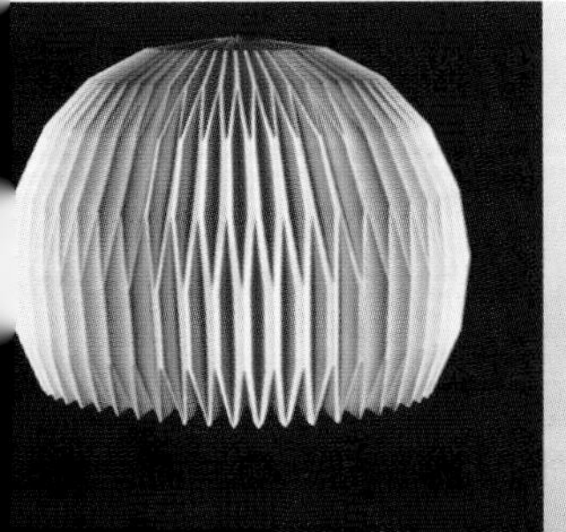

1940 Denmark and Norway occupied by Germany; exhibition *Organic Design* in the Museum of Modern Art, New York

1944 Exhibition *We Live in the Open-Air City* in Malmö

1945 Easy chair *Teak* by **Finn Juhl**

1946 Design conference of Scandinavian countries in Copenhagen; exhibition *Modern Swedish and Danish Decorative Arts* in New York; vases *Kantarelli* by **Tapio Wirkkala**; **Kaj Franck** at **Arabia**; consolidation of the Swedish welfare state

1948 **Stig Lindberg** wins gold medal at the *Triennale*, Milan; **Astrid Sampe** organizes exhibition *Textil Bilderbok* in New York

1949 The *Round Chair* by **Hans J. Wegner**; Volvo 92 by **Sixten Sason**; dinner service *Kilta* by Kaj Franck

which to this day is one of the leading ones in Europe and which remains strongly design oriented. Finn Juhl, **Poul Kjaerholm**, Borge Mogensen, **Hans J. Wegner**, **Arne Jacobsen**, **Kristian Vedel**—the new generation of Danish cabinetmakers was made up of an unsurpassed number of talented artists, but the differences in their concepts and character often remained hidden behind the catchphrase "Danish Modern." The contributions that women such as **Nanna Ditzel**, **Grete Jalk**, and **Grethe Meyer** made for the first time in history to the still mostly male-dominated field of furniture design should not be forgotten either. The excitement of new beginnings gripped furniture industry and design. The home was thoroughly cleared out and new types of furniture were developed, such as the very popular and versatile wall unit *Boligens Byggeskabe* by Meyer and Mogensen, a new kind of modular furniture that dealt the deathblow to the outmoded, old-fashioned drawing room cabinet.

Though not occupied, Sweden was culturally isolated during the war. Nevertheless, it served as a refuge for immigrants, among them numerous architects and designers; Stockholm was where they met and exchanged ideas. In the 1940s the Swedish model of the welfare state, or of providing for everybody in society, developed. Interestingly enough, the Swedes themselves called it "Volkshem" (home of the people), and of course that home had to be furnished in an exemplary way. The egalitarian principle called for a democratic design. The social democratic

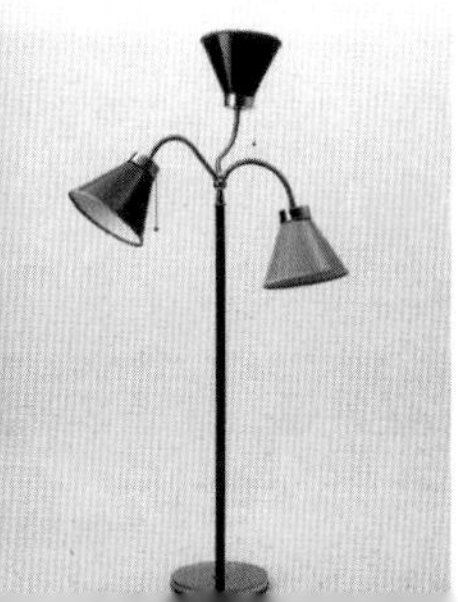

society ultimately adopted functionalism as a progressive, politically correct aesthetic. Subsequently extensive "home tests" were carried out under the direction of the art and design theoretician Gotthard Johansson. The results of these very detailed inquiries led in 1952 to the introduction of the universally admired "Swedish kitchen." The standardization was later extended to beds, tables, cupboards, and the rest of the home.

Functionalism and clarity gained the upper hand, flowery wallpaper and "period furniture" were on the way out. The spread of the enlightened taste through all parts of society seemed unstoppable. In the largest Stockholm department store, the **Nordiska Kompaniet** (NK), young couples could sign up for decorating courses. Furniture by innovators such as **Bruno Mathsson** was recommended by the government. **Sigurd Persson** designed household goods for the consumer cooperative, Kooparetiva Förbundet (KF). The ceramics manufacturer **Gustavsberg** had already been taken over by the KF in the 1930s and was putting the theory of producing more beautiful consumer goods into practice—and has been doing so since 1949 under the direction of **Stig Lindberg**, an artist, intellectual, and, like Persson, the prototype of a socially conscious and responsible designer.

In Finland also the welfare state and modernization entered into a liaison. For example, Arabia, together with the family welfare department—established in the early 1940s as part of the

"I would like to design things that are so obvious that one hardly notices them."

Kaj Franck

From left to right:

Cup production at Gustavsberg, 1950s

Floor lamp by Josef Frank for Svenskt Tenn, 1939

Dinner service *Liekki* by Ulla Prokopé for Arabia, 1958

Stig Lindberg

Silver coffeepot by Sigurd Persson, 1950s

Astrid Sampe

1950 First Scandinavian studio for industrial design founded by Sigvard Bernadotte; Kaj Franck at **Nuutajärvi**; **Arne Jon Jutrem** at **Hadeland**

1951 For the first time Scandinavians in the foreground at the *Triennale* in Milan;plywood bowl by Tapio Wirkkala

1952 Founding of the Nordic Council; chair *Myren* by **Arne Jacobsen**; wall unit *Boligens Byggeskabe* by **Borge Mogensen** and **Grethe Meyer**; *Lunning-Prize* awarded (until 1972)

1953 Dag Hammarskjold named Secretary General of the United Nations; exhibition *Scandinavia at Table* in London; cutlery Servus by **Sigurd Persson** for Kooperativa Förbundet; **Tias Eckhoff** at **Porsgrund**

ministry of the interior—produced the people's dinner service tableware, *Koti* (home), designed to "satisfy basic needs" and "cultivate good taste." The best imaginable designer was found for this task: **Kaj Franck**. Franck, a dyed-in-the-wool opponent of what he termed the "Scandinavian ideal" saw "no reason to make compromises regarding the appropriateness of articles for everyday use." His simple drinking glasses for **Nuutajärvi** and his pioneering earthenware *Kilta*, the first multifunctional dinner service systems, are masterpieces of minimalism.

Leaving a bitter war behind, Finland, still predominantly an agrarian society, experienced a wave of urbanization and was ready for the modern era and open to new and unusual solutions. That alone explains the euphoria triggered by those red, yellow, and light blue enameled coffeepots **Antti Nurmesniemi** designed in 1957 and that became cult objects. In the same year, at **Royal Copenhagen**, **Magnus Stephensen** introduced a new type of utilitarian dinner service for everyday use that could be used for food preparation as well as for serving. However, the Danish porcelain industry, so rich in tradition, found it difficult to set aside the good old coffeepot and resolutely pursue the system principle, which had long since gained a strong foothold in the furniture industry. It wasn't until the appearance of the multi-use dinner services developed by **Erik Magnussen** in the 1960s for **Bing & Grondahl** that the dining table revolution resumed.

In 1948 Stig Lindberg won a gold medal at the *Triennale* in

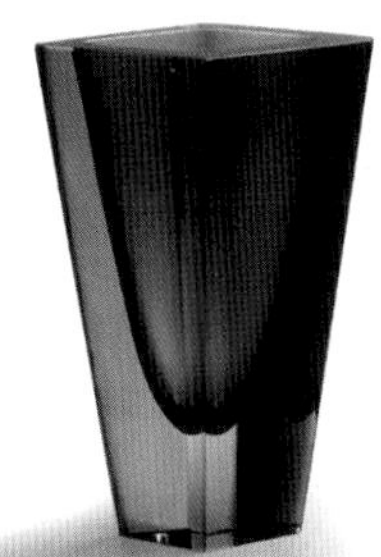

Milan. This was the first postwar *Triennale*, and it offered only a taste of the great show to come in 1951. Starting in that year, Scandinavian designers dominated the Triennale for almost two decades and were showered with prizes. The Finnish designers took home more prizes than all the others—in 1951 alone they won six great prizes, four honorary diplomas, seven gold medals, and eight silver medals. Kaj Franck also had been decorated with honors in 1951. However, the attention centered not on the master himself but on two of his fellow countrymen, the glass designers **Timo Sarpaneva** and **Tapio Wirkkala**. They were the first star designers of Europe and in their country soon enjoyed the same admiration as great artists. Sarpaneva and Wirkkala created some of the most elegant and sophisticated glass objects that stand out from everything created earlier by virtue of the fact that they no longer served any functions but were merely intended to be pure objects, pure glass art.

"Take a stone in your hand that has been smoothed by the rapids, and find in it our culture."

Tapio Wirkkala

Henning Koppel's silver serving bowl for fish, Tapio Wirkkala's plywood leaf *Lethi-vati*, Timo Sarpaneva's crystal vase *Lansetti*, Finn Juhl's *Chief Chair*, Hans Wegener's *Round Chair*, and Kaj Franck's *Kilta* have at least three characteristics in common. All were created around 1950, all belong in the shrine of Scandinavian design classics, and all were shown at an exhibition that was a complete novelty in the history of design. The exhibition *Design in Scandinavia* was extraordinary, and after its opening in 1954, it toured the entirety of the North American continent for

From left to right:

Coffeepot by Antti Nurmisniemi, 1957

Vase by Kaj Franck for Nuutajarvi, c. 1960

Kaj Franck instructs sales personnel at Arabia, c. 1950

Volvo 121 *Amazon*, 1956

Typewriter *T1* by Sigvard Bernadotte for Facit, 1959

1954 Common Scandinavian employment market; touring exhibition *Design in Scandinavia* in North America; fish serving bowl by **Henning Koppel**; stool with fan-legs by Alvar Aalto; **Vuokko Nurmesniemi** designer-in-chief at **Marimekko**

1955 Exhibition *H 55* in Helsingborg; building of suburban housing development Vällingby near Stockholm

1956 Glass collection *i-line* by **Timo Sarpaneva** for **Iittala**; Volvo limousine 121 *Amazon*, also available as station wagon; *Ericofon* by **Ericsson**; touring exhibition *Finnish Industrial Arts and New Forms from Denmark* in Germany; Lego distribution in Germany; film *The Seventh Seal* by Ingmar Bergman

three whole years. Sensational above all was the professional public relations work. Several thousand visitors on opening day at each stop were not a rarity. The high society gathered at countless dinner parties; films and accompanying courses supplemented the exhibition. America's housewives could not get over their astonishment; school children pressed their noses flat against the glass showcases; daily papers and decorating magazines reported continuously on the show.

The idea for the most successful design campaign of all times came from Elisabeth Gordon, the editor-in-chief of the magazine *House Beautiful*, back then the official organ of good taste. In her magazine, Scandinavian industrial arts had been chosen as "the most beautiful object of the year" several times. Impressed by the Scandinavian presentation at the *Triennale*, Gordon published a special issue entitled *Design in Scandinavia*. The red carpet rolled out for the Scandinavians also derived from an admiration for their politics. In the United States the concept *Sweden: The Middle Way* (after a book by M. Childs from the 1930s) for decades provided the ideal image for liberal Americans of a welfare state—the antithesis to aggressive capitalism.

Scandinavian design found acceptance not only in America's department stores and living rooms but also in its language. The catchy phrase created a myth. This was in fact the first time that all Scandinavian countries presented themselves together.

Scandinavian design found acceptance not only in

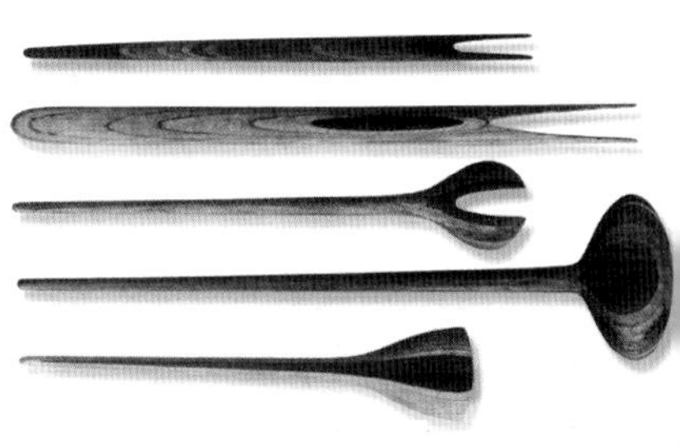

America's department stores and living rooms but also in its language. The catchy phrase created a myth. This was in fact the first time that all Scandinavian countries presented themselves together. The first pan-Scandinavian design prize, the *Lunning Prize* had been created only a few years earlier. Frederik Lunning was the head of the U.S. branch of **Georg Jensen** on New York's elegant Fifth Avenue. Incidentally, neither Kaj Franck nor Arne Jacobsen would ever have thought of calling themselves designers. Back then one spoke of "industrial artists," "artists," and "form artists." After the term Scandinavian Design had been coined, the older labels gradually disappeared.

In 1960, when CBS staged a debate between the presidential candidates Kennedy and Nixon, the broadcasting company ordered a dozen *Round Chairs* by Hans J. Wegner. This chair, simply called "the chair" in America (declared the most beautiful in the world by *House Beautiful*) was a symbol of Americans' passionate love affair with Scandinavian design. It was above all America's upper-middle class in the rapidly growing suburbs that was looking for aesthetic orientation and was glad to take up the ideal of an unpretentious, modern, yet still romantic domesticity. All things Scandinavian had both a touch of the wild and the flair of European culture. Thus Scandinavian design came to be adopted by the United States, a world power. The cultivated American way of life, legitimated in an American way through the influence of the Cranbrook Academy, became globally the first

"There is no such thing as 'the chair.' The good chair is a task one never completely masters."
Hans J. Wegner

From left to right:

Glasses *i-line* by Timo Sarpaneva for Iittala, 1956

Vuokko and Antti Nurmesniemi at the Triennale in Milan, 1960

Wooden salad servers by Tapio Wirkkala, 1956

Visitors at the exhibition *Design in Scandinavia*, in the United States, 1954

The Round Chair by Hans J. Wegner for PP Mobler, 1949

Exhibition *Design in Scandinavia*, (U.S.), 1954

1957 *Compasso d'oro* for Kaj Franck; *Chair Made of Steel and Wicker* by **Poul Kjaerholm** (won great prize at the *Triennale*); *Cone Easy Chairs* by **Verner Panton**; enameled metal coffeepot by **Antti Nurmesniemi**; Dinner service *Liekki* by **Ulla Prokopé** for Arabia; **Ingeborg Lundin's** Vase *Appel* for Orrefors; Interbau in Berlin (Hansa District)

1958 *Spanish Chair* by Borge Mogensen; easy chair *Aegget* (egg) and *Svanen* (Swan) by Arne Jacobsen; hanging lamp *Cone* by **Poul Henningsen**; exhibition *Formes Scandinaves* in Paris

1959 Dinner service for SAS by Sigurd Persson; exhibition of Timo Sarpaneva's work in South America.

style of the emerging Western affluent society. The late 1950s saw a spate of exhibitions on Scandinavian design that excluded no major country. Already in 1955 Scandinavian designers had reassured themselves of their own strength at the huge trade show *H 55* in Hälsingborg. Those were the golden years of a boom that just would not stop. Scandinavia seemed to have become a land of milk and honey and to come close to that vision of bliss **Carl Larsson** had once painted. Soon many families had their own summerhouse. An enormous number of new products was marketed. Product designers such as **Sigvard Bernadotte** and **Sixten Sason** did pioneering work. But even though their works were significant, and companies such as Electrolux conquered the new markets, this did not lead to a specifically Scandinavian use of forms.

While tubular steel was the metaphor for the modern age in the 1920s and 1930s, bent plywood now took on that role. During the 1950s no self-respecting furniture manufacturer would do without an up-to-date "form chair." During the war, lamination technology had been developed further by the U.S. Air Force. The Americans Charles and Ray Eames then designed the first shell chairs. The manufacturer **Fritz Hansen** had been working with veneer lamination for some time already. In 1952 two pioneering chair models were developed under the company's auspices, models that embodied the new three dimensional shaping in the most elegant way: Paul Kjaerholm's PKO and Arne Jacobsen's

chair models were developed under the company's auspices, models that embodied the new three dimensional shaping in the most elegant way: Paul Kjaerholm's PKO and Arne Jacobsen's *Myren* (*Ant*). It was Jacobsen's economical design that became a commercial success. More than a million *Myren* were sold. This chair is the first true industrial piece of furniture and also the icon of modern Scandinavian design. The Danish postal service immortalized the chair with the fitted waist on a stamp. Jacobsen turned the laminated chair into a kind of royal discipline in which Scandinavian designers to this day match their skills, determined each time to outwit natural laws. The 1990s in particularly have seen a veritable plywood renaissance.

After a visit to a 1959 Danish design exhibition, Poul Henningsen expressed his appreciation as follows: "many skills and elegance but not one dangerous object." The grand old admonisher opined that most things were produced because "they can be sold to America," but aside from that "the dictatorship of mediocrity" still prevailed. Henningsen had again hit the nail on the head. Toward the end of the decade Scandinavia was already on the way to losing its supremacy in international design, and Italy was about to take its place. The jeans and rock-and-roll generation rebelled against the refined domesticity that Scandinavian products embodied.

The refractory 1960s were characterized by radical ideals and the blurring of genre limits, by bold colors and sculptures,

"I believe finished products and industrial design make people more neighborly. Small things as status symbols disappear."

Arne Jacobsen

From left to right:

Arne Jacobsen

Plywood chairs by Arne Jacobsen for Fritz Hansen, 1950s

Room in the Royal Hotel in Copenhagen by Arne Jacobsen, c. 1960

Corkscrew by Nanna Ditzel for Georg Jensen, 1957

Private house by Poul Kjaerholm, 1960s

Poul Kjaerholm

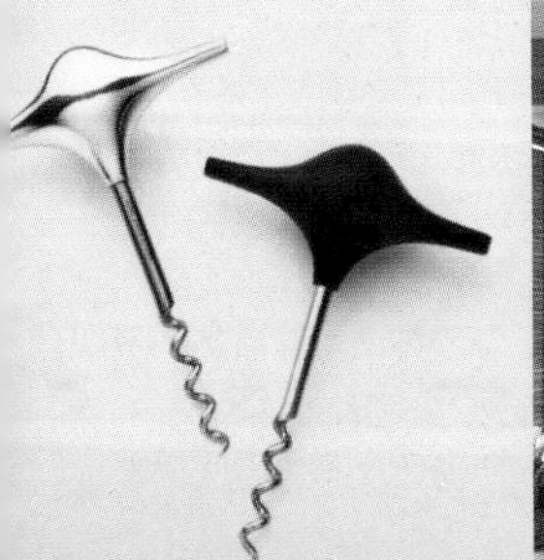

1960 *Triennale*, Milan

1961 Marimekko fashion show in the United States; exhibition *Finlandia*, Zurich

1963 Easy chair *Ball* by **Eero Aarnio**; *Plastic Foam Easy Chair* by **Aagaard Andersen**

1965 Portable radio *Beolit* by **Jacob Jensen**; Swedish "Million Program" for home-building; award of first Danish *ID Prize*; first **Ikea** store in Stockholm

1968 Exhibition *Visiona 0* by Verner Panton at the furniture fair in Cologne; founding of **Innovator** Design; last exhibition exclusively for industrial arts in Australia

1969 Olof Palme elected Swedish Prime Minister

and by happenings and environments. One artist who played with all of these elements in his works was **Verner Panton**, the Danish eccentric with international connections and perhaps Scandinavia's most visionary postwar designer. Panton, who moved to Switzerland in the early 1960s, is best-known for his freely swinging plastic chair designed in 1967. The American manufacturer Herman Miller added the chair to its product line. Another artist who could just as convincingly handle the possibilities offered by chemistry was **Eero Aarnio**, a loner from Finland. Several of the small number of plastic chairs he designed scored a great success and redefined the profession.

Panton was discovered by Percy von Halling-Koch, who was almost as ambivalent a figure as his protégé and active in the circle around *Mobilia*, a journal serving as focal point for a lively subculture. The artist **Aagaard Andersen**, who also experimented with furniture, and Nanna Ditzel, already a successful designer, were also part of this circle. Like Panton and Andersen, Ditzel had also begun working with foam and fiberglass and soon turned her back on Denmark. A deep chasm separated the bohemian furniture culture from the Danish furniture industry that had grown rich on teak. Too few ideas from the avant-garde design laboratory had a chance to be turned into actual products. Some of the most committed artists completely abandoned any business interests, among them the furniture designer and winner of the Lunning-Prize, Kristian Vedel, who went to work in

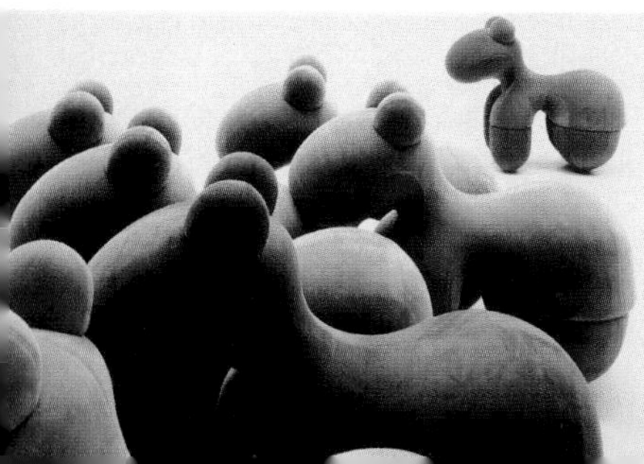

the third world and finally devoted himself to raising sheep.

Looking back on those years, Lennart Lindkvist, director of Svensk Form, wrote, "Sweden lost a whole generation of designers." The protest that had started at the universities led to contradictory results. On the one hand, industrial arts were rejected as bourgeois, but on the other hand, creativity and self-realization were at the top of the new value standards. Many a young skeptic found in industrial arts artistic and individual liberation, particularly from the fetters of industry, regarded with great reserve. The most successful Scandinavian design project of the 1960s is probably **Marimekko**, the Finnish textile manufacturer. With sassy "anti-fashion" unisex and pop patterns it first woke up its fellow country people and then blew a fresh breeze of air into a still very prudish America, where the Finnish underwear was worn by Beatniks and civil rights activists. The wave of protests on which Marimekko rode did not stop short of design institutions and plunged them into a state of crisis. Traditional organizations, such as the Landsforeningen Dansk Brugskunst, disbanded. From then on industrial artists and product designers went their separate ways. The love for America by a Scandinavia which increasingly felt itself called upon to act as the world's conscience cooled noticeably when the United States became a target for criticism. Sweden's prime minister Olof Palme participated in public demonstrations against the Vietnam War, and politicized industrial artists wove motifs of suffering Vietnamese into their wall hangings.

"Industrial arts in schools, jails, and old people's homes!"

Slogan from the 1960s

From left to right:

Easy chair *Pony* by Eero Aarnio, 1973

Plastic foam easy chair by Aagaard Andersen, 1963

Fashion show by Vuokko Nurmisniemi, 1960s

Easy chair *Bubble* by Eero Aarnio, 1968

Easy chair *Corona* by Poul Volther for Erik Jorgensen, 1961

Interlocking furniture by Börge Lindau, c. 1970

1970–1999

Comeback of the Virtues:
New Scandinavian Design

The New York Cooper-Hewitt Museum's 1982 exhibition *Scandinavian Modern Design* was the most extensive retrospective ever on this theme. A huge number of classics had been assembled for the show, and an illustrious circle of Scandinavian design authors offered their knowledge to the show catalog. Nevertheless, the event was rather a sentimental one, a grand farewell to all the wonderful things once produced by artisans and craftspeople. The exhibition was "modern" in the historical sense; names such as **Bang & Olufsen** or **Eero Aarnio** did not appear.

At the Stockholm art academy's annual spring exhibition of the students that same year, Sven Lundh, a lover of art and head of the furniture factory **Källemo**, discovered an unusual piece of furniture—a chair made of concrete. Its creator, **Jonas Bohlin**, a former civil engineer, created quite a stir with this chair because his provocation was understood: the use of the industrial material signaled a definite rejection of traditional furniture. Bohlin's action opened the floodgates to completely new concepts while also serving as an example of something very Scandinavian, namely, the power inherent in the simple and mundane. The concrete chair went into production at Källemo.

As early as 1970, after the Lunning Prize had been awarded for the last time, the once very tight Scandinavian bonds began to loosen. The decade of the oil shock, of irritation and rethinking, the 1970s brought on an identity crisis for Scandinavia's classical

"A failed experiment can be more important than a triviality."

Verner Panton

Page 74

Collection Liv by Jonas Bohlin, Exhibition in Stockholm, 1997

From left to right:

Verner Panton

Lounge *Mrs. Emmentaler* by Verner Panton, 1979

Concrete Chair by Jonas Bohlin from Källemo, 1982

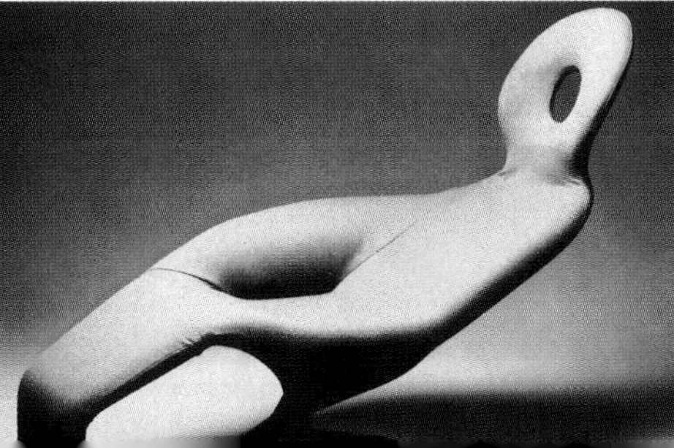

1970 **Kompan** *Spring Seesaw*

1971 **Volvo** *P 1800*; wave of mergers in Swedish glass industry; beginning of Norwegian oil production.

1972 *d-line* by **Knud Holscher**

1973 *Triennial*, Mailan and Scandinavian countries show environment for city children; Denmark joins the EU; film *Scenes from a Marriage* by Ingmar Bergmann

1974 Knife *Ideal* for disabled persons; first hit by Abba

1975 **Erik Magnussens** Thermoskanne für **Stelton**

1976 Exhibition *Nordic Industrial Design: What, Why, How?* in Oslo; Björn Borg wins at Wimbledon

1978 Chair *Ted* by **Pelikan**; exhibiton *Bang & Olufsen: Design for Sound by Jacob Jensen*, MOMA, New York

1979 **Balans** Chairs

art industry. Many designers insisted on independence and self-realization and turned their backs on industry. At the same time, many glass and porcelain manufacturers experienced an economic downturn. This crisis was accompanied by a wave of mergers and closings that left only two multinational concerns in its aftermath: **Hackman** and **Royal Scandinavia**, probably Europe's two largest design firms. The two Scandinavian giants have an imposing collection of renowned design trademarks in their repertory. While companies such as **Arabia** and **Orrefors** survived under the giants' umbrella, many other traditional names were lost, for example, **Bing & Grøndahl**.

As in other sectors of the economy, fame did not protect companies in the furniture industry against economic hardship. When the end loomed before them, renowned firms, such as **Artek** and **Fritz Hansen**, fled into the arms of powerful investors. But design-related success stories, for example, those of **Innovator**, **Stokke**, or **Frederecia** were also the order of the day. Furniture has remained the showpiece of Scandinavian design. Currently around a thousand furniture manufacturers operate in the Scandinavian countries, not counting the thousands of small workshops. Most of these the businesses are small to medium-sized, and more than half of them are located in Denmark. While only a small number of the firms—specifically those active in export—use designers to enhance the distinctiveness of their products, the export share of total sales among all Danish

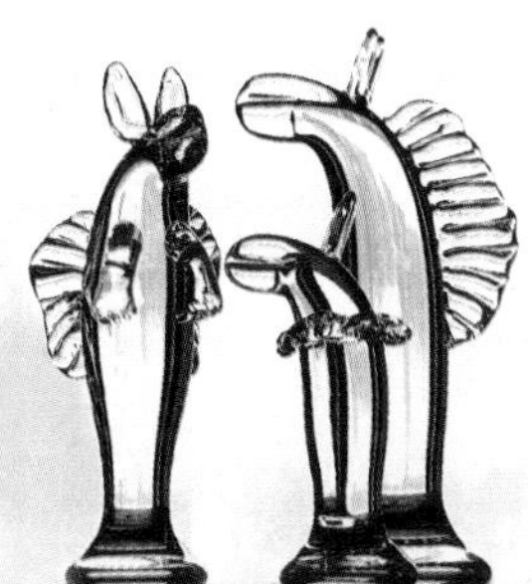

manufacturers is very high. Germany is by far the industry's largest market now, and this is also true for **Ikea**, the largest furniture group of the world. Since the 1970s this company, which moved its headquarters to Denmark for tax reasons, has earned most of its money abroad and is enjoying steady growth. In the beginning the Ikea product line was still strongly leaning toward the alternative lifestyle milieu, but in the meantime the sociological spectrum of its customers has widened, and the product line now covers almost all areas of home, thus fashioning a lifestyle labeled Swedish or Scandinavian.

"We have translated a few good ideas from contemporary design and turned them into practical products."

Ikea

With its many products reminiscent of Scandinavian design classics, the Ikea catalog has become the bible of interior design and is probably hardly less widespread than the Good Book. Ikea also exemplifies how design culture develops within a large concern, and in that regard also it is a Swedish model, for that country's economy is to a large extent shaped by industrial conglomerates operating internationally, such as **Electrolux**, **Volvo**, and **Ericsson** whose design strategies are as complex as their financial links.

The 1978 exhibition *Bang & Olufsen: Design for Sound by Jacob Jensen* at the Museum of Modern Art in New York revealed a new world of hi-fi equipment as well as a recipe for success. For while the collaboration between Bang & Olufsen and Jacob Jensen may have been a particularly lucky case, it was by no means an isolated one. This kind of alliance in small,

From left to right:

SAS Terminal in Helsinki by Yrjö Kukkapuro, c. 1980

Glass sculptures by Ulrica Hydman-Vallien for Kosta Boda, 1971

Wristwatch by Henning Koppel for Georg Jensen, 1977

Ikea store, 1970s

Beocenter 8500 by Jacob Jensen for Bang & Olufsen, 1986

Jacob Jensen

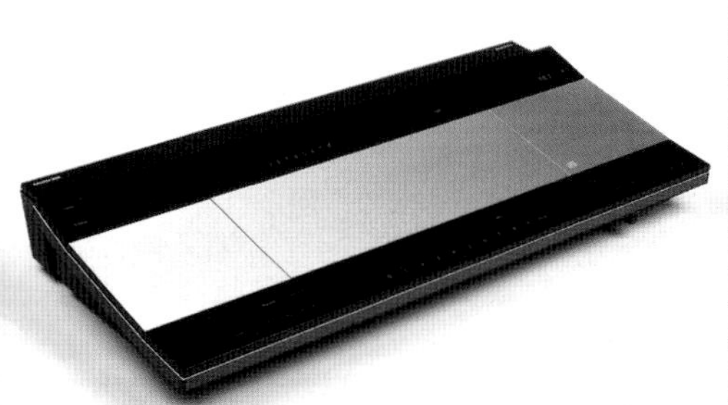

1979 introduction of Absolut Vodka

1980 **Electrolux** begins to buy up about 400 companies

1982 *Concrete Chair* by **Jonas Bohlin**; exhibition *Scandinavian Modern Design* in New York

1983 **Arabia** takes over **Rörstrand**, is taken over in turn by**Hackman** in 1990, as is **Iittala** in 1994

1985 Volvo station wagon *760*

1986 **Royal Copenhagen** takes over **Georg Jensen**; Film *Shadows in Paradise* by Aki Kaurismäki

1988 Exhibiton *Design for Independent Living* at MOMA;Introduction of European Design Prize, awarded, among others, to **Goof**, to **Kompan** in 1994, to **Fiskars** in1997

1989 Collapse of the Eastern block; economic crisis in Scandinavian countries

exclusive firms occupying a market niche through their disciplined design strategies is typical of Denmark. It could almost be called a Danish School, one that knows no recruitment problems. Already in the mid-60s Denmark had set up the ID Prize, thus creating an instrument for promoting and influencing native product design. By preference the prize was usually awarded to minimalist and functionalist design, which seemed so timeless and which had yet produced so many classics, from the watches by **Georg Jensen** to the door handles of the *d-line* by **Knud Holscher**. One of the early the winners of the ID Prize was **Stelton.** Even in the difficult decade of the seventies, that company managed to establish itself as an exclusive, upscale brand thanks to its crystal clear lexicon of forms and the close relationship between the company and its designers, in this case **Erik Magnussen.** This configuration is the secret of the company's success, and the same is true also for other firms, for **Fritz Hansen** and **Nilfisk** just as much as for **Scan View**, for example.

At the end of the 1980s the Museum of Modern Art again played the role of trendsetter. The exhibition *Design for Independent Living* presented for the first time a wider variety of public objects specifically designed for the disabled. Most of the exhibits came from Sweden, where the idea that the weaker, physically impaired members of society—the old, the sick, and the disabled—also have a right to have useful and beautiful

things. This sentiment grew out of the left-wing alternative culture, which made the welfare state possible. There, for example, basic research into the best designs of handles suitable for the disabled, was completely paid for with public funds. The designers of **Ergonomi,** the studio that initiated the developments in this direction, were the heirs of **Ellen Key** and her credo that the world can be made a better place through good design. When it became clear in the 1980s that the Scandinavian welfare model had reached its limits, the same realization also hit subsidized design.

The "made in Sweden" design for a minority was based on the application of the principles of ergonomics. The significance of ergonomics has increased considerably since the 1970s, not least of all because of the spectacular sales Scandinavian designs achieved. Among the most famous examples are **Fiskars** and Stokke; their products attained a degree of popularity that is surpassed probably only by that of the Coca-Cola bottle. Fiskars' scissors and Stokke's chairs are unmistakable icons of everyday life and for that reason are copied the world over. **Lego** and **Kompan** achieved the same success. There is hardly a child, at least not in the western hemisphere, who has not at some point come across their ergonomic toys. Here, Scandinavian design has become part of a globalized socialization experience. **Ergonomics,** that is, "the human factor," is also one of the most important selling points of the Swedish automobile industry.

"You should pay more attention to your profound Nordic mysticism. Allow more ambiguity in your designs."

Andrea Branzi

From left to right:

Plastic flatware *Hank* by Erik Magnussen, 1970s

Erik Magnussen

Jar opener for the disabled by Ergonomi, 1980

Scanner *Scanmate 11000* by Scan View, 1997

Chair *Wing* by Peter Opsvik for Stokke

Knud Holscher

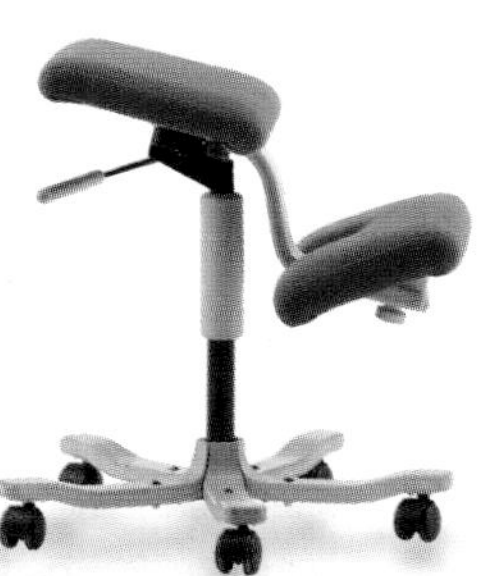

1991 Digital cell phone by **Ericsson**

1993 Chair *Trinidad* by **Nanna Ditzel; Valvomo** founded

1994 Founding of **Swecode;** easy chair BD1 by **Björn Dahlström**

1995 Finland and Sweden join the EU

1996 *Communicator* by Nokia; Copenhagen is cultural capital

1997 Royal Copenhagen takes over **Orrefors; Snowcrash** at the furniture fair in Milan; robot vacuum cleaner by Electrolux

1998 Stockholm is cultural capital; 100th birthday of **Alvar Aalto;** sofa *Flying Carpet* by **Ilkka Suppanen;** Kiasma Museum in Helsinki opened

1999 Study multimedia cellphone

2000 Helsinki is cultural capital

However, that industry now seems to have difficulty doing what it has often succeeded at in earlier days, namely, the creation of icons. Created with children in mind, pacifist, eco-friendly, and socially healthy—the correct and reliable, but also a little bit boring, image projected by Scandinavian design coincided roughly with that of Scandinavian politics.

The excited and exciting 1980s then saw the creation of precisely those "dangerous objects" Henningsen had called for. In Sweden Jonas Bohlin's and **Mats Theselius's** oblique concepts, mixed with art and philosophy, found in Källemo an inspired manufacturer. In Denmark the group **Octo** staged concept exhibitions against the prevailing one-dimensional doctrine. Nevertheless, the colorful flourishing of design remained largely a closed party and hardly noticed on the other side of the Skagerrak (Bohlin's concrete design is still not included in Vitra's famous chair collection). **Stefan Lindfors,** Finland's most prominent design rebel, was the first to turn his back on the Scandinavian self-absorption and gad about in the global village.

By the early 1990s the situation in world politics had changed completely; technology was advancing at breakneck speed, and all Scandinavian countries were in the grip of a deep economic crisis. Finland's unemployment rate rose to over twenty percent and then decreased by half in the second half of the decade. The figures in the other Scandinavian countries were similar, Norway

being the only exception because it lived on its oil reserves. But this widespread crisis did not keep the unexpected from happening. Young Swedish designers rallying around the marketing label **Swecode**—and later also **Snowcrash** from Finland—presented their products at the large fairs in Milan and Cologne, on their own steam and without asking the establishment's permission. The international design press was enthusiastic in its response as it had been in the days of Wirkkala.

That this is more than just a flash in the pan is evidenced by the widespread seething in the design industry and the formation of subversive design groups in many places, groups with names like **Panic, Raket,** or **Selle 16.** And it is further confirmed by shooting stars such as **Claesson, Koivisto, Rune,** and **Valvomo,** the second generation of young rebels. As true children of the internet, they have already created an international network as well as the Swecode Project, whose stylistic proximity to the new British design scene is obvious. These designers reveal a new purism, making full and intelligent—and sometimes ironic—use of the wealth of forms and virtues Scandinavian design history offers. These great-great-grandchildren of Carl Larsson and Alvar Aalto tend toward a cool, laconic modernity with a soft breeze of eroticism breathing through it. What remains is the still unsatisfied longing for the right life, the simple life, a longing that has accompanied us since the beginning of this century.

"Yes, less is still more"
Mårten Claesson

From left to right:

Mats Theselius

Dutch oven by Björn Dahlström from the series *Tools* for Hackman, 1998

Computer workstation *Netsurfer* by Valvomo, 1995

Rug with cross by Asplund, 1996

Chair for Gorbachev by Stefan Lindfors, 1989

Stefan Lindfors

Carafe by Ingegerd Raman for Skruf, 1993

Chair, Market, and Identity:

Contemporary Danish Design

Crafts and design are a living element of the Danish cultural heritage and the Danish identity. This is especially true for the Danish furniture classics of the 1950s and 60s, not least because of the great international attention they have received. This fact is also reflected in the language. Even in Denmark we speak of "Danish design." Although many products of "Danish design"—such as the exclusive furniture by Hans J. Wegner, Poul Kjaerholm, and Finn Juhl—were of interest only to those with money to spend, "Danish design" has a democratic appearance. It was accompanied by mass production of both furniture and objects of utilitarian art that were of similar quality but were much more affordable. Danish design thus became the credo of the Danish welfare state: prosperity for all also meant everyday articles of good quality and at prices everyone could afford.

It is not by accident that furniture above all has become the trademark for Danish design. The furniture conceived by Danish designers is clearly different from other Scandinavian furniture—perhaps due to a tradition of collaboration among artists, designers, and cabinetmakers that goes back to the eighteenth century. In the nineteenth century cabinetmakers were usually trained at the royal Danish art academy in Copenhagen. Since then the legacy of classicism is the foundation of Danish furniture art. However, the canonization of a period and its works can lead to stagnation, and thus it was not until the 1980s postmodern tour de force in architecture and design that a fresh breeze again blew through traditional Danish design, which was by then a bit stuffy and outmoded. In that decade numerous experiments which incorporated elements of historic styles released new energies, thus serving as the starting point for many young talents who have now, at the end of the 1990s, come onto the Danish design scene. Well-known designers are among most influential forces in this new beginning. For the earlier generations these are, among others, Nanna Ditzel and Verner Panton.

The central theme in Danish design is still furniture, or rather the chair—the greatest challenge for a designer. While many furniture manufacturers in the past relied on craftspeople and artisans, now only a few firms actively work together with designers to continue the tradition of producing new, experimental furniture of high quality. As the latest examples confirm, thanks to an ever increasing internationalization more and more Danish designers receive commissions from other countries, for example from Germany,

Top: Chair *701* by Hans J. Wegner for PP Mobler, 1975; bottom: wire easy chair by Mathias Bengtsson (Panic design), 1996.

England, and Italy. Recently, groups of young designers with names such as Octo, Panic, and Komplot, have drawn attention at national and international exhibitions that focus on form and concept rather than functionality.

In Denmark, during the last ten years there has been an increase in the use of both design and designers in industry. New figures show, however, that only thirty percent of Danish furniture manufacturers consult outside designers in developing new products. Because Denmark has no natural reserves for raw materials, it has concentrated on the export of finished products.

Lately, however, there has been a growing understanding of the necessity to add value to products by using designers. By now young designers' prospects for employment in industry are improving. There are at present about two thousand organized graphic designers, product designers, and artisans as well as interior designers and furniture designers in Denmark, and every year an additional three hundred complete their training.

In recent years the Danish government and its department of commerce have made every effort to induce companies to use the possibilities of design in all conceivable areas: from graphic communication to product development all the way to marketing. According to the government's 1998 plan for a new design policy, annual overall outline budgets are to be approved for financing of new initiatives, especially in the area of research and development, information and consulting, consideration of design in government agency purchasing, and financing of products with a design focus. Thanks to these initiatives design will come to play an essential role in Denmark's economic policy in the coming years.

Between the industrial design on one hand and art on the other are the artisans. They have gone through a phase in which many have turned their backs on traditional forms and function and are instead expressing themselves through paintings and sculptures. The outstanding reputation of art and the accompanying higher prestige and better pay for artists as seen in the 1970s and 80s have no doubt contributed to this, as has the widespread frustration over the limited opportunities to sell craft products intended for everyday use—opportunities that were cut back even further by cheap imports. Now, at the end of the twentieth century, a counter-movement has established itself, a kind of neo-realism in which the artisan, based on the experiences and activities of his daily life, creates everyday articles of great simplicity and sensitivity from classic materials, for example, glass, ceramics, and textiles. A series of everyday objects developed by four artisans for Royal Scandinavia exemplifies this new movement. In the exhibition catalog for a show of their works the group formulated its goals as follows: "It was our goal to show objects whose purpose was neither practical, nor time-saving, neither affordable nor expensive. Instead, these objects are intended to convey the pleasure in thinking about their significance and content and to make manifest through all this the material." In this tension between design, craft, and architecture lies great opportunities for the continued strong development of Danish design.

Bodil Busk Laursen
Director of the Danske Kunstindustrimuseum, Copenhagen

Between Aalto and Nokia

Contemporary Finnish Design

Finnish design at the end of the millennium is characterized by internationalization and a wide variety of forms. As a result of the recession in the early 1990s, development and launching of new products decreased. By now the situation has changed again, and companies are again investing in product development, and calling increasingly on designers. Internationalization occurs in two ways, when Finnish designers work with foreign companies and when Finnish manufacturers use foreign designers. Young designers benefit from the opportunity to work directly with industrial clients. All in all, Finnish design is increasingly moving from its peripheral position toward the center of Europe.

National and regional characteristics will become even more significant, particularly in view of the growing international competition, for when products are technologically and functionally almost identical, differentiation occurs above all through their design. In this connection the unique national characteristics of products can become a key factor. Among the traditional strengths of Finnish design are its austere, functional lines that are enhanced by the economic use of materials. Practical usefulness and an aesthetic free of fashion trends as well as a natural beauty inherent in the products—these are the main features of the Finnish design legacy. There are numerous examples of design products created in this spirit that were at first considered avant-garde but later rose to the status of design classics and continued to be produced for decades thanks to their huge popularity. Probably the best known example is the vase Savoy by Alvar Aalto, which has been in production for more than sixty years.

Despite the successes of the past there is an urgent need for innovation. A phenomenon typical of the 1990s is the large number of designers who have early on in their career achieved a certain renown. A successful presentation at the international furniture fair in Milan—such as the one of the Snowcrash design team in 1997—signals a trend offering a unique lifestyle, and a characteristic philosophy and concepts. At the same time, the efforts to gain international attention also serve to elicit a response at home.

One of the disciplines with high growth rates is industrial design. The pillars of the Finnish economy—the timber and metal industries and the dynamic telecommunications

Vase *Kantarelli* by Tapio Wirkkala for Iittala, 1946; Ski poles by Creadesign for Exel, 1994

exel
exel

sector—have a great demand for design services. Finnish products are popular all over the world—and not only forest and paper machinery but also cell phones and (winter) sports equipment. Nokia, Valmet, and Polar Electro exemplify the successful use of design in combination with advanced technology.

In Finland as everywhere else in the international scene, one of the leading motifs of the late 1990s is Nordic modernism, characterized by pure lines and practical usefulness. Modernist trends are still alive and well and even give rise to new classics, such as Heikki Orvola's vase *Carambola* of 1996 with its plain and yet expressive style.

Simplicity and closeness to nature are among the contemporary motifs that will continue to grow in significance. The theme of nature is a lasting and increasingly important one; in particular, it is characteristic of the crafts. An example of this is Maisa Turunen-Wiklund's 1998 wrap jewelry created from threads in which simplicity is combined with a sensitive observation of nature.

Other current characteristics of design are lightness and translucency. Lightness in particular is expressed in the choice of structures and materials: thin textiles, paper, and translucent plastics give form to the striving for "weightlessness." The room dividers designed by Ritva Puotila in 1997 are transparent—truly an expression of the spirit of our time. With the use of simple paper cord, a sophisticated and timeless aesthetic creation was produced.

The most austere form of Nordic modernism is minimalism, which reduces structure and material to the absolute minimum. The purist plainness is expressed in the traditional crafts (furniture, ceramics, glass) as well as in the manufacturing of individual pieces or small lot sizes. The chair *The Hard A* designed in 1996 by Jouko Järvisalo exemplifies this principle of utmost economy. In design, as in other sectors of industry, high technology plays an ever more important role. The information society requires constant actualization of technological possibilities, the competition is merciless, and products quickly become obsolete. Product development demands a great deal, and design facilitates the effective use of technology. The cell phones by Nokia, the second largest manufacturer of mobile telephones in the world, serve as a clear illustration of this development.

Another design theme of the late 1990s is the revival of the 1960s. Pop has its comeback in strong colors, soft shapes, and a return to lifestyles emphasizing the community. Other rediscovered elements from the 1960s are the modular structures and the mix-and-match possibilities they offer. For example, in the pruning shears *Clippers* by Fiskars, modern technology and the colorful pop world merge successfully.

What then is the emerging trend? The changing and increasingly international lifestyle also leads to changes in the use and content of products. Fickleness and transience are the predominant characteristics of the modern world, and products such as Stefan Lindfors's *EgO* coffee cups take this new lifestyle into account. In spite of all internationalization, the elite of contemporary Finnish design stand firmly by the continuity of Finnish tradition—the latest example: Snowcrasher Ilkka Suppanen took his cue for his divan *Flying Carpet* from the economical and soft lines of Alvar Aalto.

Anne Stenros
Director of the Design Forum Finland, Helsinki

Antorage in Chaotic World:
Contemporary Norwegian Design

Norway has always been the junior partner in the Scandinavian design club, and there are probably several explanations for this. Our design environment was smaller, our mass production less developed, less aggressive, and moreover it shied away from experiments. We have created no core areas that could serve as a matrix for a typically Norwegian school of design. In contrast to Denmark's furniture production in birch and teak, Sweden's glass industry, and Finland's architecture, we have lacked a focus. In addition, we have neither had sufficient resources to conduct international marketing campaigns nor sufficient critics proficient in foreign languages who could have presented our strengths to foreign observers. The production of consumer goods played only a minor role in Norway's impressive economic and technological development in recent decades. Norway's current position in modern technology and process logistics is based on its petrochemical industry. Apparently nobody else is our equal when it comes to blowing up tunnels or building bridges. This one-sided orientation, however, has left other resources and creativity unused instead of being employed with a view to the strong international influence our designers had in the 1950s: the manufacturing of products for house and home.

In the twentieth century Norwegian design grew out of a mutual fertilization of craft-oriented studio production and industrial production in small lot sizes. Designers have remained conscious of the folklorist tradition, and that has influenced the form and choice of materials and techniques. There was hardly a difference between the artist designing a piece of furniture and the people manufacturing its components and assembling them. As a result furniture design had an inner strength and purity.

These connections to folklore and applied art and their uneasy alliance with industrial methods of production have perhaps offered us a starting point for the creation of a characteristic national lexicon of design. In a world that is evidently focused on the mass production of trivialities—with design and quality of materials replaced by surplus, semi-finished items, and imitations—the Norwegian tradition of design will be able to offer a combination of innovative design and genuineness of materials.

It is still Norwegian design's special strength to be able to pour egalitarian and democratic ideals into forms suitable for production. Thus its unique characteristic is the combination of a design tradition with social ideals: it offers genuine materials, skilled

Besteck *Chako* von Tias Eckhoff für Norsk Stålpress, 1984; Strickjacke *Rosa heimafrå* von Ellinor Flor, 1984

craftsmanship, simplicity of details, a steady hand in the design, ecological awareness, and functional clarity; it meets the demands of ergonomics and is obviously user-friendly. This list of advantages may not yet grant Norwegian designers admission into the international design heaven, but it can serve as a valuable anchorage in a chaotic world.

The strength of contemporary Norwegian design lies—even more so than in the 1950s and 1960s—in its willingness to break new ground. The old paths lead us to what is well known and familiar: one of them takes us to the elitist design world filled with imaginative fashions, phenomenal innovations, and functional deficits; the other path ends at a pile of mass-produced, disposable products. The middle ground between these two extremes raises ethical problems that must be taken seriously. Here ecological awareness calls designers to a new simplicity, a willingness to take responsibility in the context of production, and a renewed focus on economic usefulness and purity of the materials. The great challenge Norwegian design currently faces is to find an impressive technological and artistic solution that meets the requirements of this incontrovertible conviction. To meet this challenge, young Norwegian designers are developing an invigorating, fresh approach based on principles that will also increasingly apply in the world beyond our borders.

Peter Butenschon
Direktor of Norsk Form, Oslo

The Second Phase of Modern Design

Contemporary Swedish Design

Swedish design runs like a reliable wool thread through the history of design. In the mire of design trends it has always stood firm. It is appreciated all over the world because of its functionality and its safety—less so because of its beauty, splendor, or glamour. With qualities such as honesty and reason it has not been possible to create a spectacular and fashionable presence in the arena of international design. Swedish design products are manufactured with great care from the best raw materials, which has earned them a reputation for high quality. Moreover the pure materials, often untreated and in their natural colors, have lent Swedish design an aura of ecological awareness. (A reputation that is not entirely deserved. The Swedish environmental protection regulations are not as strict as, for example, the German ones.)

And then all of a sudden "Swedish" becomes the new catchword for international designers after "Provençale" or "Country" have become worn out, and this time "Swedish" does not refer to ball bearings, Volvo, or sex massages. No—ever since international home decor magazines printed emotional descriptions of eighteenth- and nineteenth-century interiors of Swedish castles, the "Gustavian" style, the style of Swedish King Gustav III, has experienced a revival. People everywhere lounge on wooden chairs dyed with linseed oil in rustic Louis XVI-style with seats in pale-green striped cotton, and chic apartments in Manhattan or Paris must contain at least one kitchen bench painted gray with checkered, round cushions on the armrests.

The international voice of the Swedish home, Ikea, joined this trend with a whole series of copies approved by the Swedish Office for Antiquities. At Ikea one can buy a complete interior decor in the style of the eighteenth century—from flatware all the way to a four-poster bed with canopy—at affordable prices. And then the artist couple Carl and Karen Larsson made a comeback. Their turn-of-the-century house in Sundborn was dismantled and taken to London, where it was exhibited with great success in the Victoria and Albert Museum. Around the world the home decor press copies Carl Larsson's edgings and the embroidered tablecloths of Karin Larsson with great enthusiasm. This attention to all things Swedish is very pleasant, of course. However, it is mostly a focus on styling and thus constantly needs new props to keep it alive. As it turned out, this Swedish trend was only a warm-up exercise; with its collection PS Ikea launched a contemporary continuation of all this "Swedishness." At about the same time, Swecode, a group of young manufacturers and designers, presented exactly this kind of design on the international scene. Then, in 1998, Svensk Form and a consortium of log house manufacturers demonstrated what a modern log cabin could look like. The prototype *Vistet*, erected beside the Nordic Museum, consisted of eight-inch logs and was furnished by a number of young designers. The home of the future can be a solid log cabin, which is easy to assemble and move.

This example is indicative of the "second Swedish modernism" Andrea Branzi had noted already in 1989. It is the legacy of both Sweden's poverty during the eighteenth and nineteenth centuries, which reduced the gilded continental building style to an ochre-yellow, rural style, and of the prosperity of the twentieth century, whose catchwords were planning, social equality, and affordability. The new generation of Swedish designers obediently followed their tradition, offering function, cunning, and clarity in their designs. When backed by big companies, such as Ikea, designers can also afford a touch of disarming ingenuousness. The *PS* collection is like a bright dream of life in modernist Elysian fields. This dream will never again become reality. When the world presents itself at the Expo 2000 in Hanover, it will be a completely different one than that celebrated in 1900 in Paris. Back then the affluence of industrial society was just beginning; today most people predict a future of poverty and isolation for themselves.

Thus it is no accident that young designers want to revive that earlier, beautiful vision. I see their designs as symptoms of those changes all of our culture has to undergo, and I believe that the Swedish way to deal with design has a good chance to succeed in the midst of these changes. Strictly functional, economical in its use of material and in production, and supported by a distribution geared toward the most effective use of resources, it is in a good position to become very important. Swedish reason and cunning, Swedish proportions and awareness will become exports during the restoration of the decaying consumer society. That functional gray wool thread, its warmth, reliability, durability will be more in demand than ever before. This is not to say that this Swedish wool thread could not also benefit from a little splendor and glamour

Ulf Beckman

Editor-in-Chief *Form*, Stockholm

Cell phone *GSM* by King-Miranda for Ericsson, 1994; coatrack *Quasimodo* by Jonas Lindvall, 1995

ERICSSON
PWR SERV
CLR
1
ABC
2
DEF
3
GHI
4
JKL
5
MNO
6
PQR
7
STU
8
VW
9
XYZ
0
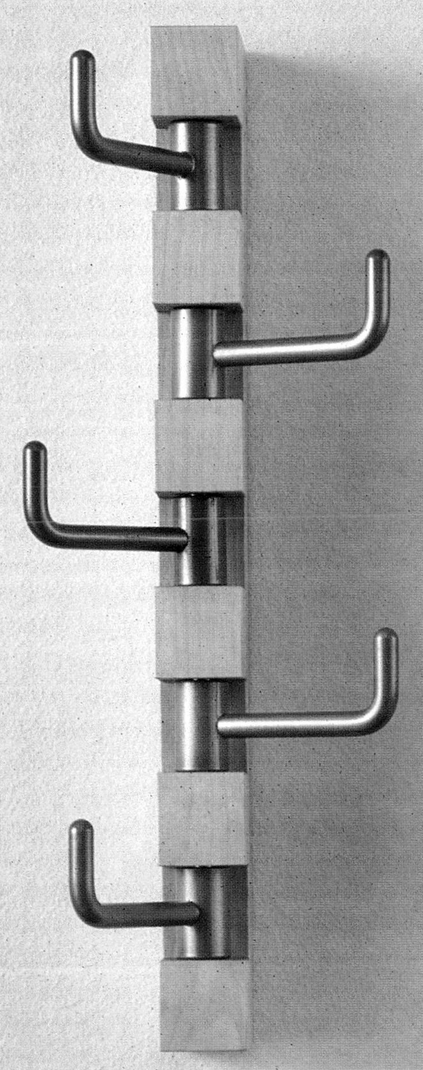

Medicine cabinet by Thomas Eriksson for Cappellini

Page 97

Wire-cone easy chair by Verner Panton for Plus-linje

Directory

From Aalto to Zero

Alvar AALTO

Architect, Furniture Designer, and Glass Designer / Finland

1898 Born in Kuortane near Jyväskylä

1921 Architecture diploma

1923 Architect in Jyväskylä, later in Turku (1927) and Helsinki (1933)

1924 Marries the architect Aino Marsio (d. 1949)

1927 Wood experiments; library in Viipuri (until 1935)

1928 Congrés International d'Architecture Moderne (CIAM)

1929 Hospital Paimio (until 1933)

1932 Furniture marketed through Wohnbedarf AG, Zurich

1933 Exhibition in the Fortnum & Mason department store in London; *V. Triennial*, Milan

1934 Patent for L-shaped legs (1935 for the first cantilever wooden chair)

1935 Founding of **Artek**

1937 Finnish pavilion for the Paris World's Fair

1938 Exhibition at the MOMA, New York

Page 99

Cantilever chair, 1932

In 1932 a sofa with a tubular steel frame came on the market, and soon became known in Europe as the "Aalto Sofa." One of the first flexible pieces of furniture, it had a backrest that could be tilted at various angles. Lowering it into the horizontal position turned the sofa into a bed. This folding sofa—which had only limited success at the cash register because the mechanism did not always work—was designed by Alvar Aalto, one of this century's most innovative architects and designers. On the occasion of his 100th birthday in 1998, no less than a dozen exhibitions presented his very voluminous work. In almost all his projects, among them universities, hospitals, concert halls, town halls, and whole cityscapes, he had everything under his control, from the overall plan all the way down to the doorknobs. Many of his design objects thus were created as byproducts of extensive building projects.

Beginning in the mid-1920s, he worked closely with his wife, the architect **Aino Aalto;** often their individual contributions to a design are hard to tell apart. Though at first an adherent of Nordic classicism, Aalto soon came into contact with the new radical trends from Central Europe. He became friends with the Bauhaus artist László Moholy-Nagy and attended the CIAM-Conference of progressive architects in Frankfurt, Germany. This forum for social utopias supported the young humanist in his ideas, which met with only a very lukewarm response back home. In 1927 Alvar Aalto began to experiment with glued and bent wood, inspired by Thonet furniture and the technique of a company in Estland that manufactured, among other things, plywood seats for streetcars. When Aalto was awarded the contract for a hospital in Paimio in 1929, he used this technique for a series of chairs. The hospital, designed along daring functionalist lines, became a laboratory for the design genius. In his furniture designs Aalto at first went

in for tubular steel, which was back then the quintessence of modern style, as for example in the easy chair *40.* But already for the subsequent model *41*, also called *Paimio* (illustration page 12), he decided on a pure solution in wood, exploring the potential of the material here for the first time to its limits. This "first soft wooden chair," conceptually close to Marcel Breuer's 1925 easy chair *Wassily*, is Aalto's masterpiece, his first true innovation as a furniture designer. The chair was revolutionary above all because it combined a runner-like frame and an S-shaped, springy seat of bent plywood. These days no design museum wants to be without the *Paimio* easy chair, which stands out both because of its seating comfort and its strong sculptural effect.

Aalto's stroke of genius not only rehabilitated the old-fashioned material wood but also revealed it as a "form-inspiring and profoundly humane material." Moreover, designing in wood also made sense economically, especially as birch, Aalto's preferred material, is omnipresent in Finland. It was certainly no accident that he developed this successful design as a "furniture style for the sick." The Aaltos considered tubular steel "too hard" for the patients, both physically as well as psychologically. Instead, they created a soft design based on the needs and expectations of the user. In the process the perfectionist designer also paid attention to seemingly minor matters, such as clever door handles on which the nurses' aprons would not get caught. The easy chair *42,* the first cantilever chair in wood and

1939 Finnish pavilion for World's Fair in New York

1946 Teaches at the Massachusetts Institute of Technology (until 1948)

1952 Marries the architect Elissa Mäkiniemi (d. 1994)

1963 President of the Finnish Academy

1964 Technical University in Helsinki built

1976 Died in Helsinki

1988 Opera house in Essen completed

1998 5th exhibition at the MOMA, New York

Stool *54*, 1937

Lecture hall of the Viipuri library with stool *60*, 1935

Aalto's response to Ludwig Mies van der Rohe, created a sensation. Its seat hangs between C-shaped frames of laminated birch that appear very slim and lightweight because they support hardly any weight at all—easily one of Aalto's most elegant seat designs. It was followed by the cantilever lounge *43,* whose exciting wavy silhouette and precarious equilibrium were clear signs that the designer had taken his material to its limits, and finally by the lounge **406,** a commercially successful variation of the same principle.

In the very productive years between 1929 and 1936 Alvar Aalto designed not only the by now world-famous *Paimio* furniture but also completed another large project, the library in Viipuri, now in Russia. He was not the only one who considered the stool 60, intended for the lecture hall, one of his most significant contributions to furniture design. The three L-shaped legs, essential details, are a stunningly simple and stable solution to the age-old dilemma of the precarious connection between vertical legs and horizontal seat. Aalto later expanded this approach with Y-shaped legs as well as with fan-shaped legs, reminiscent of medieval fan vaulting; both were more costly solutions than his first one. Pliable wood was the ideal material for the plant shapes Aalto preferred, the irregular "Aalto-lines" that became his trademark because he repeated them in all kinds of materials: in the outer walls of a civic center as well as in the curved glass of a vase. The amoeba-like, wavy lines for which the art connoisseur Aalto took his cue from avant-garde artists like the sculptor Hans Arp symbolized the turn to a less linear and more humane, softened functionalism "made in Scandinavia." The oversize wall of the Finnish pavilion at the 1939 New York World's Fair was faced with timber and caused quite a stir—and brought the international breakthrough for Aalto. It provided a

Umbrella Stand *115* for Artek

public symbol for the new style and in its way was the precursor for the later kidney-shaped tables.

Always aware of the necessity for economy and standardization, Aalto saw the endless possibilities organic shapes offered. They were a chance to avoid triviality. In his words: "The world's best standardization committee is nature itself, but in nature standardization occurs mostly in the smallest unit, the cell. The results are millions of flexible combinations in which no stereotype can be found." Glass, a liquid medium that can take on any conceivable shape, fit in very well with Aalto's use of organic shapes. Unlike his furniture, his glass objects were created almost exclusively for various competitions in which both Aaltos participated frequently. In addition to the famous vase Savoy (its original name was "Lederhosen of an Eskimo Woman"), better known in Finland than the national coat of arms, he designed such original and useful objects as decanters and cocktail plates in various versions.

Products

1929 Stacking chair in solid and laminated birch

1931 Easy chair *40*, tubular steel and bent plywood; easy chair *41* (also called *Paimio*)

1932 Easy chair *42*, first cantilever chair in wood; glasses *Bölgeblick* by Aino Aalto (now Aino Aalto for **Iittala**)

1933 Vase *Flower from Riihimäkr*, stool *60* with L-shaped legs

1935 Chair *65* with L-shaped legs

1936 Vase *Aalto-Flower*, Lounge *43*, 1936

Easy chair *400* for Artek, 1936

Page 103

Vase Savoy, 1936

Lounge *43*, 1936

1936 Vase *Savoy* (also called *Aalto*); lounge *43*; easy chair *400*; serving trolley *900*

1938 Easy chair *406* (final version in 1947)

1947 Chair *612* with Y-shaped legs

1954 Stool X *600* with fan-shaped legs; Ceiling light *331*

1956 Floor lamp *810*

An integral part of the Aalto's architecture is his artificial lighting, designed to imitate natural daylight as perfectly as possible. Though he designed a large number of lamps, only a few of them went into production. Alvar Aalto, one of the most important architects of the modern age and the godfather of Finnish design, was the first Scandinavian designer to achieve international fame, recognition that paved the way for the "Nordic" boom of the 1950s.

Ceiling light *331*

Floor lamp *A 805* for Artek

Eero AARNIO

Furniture designer / Finnland

"Design a plastic chair" was the task **Asko,** Finland's greatest furniture house, gave Eero Aarnio in the early 1960s. Back then Asko was better known for its extensive forest estates than for its furniture, but that was to change. What Aarnio accomplished during his 1962 summer vacation, with the use of plenty of newsprint and paste from the drugstore, was a seat of a totally new generation. It anticipated by several years similarly innovative concepts, like the *Panton* chair or the inflatable easy chair *Blow* by Gionatan De Pas. *Ball,* a fiberglass ball cut open in the front and padded on the inside, rests on an iron base (illustration page 22). With a diameter of about 40 inches, it looked imposing but also provided those sitting in it with an unusual experience. They practically disappeared into the chair as though into a cave and could dangle their legs as well as their souls. The ball-shaped easy chair was nothing less than a mini-environment, a resting place shielded from the outside world. Many an owner who did not want to entirely give up contact with

1932 Born in Helsinki

1954 Studied design in Helsinki (until 1957)

1962 Designer in Helsinki

1968 Booth for **Asko** at the Cologne furniture fair

1969 Design prize of the American Institute of Interior Design (A.I.D.)

1991 Participated in the exhibition *Masters of Modern Design*, New York

1997 Third reedition of his "classics"

Easy chair *Pastilli*, 1967

Products

1961 Wicker chair *Jattujakkare*

1963 Easy chair *Ball* made of polyester reinforced with fiberglass (also called *Thunderball, Bomb,* or *Globe*)

1966 Easy chair *VSOP*

1967 Easy chair *Pastilli;* shelving system *Disco*

1968 Seating furniture *Serpentine;* easy chair *Gyro;* seating furniture *Bubble*

1971 Easy chair *Tomato*

1972 Stacking chair *U-023* made of polypropylene

1973 Easy chair *Pony*

1979 Easy chair *Avec*

1981 Seating system *Kimara*

1991 Table *Screw*

1993 Easy chair and table *Dolphin*

1998 Easy chair *Formular* (prototype)

the outside world installed stereo loudspeakers in the chair or, as did Aarnio, a telephone, thus underscoring the seat's resemblance to a space capsule. The strange object was a sensation at the Cologne furniture fair in 1966. Orders poured in from all over the world, and the New York Times devoted an article to the chair. This worldwide response catapulted the young designer, who had just set up on his own in Helsinki, into big business. Aarnio followed this initial success with a series of plastic furniture: home décor sculptures with pithy names such as Pastilli, Bubble, and Tomato. The red easy chair Tomato marked Aarnio's turn to pop design, making him a kind of commercial Claes Oldenburg for the living room. Another object, also oversized, is the table Screw designed in the 1990s.

Eero Aarnio's early designs are veritable focus points in which the experimental trends of the 1960s meet, from the use of shocking colors, the easy and unconcerned handling of plastics, and the dissolution of hitherto valid design conventions. For example, the designs exhibit a consistent preference of organic forms for which plastics were especially suited. In Aarnio's chair designs this nexus of different trends ultimately led to the fusion of seat, frame, and legs into a unity. In addition, plastic furniture was perfect for the new trend toward a flexible decor and lifestyle: it could be used outdoors as well as indoors, and it practically called for an unorthodox sitting posture. A critic praised the easy chair *Pastilli* as "comfortable to sit in. You can bounce on it, you can change your position without getting up, and you do not have to worry about damaging your rugs or other floor covering." *Pastilli*, a modern variation of the rocking chair, looks like a hard candy into which a thumbprint has been pressed. It is another one of Aarnio's conceptual masterpieces and his second invention, at an early stage in his career, of a new type of furniture. At the 1968

Cologne furniture fair (where the Dane Verner Panton also staged a spectacular event in plastics) Aarnio built an installation for the Asko booth consisting of a 50-foot-long zigzag path of *Pastilli* easy chairs. Even though Aarnio's polished, industrial style was tantamount to an attack on the successful Scandinavian design of the 1950s, he also managed to continue that tradition in his rounded shapes, "a natural use of a non-natural substance," so to speak. Overnight Aarnio's furniture became an icon of the new consumer culture. Soon no film director wanted to do without these props of the future space age.

However, the 1973 oil crisis made it clear that the future would probably not be made completely of polyester. The production of Ball was halted in 1979 (and for a brief time restarted in 1984). As prior to 1962, Aarnio turned to natural materials without losing his pioneering spirit. In the early 1980s he was one of the first to design furniture on screen. Although Ball and Pastilli have been among the standard items at many design retrospectives, they were not included as classics but as curios, like the cast-off bell-bottoms dating from the same era. It is only since the nineties' recycling of the 1960s as a lifestyle that Eero Aarnio has experienced a comeback. Now his early designs are in production again together with new plastic furniture designed since then.

From left to right:

Easy chair, 1967

Table *Parable*

Chair (prototype), 1998

Easy chair *Form,* 1998

Pages 108/109

Tables *Dolphin,* 1993

Table *Screw* for Adelta, 1991

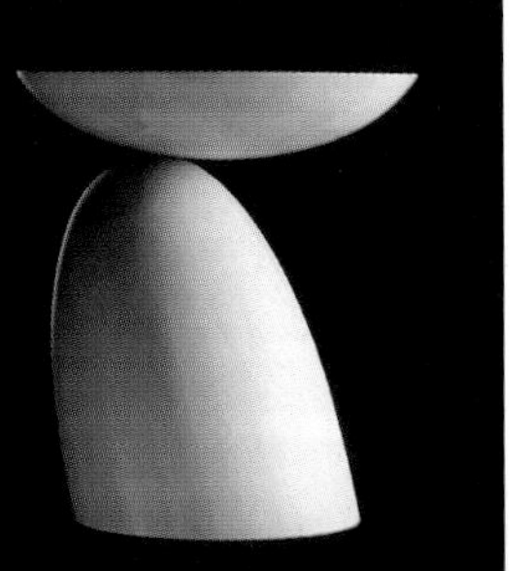

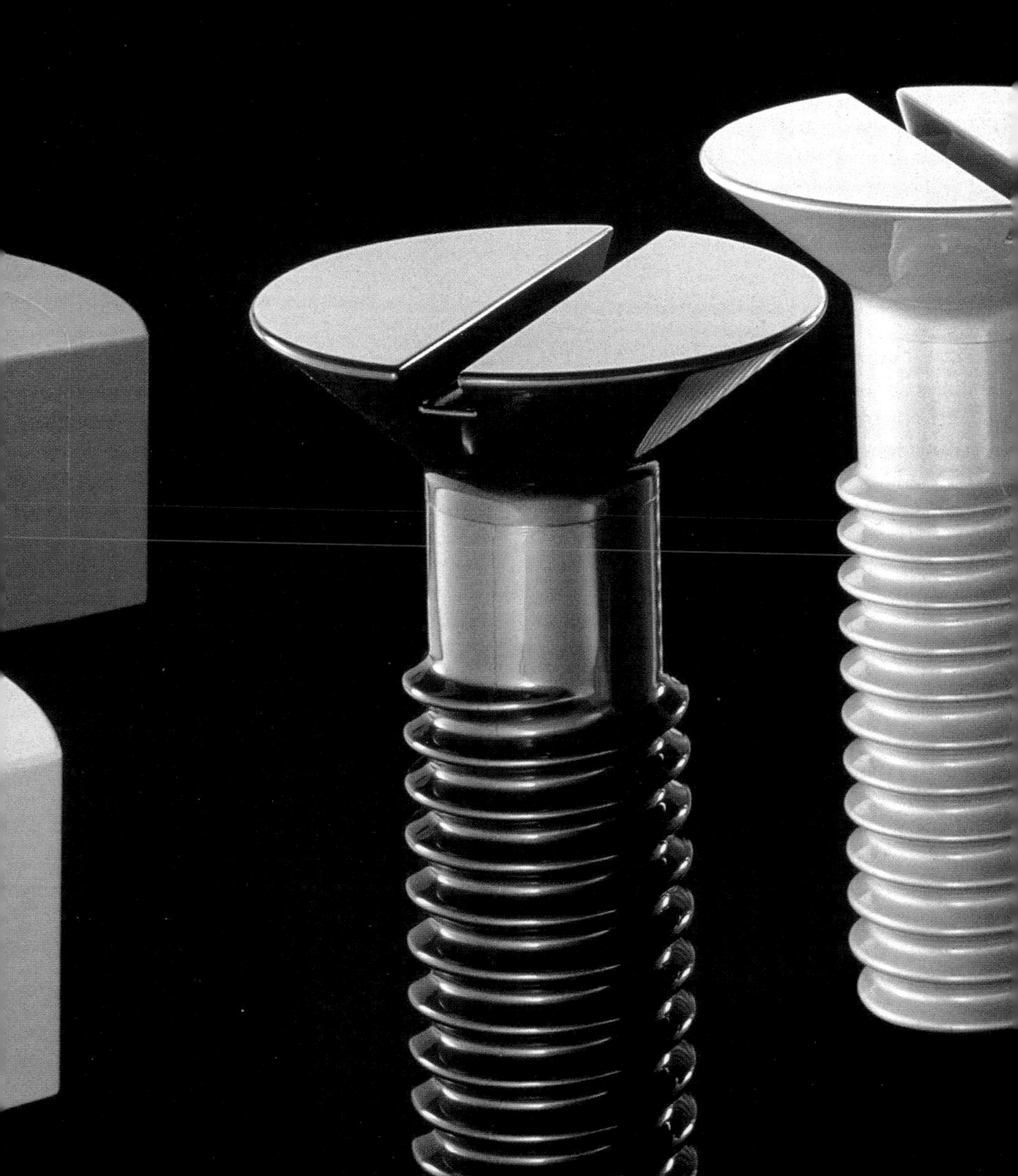

A&E DESIGN

Studio for Product design / Sweden

A & E Design AB, Stockholm

1968 Founded in Stockholm by **Tom Ahlström** and **Hans Ehrich** (since then twelve times recipient of prize for Outstanding Swedish Design)

1982 Interdesign founded

1987 Designer of the year

1998 Anniversary exhibition

A & E achieved its commercial breakthrough with an everyday object that had always been made of wood—a dishwashing brush. A&E used plastic. The practical material was perfect for A & E's clear lines and shapes and strong colors. Black, white, and fire-engine red are still the company's signature colors. **Hans Ehrich**, a French car enthusiast and wearer of self-designed, made-to-order suits, is the grand master of Swedish product design. In the late 1960s he opened a design studio with his partner **Tom Ahlström,** just when Scandinavia's classical design seemed to be at its end, when protest and criticism of capitalism appeared to have reached their zenith, and many design students deserted into the putative freedom of crafts.

A & E represented the counter-model to this situation. Polished models from the in-house workshop and detailed documentation on product ergonomics became the hallmark of the two design perfectionists. Like only a few of their Swedish colleagues, these two also made a name for themselves on the

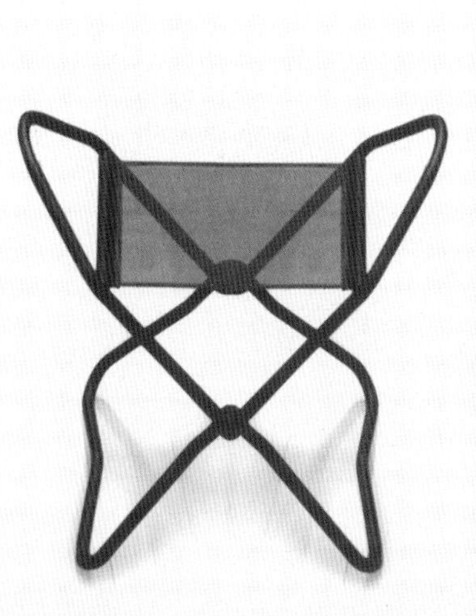

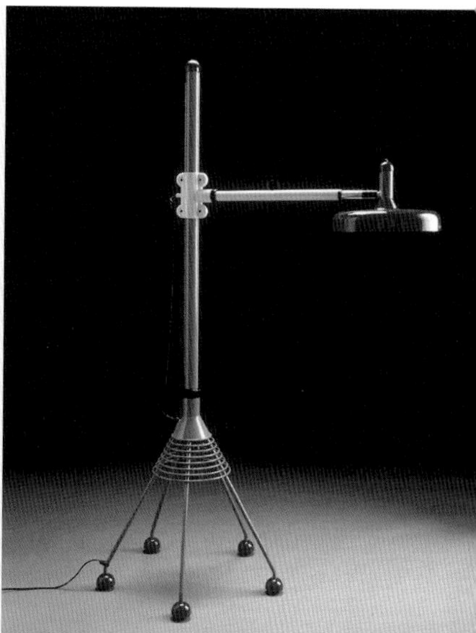

international scene. As declared functionalists, they prohibited any kind of decoration and worked strictly "geometrically"—in stark contrast to the organic aesthetics of their colleagues. The two inseparable artists designed a huge number of inconspicuous but effective everyday things, items most consumers pick up at one time or another, for example, milk bottles and toothbrushes. Among other useful devices, they also designed a tear-off roll for numbers, which has proven as handy at the employment office as at the supermarket cheese counter.

From the beginning they focused on designing aids for the frail and infirm. Prizes were heaped upon A&E, among others the prize for Outstanding Swedish Design (a dozen times). A showpiece from their latest production is the folding stool *Stockholm*, a mobile piece of furniture for all occasions. Originally intended for the national museum, it is now a portable seat for stressed-out art lovers all over the world. It is also available in fire-engine red, of course.

Products

1970 Plastic chair *Bam Bam*
1974 Dispenser *Turn-O-Matic*
1975 Dishwashing brush *Jordan*
1983 Floor lamp *Stella Polaris*
1995 Folding stool *Stockholm*
1998 Bath board *Fresh*

From left to right:

Folding Stool *Stockholm II*, 1995

Floor lamp *Stella Polaris*

Dishwashing brush *Jordan 1230*

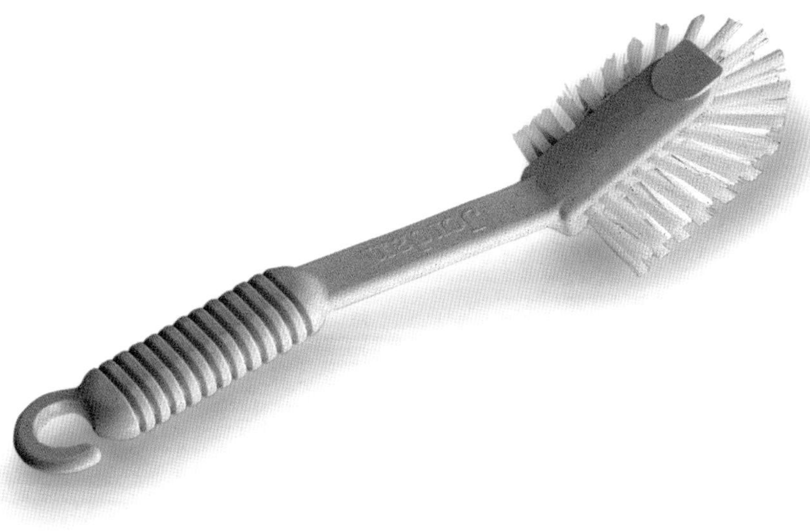

ABSOLUT

Alcohol Manufacturer / Sweden

V&S Vin & Spirits AB, Stockholm

1906 Distillery founded in Åhus

1922 Alcohol monopoly (V&S)

1957 V&S exports Explorer Vodka, bottle design by **Sigvard Bernadotte**

1979 Subsidiary Absolut Company introduces Absolute Pure Vodka, bottle design by **Hans Brindfors** (after a lawsuit in the United States it is renamed Absolut Vodka)

1980 Advertising slogan *Absolut Perfection*

1985 Art campaign, later also fashion and photography

1996 Design award of the U.S. glass industry for the Absolut bottle

1997 Advertising campaign "Absolut Cities;" new company building in Åhus

The success was so unbelievable that those involved argued in Sweden's press over who had earned it. The facts: sales shot up in the first ten years from 220,000 gallons to 5,500,000 gallons and has doubled again since then, making Absolut one of the ten best-selling brands of spirits in the world. It is also the only one whose bottle design played a role from the very beginning. In the late 1970s the alcohol concern V&S discovered a market niche for upscale liquor in North America and decided to save an old distillery in Åhus in southern Sweden from its end. V&S thus gave birth to its current subsidiary, Absolut. Back then, market analyses (and the example of Bacardi) indicated a trend "to white as opposed to brown liquor." V&S thereupon created a new product whose purist profile was patched together from historical set pieces.

The brand name—"Swedish Blond" and "Royal Court" had been discarded—was borrowed from "Absolut Rent Bränwin" (Absolutely Pure Spirits), a high-proof product of the nineteenth century. The shape of the bottle also comes from the past and is modeled on medicine bottles, as they were known in pharmacies. The Absolut bottle appears solid and heavy, but because of its cylindrical simplicity, its transparency (no pasted-on label), and its distinctive shape, it cuts a very elegant figure. Pure, strong, blond, Swedish—so runs the chain of associations.

The designs were developed by Hans Brindfors, an advertising artist who also refurbished the images of SAS and Ikea. The success in America took on sensational dimensions when the yuppie generation accepted Absolut in the 1980s as a cool lifestyle drink. An advertisement contributed by the late Andy Warhol (captioned "Absolut Warhol") sparked the marketing campaign. To date the pop master has been followed by more than four hundred artists, mostly from the United States, as well as by a series of additional campaigns that helped the company to successfully occupy the cult-filled region between art, advertising, and fashion. They have also staged "events" and thus stayed in continuous, attractive communication with the public, and more recently, on-line.

Absolut's marketing is all about design, for most of the advertisements are original and contemporary picture puzzles featuring the distinctive outline of the bottle. The 40- to 50-percent-proof grain distillate from the province Schonen today has cornered more than 60 percent of the U.S. vodka market, and it is the only product ever to win both an "Effi" and a "Kelly," two sought-after trophies of the U.S. advertising industry. At the same time, the company offers a lesson in entrepreneurial courage. Within the company the idea to export Swedish vodka—V&S had already foundered in such an undertaking once before, in the 1950s—had long been considered a crackpot idea.

Bottle prototypes and current Absolut bottle, 1979

Sari ANTTONEN

Furniture and Exhibition Designer / Finland

1966 Born in Helsinki

1986 Studied cabinetmaking (until 1988)

1990 Studied design in Helsinki

1994 First prize in the **Ikea** competition

1995 Designs **Marimekko** store with **Antti Eklund**

1996 *Finnish National Prize for Young Artists,* architecture prize for project Eco-Logis, Paris

1997 Founds **Reflex Design** together with Nicolas Favet

1998 Designs opening exhibition for Kiasma art museum, Helsinki Products

1995 Chair series *Tubab*

1996 Cabinets *Superheroes*

1997 Upholstered furniture *Prêt-a-porter,* room divider *Hotpants*

1998 Drinking glass, *Kiasma;* chair Kiss for **Piiroinen**

A red television set on crooked legs, rolling shelves, and a floor lamp with a bird's foot: the furniture group *Trinity* is one of those "merry product families" Sari Anttonen has included in her program. The expressionist designer, who graduated from an anthroposophical high school, completed an apprenticeship as a carpenter, and has a fondness for Gaetano Pesce's "totally absurd things," wants to draw out the hidden meanings of everyday objects. For the curious designer, furniture is not so much inanimate objects as personalities entering into relationships with each other and telling stories; in other words, it is like her *Superheroes*—a series of amorphous cabinets of a flexible material that look escapees from a comic strip. Another example of her concept is the chair series *Tubab (Paleface)*—handmade, individual pieces she assembled in Senegal from recycled sheet plate and local textiles. Anttonen is a typical representative of Finland's new designer vanguard, leaping with ease over cultural and genre boundaries and playing with the fragments of our disintegrating society. Her latest works are the environmental house Eco-Logis and a bent drinking glass for visitors at the Kiasma art museum in Helsinki. Since Sari Anttonen founded the Franco-Finnish joint venture **Reflex Design** with the architect Nicolas Favet, Paris is her second home.

Cabinets *Superheroes*

ARABIA

Keramikhersteller / Finnland

"Just as all Americans know who is playing for the Giants, so all Finns know who the designer at Arabia is"—or so common parlance has it. At least Helsinki's design students know it because their institute is located in the tradition-conscious firm's factory building. Arabia was founded in the late nineteenth century as a branch of the Swedish porcelain manufacturer **Rörstrand.** The new establishment was part of a plan to open up the huge Russian market for plates and cups starting from Finland (which back then was still a part of the Czar's empire). Within only a few years the company supplied at least half the Finnish demand. At first, simple glazed stoneware was produced, and while it left something to be desired in terms of artistic originality, the company—by now Finnish—was commercially remarkably successful. During the expansive 1920s, the firm bought up several of its competitors. With a length of 374 feet, the new factory's kiln was the longest in the world at that time. In the late 1930s Arabia had about one thousand employees and was Europe's leading ceramics manufacturer. "It is

Arabia Designor Oy AB, Helsinki

1873 Founded as subsidiary of **Rörstrand**

1896 Thure Öberg is first artist hired

1916 Company becomes Finnish after several changes of ownership

1927 Buys up porcelain factory Lidköping

1929 Largest kiln in the world

Bowl *24h* by Heikki Orvola

1932 **Kurt Ekholm** artistic director (until 1948), sets up studios for artists, and founds the museum

1937 New factory buildings

1946 **Kaj Franck** designer-in-chief (until 1978)

1947 Taken over by the Wärtsilä concern

1983 Buys up Rörstrand

1988 Introduces collection *Pro Arte*

1990 Taken over by **Hackman** concern (in 1994 united with Rörstrand, **Gustavsberg,** and **Iittala** in Designor Oy)

1998 Exhibition for the company's anniversary Products

1900 Ceramics *Fennia* (Gold medal at the Paris World's Fair)

1936 Service *Sinivalko* by Kurt Eckholm

Page 117

Vase by Kati Tuominen

Cup and pitcher *Storybirds* by Kati Tuominen, 1995

Cups *EgO* by Stefan Lindfors, 1997

hard to imagine what the Arabia product line looked like," applauds **Kaj Franck as** late as 1946—nothing but "copies of Swedish models produced from English and French models." Nevertheless, the products' aesthetic quality had already improved considerably even before the war. This was due to the efforts of **Kurt Ekholm,** who had been in charge of design at Arabia since 1932. The young, dynamic Swede—he was only twenty-five at the time—set up studios as "labs" for creative pottery in the midst of the factory. The company's present-day design department developed out of these studios. Ekholm contributed a series of functional designs to the new, modernized profile of the company, for example, the everyday dinnerware set *Sinivalko.* Arabia thus became Finland's industrial and artistic center for ceramics.

Shortly after World War II, about thirty pottery artists were employed, far more than in any other Scandinavian company. In 1945 Ekholm hired Kaj Franck, who soon took on the role of designer-in-chief—and this marked the beginning of Arabia's most innovative phase. Franck's basic idea was to mass-produce beautiful, multi-use everyday goods. In 1946 he designed the dinnerware set *Koti* (*Home*) for the Finnish family welfare agency, taking into account the needs of poor extended families in the country, thus setting a trend. Born out of necessity, his design ideas pointed the way ahead and were economical. The famous dinnerware set *Kilta* (now called *Teema*) in time conquered Finland's kitchen cupboards.

Franck's congenial team also included young designers, such as Saara Hopea and **Ulla Procopé;** the latter's dinnerware set *Liekki (Flame)* not only became famous but also sold very well for several years. Arabia's simple and solid products have had a decisive influence on the world's image of Scandinavian product design. In the 1970s and 1980s the company went through hard

times, both in economic and conceptual terms, that were accompanied by waves of mergers. It is ironic that Arabia bought up Rörstrand, its former parent company, only to then be integrated into the **Hackman** empire (now a division of Designor Oy).

The factory fires about 30,000 pieces per day and is also doing very well with the funny Finnish "Mumin" figurines. It now has three designers permanently on staff and thus continues on the road to success. Even famous designers without background in ceramics, such as Fujiwo Ishimoto, who lives in Helsinki, and Stefan Lindfors, who lives the greatest distance away from Finland, work part-time in the Arabia studios. In the late 1990s the company won several sought-after design prizes at the Frankfurt "Ambiente" fair for its products, among them a dinner service by the Franck's former pupil Heikki Orvola. This service, *24h,* is a kind of *Kilta* of the 1990s that met with an even better response abroad than at home.

1953 Service *Kilta* (discontinued in 1974, reissued in 1981 as *Teema*)

1958 Dinnerware set *Liekki* by **Ulla Procopé**

1994 Pitchers *Storybirds* by **Kati Tuominen** (design prize of the *Ambiente* fair; 1997 awarded for the dinnerware Service *24h* by **Heikki Orvola**)

1998 Service *Tilda* by **Pia Törnell**; anniversary dinnerware set *EgO* by **Stefan Lindfors**

Vase *Pro Arte IV* by Heikki Orvola

ARCH DESIGN

Studio for Furniture and Product Design

The studio of **Barbro Kulvik** and **Antti Siltavouri** is located in the solitude of the Finnish countryside. The prominent designer couple lives and works at Fiskars, Finland's oldest metal factory that has developed into a tourist destination (see Guide). Barbro Kulvik, former editor-in-chief of the magazine *Form Function Finland,* designs wooden and metal furniture, such as the ultralong and ultralightweight extreme table *One Wing,* of airplane veneer and standing on V-shaped steel legs. Echoes of the rural surroundings reverberate in her floor lamps *Milky Way,* plastic objects shaped like pitchers with handles. Antti Siltavouri works on typically Finnish things, such as heavy-duty vehicles for the lumber industry and an ice resurfacing machine. In addition, the former executive member of the International Council of Societies of Industrial Design has worked on variable shelving systems. Since 1993, a colony of creatives—industrial designers as well as artists—has begun to gather around Arch Design.

Arch Design Oy

1989 Arch Design founded

1993 **Fiskars** artist community started

1999 Exhibition *350 Years Fiskars*

Products

1991 Ice resurfacing machine *Serv Ice* by Antti Siltavouri

1993 CD-rack *Hook* by Barbro Kulvik for Fiskars

1996 Shelving system *Pergamentti* by Antti Siltavouri

1997 Table *One Wing* by Barbro Kulvik

1998 Light therapy lamp *Lux mea Lex* by Barbro Kulvik

Left: Lamp *Kaamos (Light Shower)*

Right: Floor lamp *Milky Way*

ARTEK

Furniture Manufacturer and Furnishing House / Finland

Artek Oy AB, Helsinki

1935 Founded in Helsinki

1936 First exhibition with rugs from Morocco

1945 Swedish subsidiary founded

1950 Opening of gallery

1963 Merger with Billnäs, **Alvar Aalto** withdraws from company, Elissa Aalto remains head of the company (until 1977)

1976 Ben af Schultén artistic director

1997 Taken over by Proventus Design; collaboration with **Valvomo** and **Raket**

Products

1995 Re-issue of easy chair *40* by Alvar Aalto (1931)

1996 Chair and table *626/826* by Vesa Damski

1997 Lamps *JL2P/JL2L* by **Juha Leiviskä**

1998 Table *Yotu* by Hanspeter Weidmann; chair *Droppe* by Valvomo

One evening in October 1935, when the Aaltos were having dinner with friends, the conversation turned to orders from England that had piled up in part because nobody in the furniture factory knew English and in part because **Alvar Aalto** did not answer letters. That was the impetus for the founding of Artek, a separate company that was to market Aalto furniture and promote a contemporary lifestyle. Artek fulfilled its task, in part because Marie Gullichsen was one of the dinner guests that evening. She was a wealthy art lover, who dreamed of bringing modern art to Finland. Already in 1937 she had shaken hands with Fernand Léger, who was giving a lecture on French painting in connection with an exhibition.

Artek developed into a cultural forum. By the end of the 1930s the furniture collection was as good as complete. However, Artek's business success was not as "timeless" as Aalto's designs. A lull in the 1960s forced the company to expand its product line, and that prompted Aalto to withdraw from the company out of loyalty to his principles. Under the leadership of Ben af Schultén the company has returned to its former purism but lately is also increasingly seeking contacts with young designers, for example, **Valvomo.** Production of Aalto discoveries are still possible, even belatedly; for example, the easy chair *40,* an early hybrid with a birch shell on tubular steel.

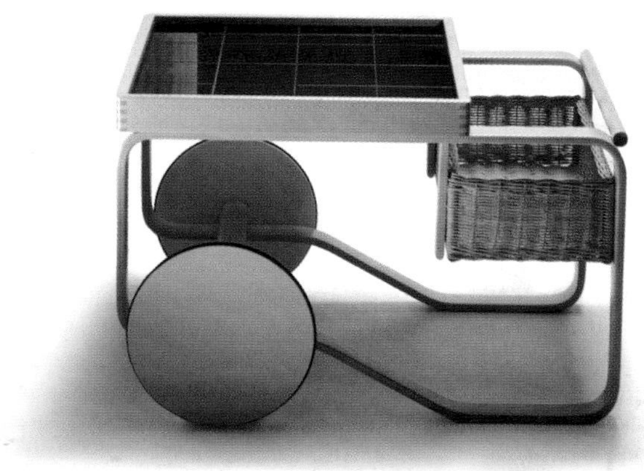

Serving trolley *900* by Alvar Aalto, 1937

Gunnar ASPLUND

Architect and Furniture Designer

As **Alvar Aalto** wrote in the obituary for his friend, "His closeness to nature, including human beings, was evident in all his projects." Gunnar Asplund is considered Sweden's most important architect of the twentieth century. His early works, such as Stockholm's South Cemetery, had a classicist cast. Asplund followed Danish models such as Thorvald Bindesbøll, then turned for a short time to a Bauhaus-inspired functionalism, especially following his work on the Stockholm Exhibition in 1930. This "battle of the styles" is also evident in his furniture. In 1917 he contributed a room to the Hemutställningen (Home Show) whose simple furnishings were reminiscent of rustic furniture, and a decade later he drew attention at the Paris art-deco show with his elegant armchair suitable for a boudoir. In 1930 he constructed chairs and easy chairs with a tubular steel frame. One year later he co-authored a modern arts manifesto and wrote, "There is no need for old cultural forms."

1928 Completed city library of Stockholm

1930 Architecture for Stockholm exhibition

1931 *Acceptera-Manifest* calls for functionalism

Products

1925 Armchair for Cassina

1926 Ceiling light *AV* for **Gärsnäs**

1930 Chair *GA 1* and easy chair *GA 2* for **Källemo**

Armchair, 1925

Round ceiling light for Gärsnäs

ASPLUND

Manufacturer of Furniture and Rugs / Sweden

Asplund, Stockholm

1990 Founded in Stockholm as a furniture gallery

1995 Marketing through **Swecode**

Products

1995 Book support by **Thomas Eriksson;** rug *O* by **Matz Borgström;** candlestick *Lucia* by **Thomas Sandell**

1997 Rug *Rug on Rug* by **Jonas Bohlin;** towel table by **Helene Tiedemann**

1998 Rug *X5* by **James Irvine;** rug *Maze* by **Tom Dixon**

A white wool rug with a fringed rectangle as though scrawled there by a child, a slim wooden table with a rack underneath for tablecloths, a book support that cannot fall over: like these, many Asplund products are amazingly simple. They are articles of practical value and, nevertheless, appear like code symbols pointing beyond themselves: design as metacommunication. This is particularly true of the rugs, by now a hallmark of the company, as in the case of **Jonas Bohlin's** *Scribbling* (fringed rug or carpet). Matz Borgström's *Zero,* a circular rug with a whole in the center, is also both object and signal at the same time, negating itself, so to speak. Renowned designers from beyond Sweden's shores, such as the British Tom Dixon, contribute their share of similarly cryptic creations. In the early 1990s—when the forerunners of the new design wave had just reached Sweden's capital—Christian and Thomas Asplund opened a furniture gallery. The two brothers, one of them a bank clerk, the other an art dealer, wanted to produce experimental pieces of furniture. Their principle to which they hold fast: it's better to reduce production runs than to make aesthetic compromises. Their enterprise has developed into one of the more noble among Stockholm's new design houses. The principles remained unchanged, but by now the production runs may also be a bit bigger.

Rug *O* by Max Borgström

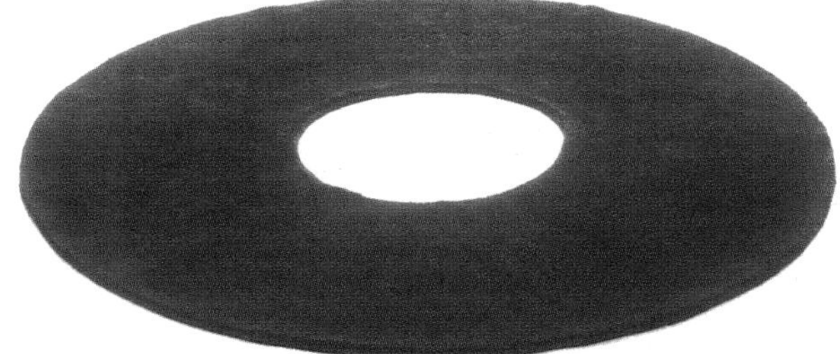

Page 123

Towel table by Helene Tiedemann

Rug by Carouschka

Stool by Thomas Eriksson

18-483
3·01

Åke AXELSSON

Furniture Designer and Interior Designer / Sweden

Galleri Stolen AB, Stockholm

1932 Born in Visby

1962 Freelance furniture designer

1963 Works for **Gärsnäs**

1970 Workshop in Vaxholm; teaches at the Konstfackskolen, Stockholm

1988 Founds own marketing company **Galleri Stolen**

1991 Buys chair factory for production

1997 Exhibition *39 Chairs*

Products

1963 Stackable chair S 217

1978 Easy chair *Vaxholmaren*

1984 Chair *Linnea* (No. 2 1990)

1994 Easy chair *Gustav* (No. 1–3)

The committee awarding him a prize for his chair *Anselm* in 1997 explicitly confirmed his "austerity." Åke Axelsson, the son of a small farmer, had experienced living from hand to mouth firsthand and learned cabinetmaking from the bottom up. Axelsson, who graduated from the art academy at the age of thirty, came to design only in 1968 when he presented experimental furniture in a one-man show and "for the first time dared to express himself."

While the critics were enthusiastic, the furniture industry remained unmoved. Axelsson's first chair had gone into production in 1963 at **Gärsnäs** (a company for which he worked for many years). Then the designer moved to the country, wanting to "develop new furniture on the basis of classical traditions" (much like **Kaare Klint**). For this purpose he traveled to London to study Egyptian and Greek chairs in the British Museum.

Again and again he varied the models he developed, often drawing upon traditional examples, such as rustic chairs or café-style seating à la Thonet, and over time accumulating an astonishingly far-ranging œuvre. Many called Axelsson the new **Bruno Mathsson,** probably because he is a similarly single-minded oddball. Having already taken the marketing of his works in hand, Axelsson also purchased a production facility in the early 1990s, thus getting closer to his goal of environmentally sound production on a small scale informed by personal contact between producer and buyer. Without exception, his chairs are lightweight and ergonomic and express the idea of the simple life, engraved into the Swedish popular mind since Carl and Karin Larsson's exodus from the city. The vanguard of young Swedish designers who now insist on a new restraint, has long since accepted the strict Axelsson as its father figure.

Page 125

Chair and bar stool

Oak bench *Robertsfors*

(all for Galleri Stolen)

BALANS

Group of Furniture Designers / Norway

1978 **Svein Gusrud, Hans Christian Mengshoel, Peter Opsvik,** and Oddvin Rykken develop ergonomical chairs

1979 *Balans* chairs at the furniture fair in Copenhagen

1984 *Design Export Prize*

1986 *Jacob Design Prize*

The new seating that came on the market in the 1970s as—in the typical jargon of that era—"furniture for alternative sitting positions" not only radically changed Norway's furniture industry and furniture design, but was also very good news for the overtaxed spines of office workers. As is the case with many inventions, the anthropometrically balanced seat is the result of collective creativity. The Norwegian **Hans Christian Mengshoel** came up with the idea that the traditional, static chairs and the equally static European sitting posture they enforce needed to be reformed. Mengshoel, a champion of ergonomically correct sitting, owns the basic patent and the copyright for the *Balans* trademark.

The initiative for the technical realization of the sitting reform came from a fellow Norwegian, the furniture designer Oddvin Rykken. Together with Mengshoel he formed a team that included their colleagues **Peter Opsvik** and **Svein Gusrud.** Under the name *Balansgruppen* the four soon developed, more or less jointly,

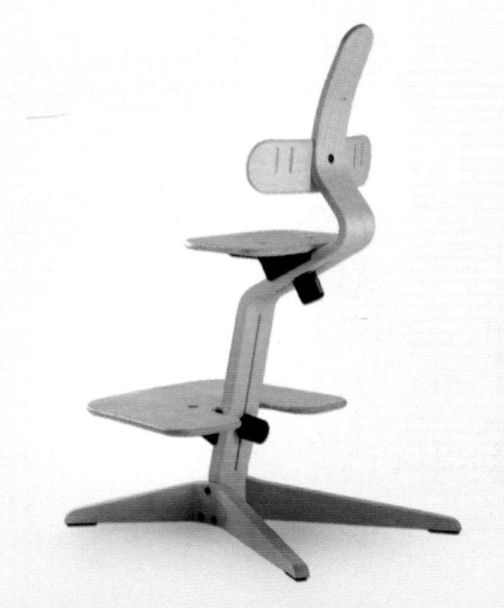

Children's chair *Sitti* by Peter Opsvik for Stokke

Chair Balans *Activ* by Svein Gusrud for Balans

highly innovative seating furniture, featuring a total of twenty-five models. The current extensive product line is based on the original principle and covers the whole gamut of seating: from office chairs on wooden runners to upholstered furniture all the way to folding stools.

The consistently realized concept has sometimes led to rather complex constructions. The strictly functional arrangement of the supporting elements has given the "seating machines" a unique space-shaping, aesthetic design with zoomorphic features. The group's most famous chairs—probably because they are so unmistakably different from the usual bottom-centered seating—are those that require sitting on one's knees, a posture that relieves the strain on the spinal column (illustration page 37). However, *Balans* users are not limited to only one position. After all, the point of the new design was the movability and changeability of the constellation person-chair. The first prototype was introduced in 1979 at the furniture fair in

Products

1979 Chair *Balans Variable* by Peter Opsvik

1982 Chair *Balans Activ* and prototype for Busse by Svein Gusrud; collapsible stool *Balans Basic* by Oddvin Rykken

1984 Chair *Balans Duo* by Peter Opsvik

Rocking chair *Hippo* by Wolfgang Rebentisch for Stokke

Copenhagen and hit the office chair market—not known for being avant-garde—like a bolt from the blue. To date, more than a million *Balans* chairs have been sold. The relaxation furniture is also increasingly used in offices and hospitals.

The group's most famous brand is **Stokke,** but it also has lots of no-names. Numerous instances of plagiarism have for some time been making life difficult for the originals from Norway. Nevertheless sales are still growing because the idea of the sensible and yet casual seating culture has long since moved from the office to the home. One *Balans* project is still on the drawing board: if the Norwegian sitting reformers have their way in the future, then public transportation users will also be able to sit perfectly ergonomically. Plans for completely relaxed riding on buses and trains are already in the works.

Rocking chair *4014 Gravity* by Peter Opsvik for Stokke

BANG & OLUFSEN

Manufacturer of Phonographs and Televisions / Denmark

In 1954 the critic **Poul Henningsen** described a radio manufactured by Bang & Olufsen as, "a monster with a bloated belly, an insult to people who like modern furniture." It took another decade before the company, already distinguished as a top brand in prewar Denmark, would find its way to an original product design. Henningsen's unequivocal criticism was not heeded until the company experienced a downturn in sales in the early 1960s.

B & O learned from the Danish furniture industry, which exported its modern design all over the world. The turning point came in 1963 when the company hired creative talents, for example, the renowned industrial design firm **Bjørn & Bernadotte** and their former staff member **Jacob Jensen.** With the miniradio *Beolit 500* (with buttons for preselected stations) and the stereo radio *Beomaster 900* the company bid farewell to the complacent 1950s. The flat boxes with their geometrically arranged operating buttons called to mind the orderly design of the German hi-fi

Bang & Olufsen Holding A/S, Struer

1925 Founded by **Peter Bang** and **Svend Olufsen;** radio with power cord

1931 First Danish sound film recorded with B&O equipment

1939 *Beolit* (first use of the prefix "Beo")

1948 First tape recorder, later also television sets and table telephones

Radio *Beolit 39,* 1939

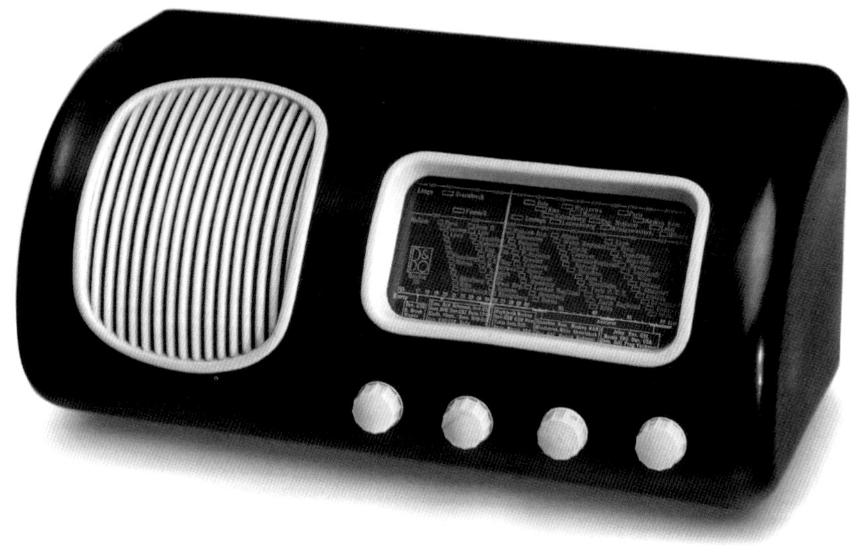

1963 Collaboration with designers, especially **Jacob Jensen**

1966 Danish *ID Prize* for portable radio *Beolit 500* (until 1994 twelve additional prizes)

1968 Expansion of international sales

1978 Exhibition *Bang & Olufsen: Design for Sound by Jacob Jensen* at the MOMA, New York

1990 After years of losses, twenty-five percent of company taken over by Philips

1992 New management

1997 Repurchase of the Philips shares; collaboration with **Ericsson**

Products

1934 Audio cabinet *Hyperbo 5 RG* with tubular steel frame

1939 Radio *Beolit 39* made of Bakelite

producer Braun. The elegant wooden housings, however, were a Danish ingredient. While in 1960 more than ninety percent of sales were to domestic customers, by the mid-1970s two of every three products were sold outside Denmark. B & O has become an international brand and achieved cult status, especially because of its strict design grammar, at times applied so rigorously that it has almost become a synonym for Danish design (and all that without a design department): ruler-straight lines, hard edges, flawless surfaces, and sparse graphics.

For more than three decades, Jacob Jensen, who had advanced to the status of mastermind, was responsible for the supple minimalism. The cube-shaped portable radio *Beolit 500* and the stereo system *Beolab 5000* (made of individual components) already distanced Jensen irrevocably from the old-fashioned radio as a piece of furniture. The operating-button-turned-slide-rule (illustration page 20), a detail recurring in many B & O designs, represented the merger of mathematical

Portable radio *Beolit 600* by Jacob Jensen

Page 131

Top: CD player *Beocenter 2300* by David Lewis, 1990s

Bottom: Stereo system *Beolab 5000* by Jacob Jensen

1964 Stereo radio *Beomaster 900* by Henning Moldenhawer
1965 Battery radio *Beolit 500* by Acton Bjørn
1965 Portable radio *Beolit 600*
1967 Stereo system *Beolab 5000*
1969 Receiver *Beomaster 1200*
1972 Record player *Beogramm 4000* with tangential arm all by Jacob Jensen
1976 Receiver *Beomaster 1900*
1986 Television *MX 2000* by **David Lewis**
1991 Stereo system *Beocenter 8500*
1993 Audio-video system *Beosystem AV 9000* by David Lewis
1997 CD Player *Beocenter AV5*

exactitude with elegance, a duality that made B & O sets objects of reverence even though the aseptic surface was not always wrapped around the latest technological developments. Today as a very reputable, elegant, medium-sized company with 2,300 employees, Bang & Olufsen virtually has a monopoly on the highly solvent hi-fi elite. In the early 1990s the company still ran up losses and was close to ultimate liquidation. With a management change in 1993 B & O succeeded in reinventing itself (including a renovated CI). The Armani among audio equipment suppliers offers sound chambers for the country houses and penthouses of the world and now earns every third krone from custom-made systems. With in-house designers such as Englishman **David Lewis** and **Steve McGugan** from Scotland, B & O still follows the old recipe of extravagant understatement mixed with 007-comfort, for example with intelligent components such as the remote-controlled active boxes *Beolink.* However, the company creates not only sound equipment, but "audio-visual architecture" all the way to the living room classicism of the *Beosystem AV 9000.*

Loudspeaker *Beolab 3500,* 1990s

BENT KROGH

Furniture manufacturer / Denmark

Krogh, the company's founder, belongs to the old school of Danish furniture manufacturers. Four decades ago he began with such solid, basic objects as school desks and outdoor furniture, in his preferred material, steel. Today the product line ranges from basic furnishings to original high-design. Engaged since the 1980s in the highly competitive contract business, the company has made a name for itself with unorthodox materials. Those crossing the Great Belt by ferry can sit on *Opus,* an all-weather chair with a sturdy steel frame and a rubber back. *Opus* is only one of a whole series of space-saving, usually stackable chairs. Also included in the product line are the steel shelves *Transit,* which can be mounted without any tools, and the table series *Lobster* offering conference seating in variable arrangements. Krogh relies on collaboration with well-known design studios such as **Friis & Moltke, Pelikan,** and **Komplot** (which created the company logo). And with **Niels Jørgen Haugesen's** teak models *Xylofon* outdoor furniture is also still on the agenda.

Bent Krogh A/S,
Skanderborg

1960 Founded by Bent Krogh

1984 First designer furniture

1995 *Danish Furniture Prize*

Products

1984 Steel furniture system *Transit* by **Pelikan**

1988 Shelves *Columbus* by **Niels Gammelgaard**

1989 Table *Lobster* by **Komplot**

1994 Chair *Opus* by Pelikan

Deck chair *Xylofon* by Niels Jørgen Haugesen

Sigvard BERNADOTTE

Silversmith, Product Designer, and Furniture Designer / Sweden

1907 Born in Stockholm

1926 University at Uppsala, later art studies in Stockholm and Munich

1930 Silverwork for *Georg Jensen;* participation in the Stockholm Exhibition

1933 Assistant director at Ufa, later at MGM

1944 Consultant for Illums Bolighus, Copenhagen

1950 Trip to the United States; founds **Bernadotte & Bjørn** Industry Design (B&B) in Copenhagen

It is not without a certain irony that one of the first Swedes to implement the socialist postulate of "beauty for all" had spent his childhood in the royal palace. The blue-blooded Prince Sigvard, a son of King Gustav VI, an aesthete who had wanted to become an actor but, upon the advice of his parents, decided to study "something useful," broke new ground for Scandinavia's industrial design. Among his most famous products are office equipment and practical kitchen utensils made of plastic, items that soon became indispensable in all Scandinavian households. In addition he designed high-tech products, such as a videophone for **Ericsson** and a miniradio for **Bang & Olufsen.**

Even at the beginning of his career, the wide range of his activities is astonishing. In the 1920s he worked as silversmith, textile artist, bookbinder, and scene-painter. In the 1930s the crackerjack traveled through Africa, completed additional studies in Munich, and cultivated his predilection for film—first at the Ufa studios and then in Hollywood. He arrived at a fork in the road in

1950 during a trip to the United States when he met the design elite of the then leading industrial nation. Inspired by the American way of design he founded that same year an office for industrial design in Copenhagen together with the Danish architect **Acton Bjørn.** Theirs was the first and for a long time the only such design studio in Scandinavia. Among Bernadotte's first employees was **Jacob Jensen,** whom he taught the basics of design as well as polite manners. Bernadotte was the Swedish Henry Dreyfuss. At the end of the 1950s "B&B" had eighteen employees, among them designers from the United States, England, and Germany. Bernadotte was so popular his signature was put on products; it is probably safe to say that his noble birth was not a hindrance to his growing popularity. A sophisticated, polished designer who could work today on a snow-scooter, tomorrow on a fashion collection, and the next day on the furnishings for a luxury liner gradually became more of a manager than an artist. Back in Stockholm the office of the design count merged at the end of the 1960s with a British company. When the new entity ran into the red even though business was flourishing and was finally liquidated, it signaled the end of an era—one in which industrial design grew out of its infancy.

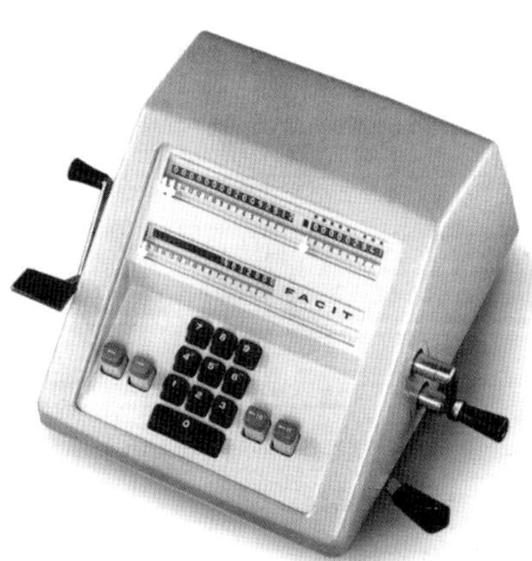

1953 Book *Industrial Design: Modern Industrial Formgiving*

1956 Works for **Bing & Grøndahl** and Rosenthal

1958 B&B branch in Stockholm

1961 President of the ICSID (International Association of Industrial Designers)

1964 Founds design studio in Stockholm

1998 Retrospective at the National Museum in Stockholm

Products

1939 *Bernadotte Flatware* for **Georg Jensen**

1950 Plastic bowl *Margrethe*

1952 Table calculator for Facit (first sales success)

1957 Typewriter *Facit T1*

1959 Dictaphone *Agavox*

1964 Portable radio *Beolit 500* for **Bang & Olufsen**

1966 SAS flatware and dinnerware set

1970 Forklift *GM*

1971 Videophone for **Ericsson**

Plastic bowls *Margrethe*

Table calculator *Facit CM2-16*

Thea BJERG

Textile Designer / Denmark

1960 Born in Copenhagen

1983 Studied design in Copenhagen (until 1987)

1987 Opened studio

1992 Industrial Arts Prize (Hetsch Medal) in bronze (1994 in silver)

1995 Book *Thea Bjerg No. 1–44 Textiler*

1998 Participation in exhibition, *New Textile Techniques,* United States

Products

1993 Hand-printed silk scarves

1994 Laminated fabric *Wave: Pearl-white;* laminated fabric *Circles: Peacock-blue*

1998 Textile print *Gauffré,* silk synthetics

Usually, the fabric selection is "rather dull," opines Thea Bjerg, and consequently there is "a great demand for new materials," she says, and that is what this newcomer from Copenhagen has been experimenting with for some time. Her showpiece products, complex "laminated textiles," were already admired at numerous exhibitions and have since become an insider tip in Denmark. They are manufactured using a traditional process Bjerg has improved upon in years of painstaking detailed work to give silk fabrics a three-dimensional depth.

In preparation for this task, Thea Bjerg has looked around in many countries and in many weaving mills and now plays her daring games with Europe's silk culture. For example, when the whites of her fabrics blend into color nuances such as "oyster" or "champagne," images of the former pomp of the courtly wardrobe come to mind immediately. The improvised, irregular fine textures of her shimmering fabrics constantly create new scenes of light and shadow: a ruffled labyrinth-like intertwining of folds and forms. She calls this "fabrics in movement." If this fine texture serves as background for secular motifs such as stylized medals or spark plugs, then pop and baroque enter into a shrill liaison. And Bjerg's story also has a Danish punchline. A medium-sized weaving mill, counting on export opportunities, does what for a long time nobody considered possible: it takes Thea Bjerg's slightly decadent textile creations all the way to production.

Fabric *No. 11*

Page 137

Fabric *No. 33*

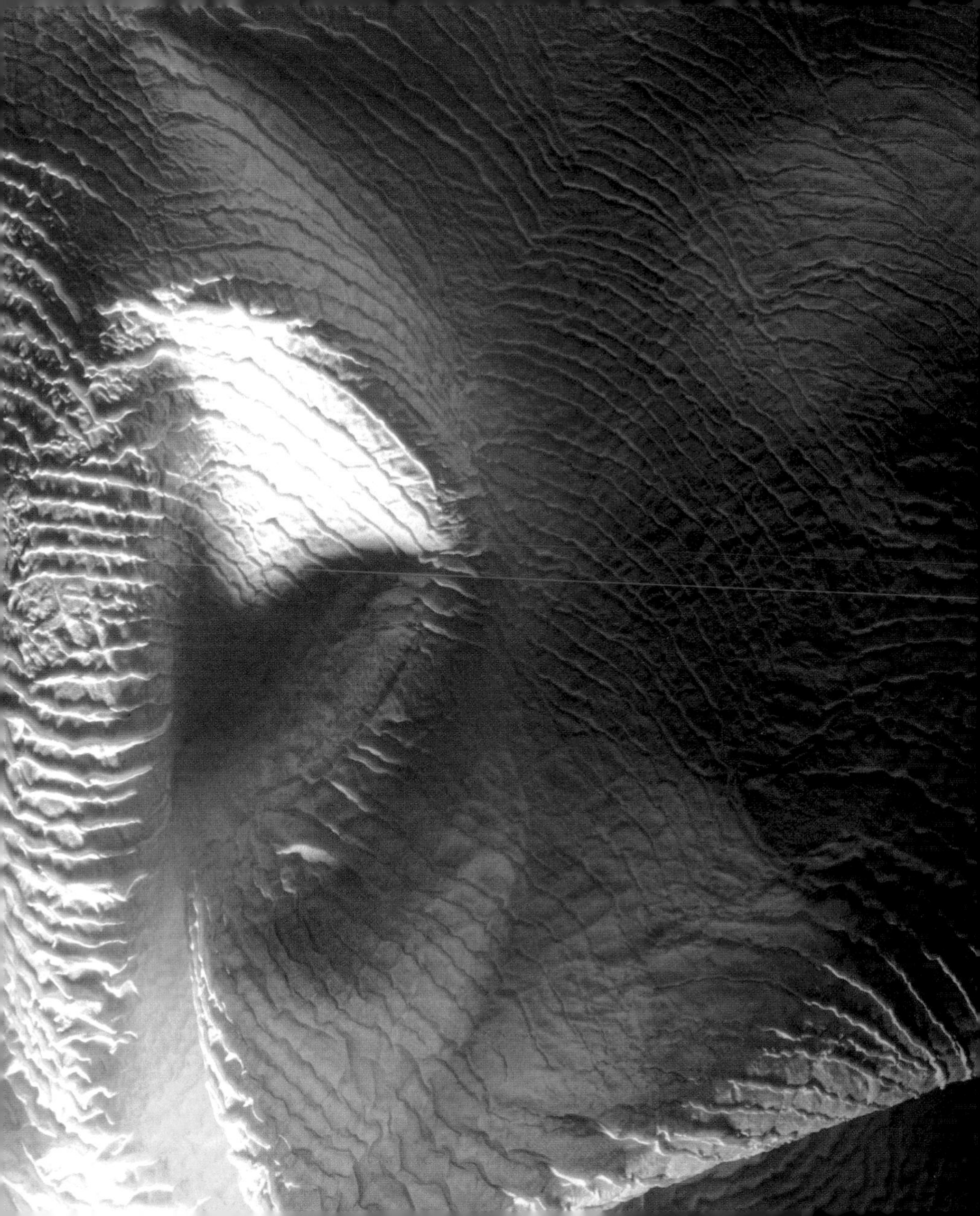

Christian BJØRN

Product Designer and Industrial Designer / Denmark

1944 Born in Copenhagen
1969 Art academy, Copenhagen (until 1974)
1974 Design Studio, Copenhagen (with Henrik Jeppensen and Nils Toft)
1979 *ID Prize* (until 1997 nine more times)
1997 Awarded European Design Prizes together with **Oticon** and **Bates**

Products
1995 First-aid box; sweeper *SW 650* for Nilfisk
1997 Garbage transport system for Bates

What do a garbage can and a hearing aid have in common? Both are usually hidden and seem to be off-limits for designers. However, in 1997 a garbage removal system and a hearing aid system each received an EU Design Prize, and Christian Bjørn's design studio had a hand in the development of both. With technicians he developed a new, integrated concept for household garbage for the company **Bates.** Bjørn's design was based on the use of paper bags and allowed waste to be disposed of with a clear conscience. The hearing aid he developed for **Oticon** was the first digital compact hearing aid in the world and broke new design ground.

Both projects required interdisciplinary collaboration. As needed, freelance specialists are added to his permanent staff of five. Therefore his unusually diversified product range extends all the way from the development of electronic high-tech instruments to service concepts and to architectural solutions and graphic interfaces.

Hearing aid *Digifocus* for Oticon, 1996

Garbage transport cart for Bates

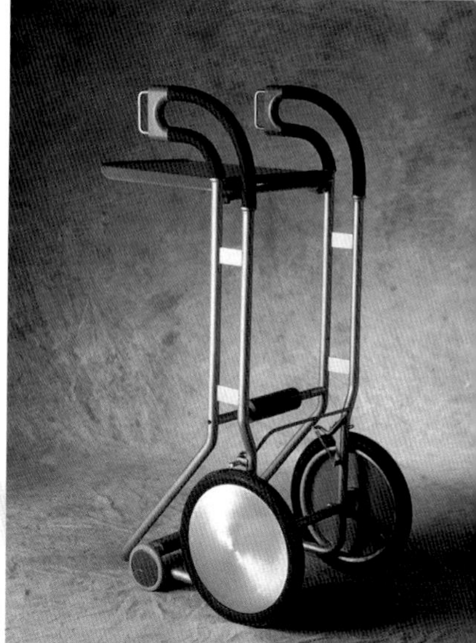

BLÅ STATION

Furniture manufacturer/ Sweden

In the early 1980s Börge Lindau—then still working with Bo Lindekrantz—designed a dining and conference table that could also be used as a table-tennis table. Among Sweden's furniture community the two designers back then were considered an unbeatable pair. Later Lindau—whose signature is Blå—moved to the country in southern Sweden, and from those greener pastures he now directs his own furniture factory, a family-owned firm to which his son Johan has also contributed designs. The basic idea has remained the same: Extravagant concepts plus quality. His preferred materials are birch and steel. Outside designers complement the company's program. The award-winning bench Söndag, equally suited for churchgoers and lovers, was designed by Annette Petersson, and the lightweight (because riddled with holes) folding chair Cheese is by Josefin Larsson. Blå's furniture can be found in many Swedish restaurants but also in reception and areas administration buildings, such as that of the manufacturer Absolut.

Blå Station AB, Åhus

1984 Founded by **Börge Lindau**

1986 First Blå-Furniture

Products

1990 *Beplus* Börge Lindau

1995 CD-holder *Musikal*; seating system *Gate* by Johan and Börge Lindau

1996 Chair *Cheese* von Josefin Larsson

Chairs *Common One B40* by Börge Lindau

Bench *Söndag 065* by Annette Petersson and Lotta Josefsson

Jonas BOHLIN

Artist, Furniture Designer, and Interior Decorator / Sweden

1953 Born in Stockholm

1974 Works as civil engineer

1976 Studies interior design at the Konstfackskolen in Stockholm (until 1981)

1981 Freelance designer; works for **Källemo**

1985 Cofounder of the gallery Mobile, Stockholm

1988 *Georg-Jensen Prize*

1989 Designed restaurant *Tranan* together with **Thomas Sandell**

1991 Cofounder of design training at the Beckman School, Stockholm

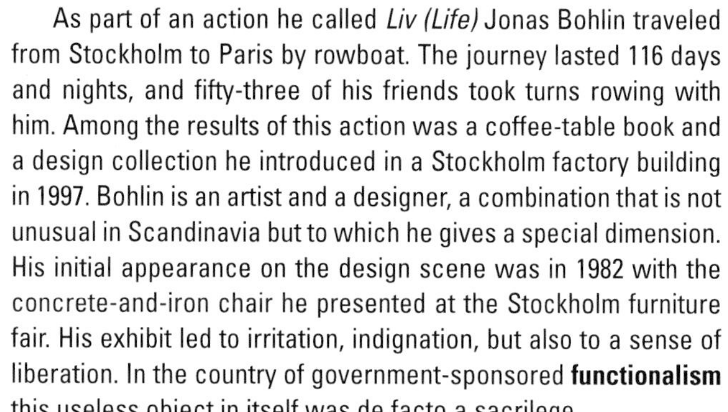

As part of an action he called *Liv (Life)* Jonas Bohlin traveled from Stockholm to Paris by rowboat. The journey lasted 116 days and nights, and fifty-three of his friends took turns rowing with him. Among the results of this action was a coffee-table book and a design collection he introduced in a Stockholm factory building in 1997. Bohlin is an artist and a designer, a combination that is not unusual in Scandinavia but to which he gives a special dimension. His initial appearance on the design scene was in 1982 with the concrete-and-iron chair he presented at the Stockholm furniture fair. His exhibit led to irritation, indignation, but also to a sense of liberation. In the country of government-sponsored **functionalism** this useless object in itself was de facto a sacrilege.

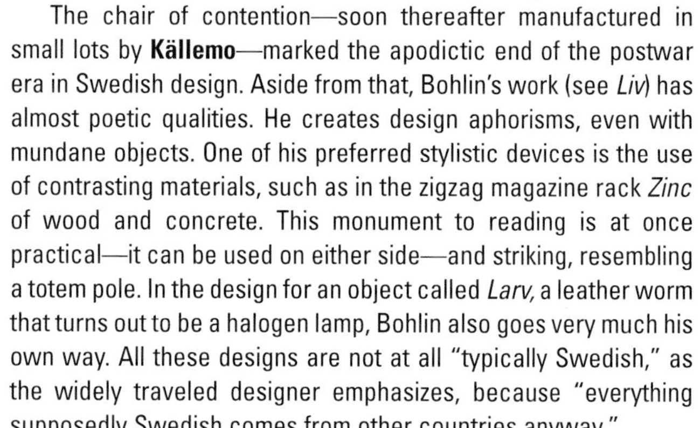

The chair of contention—soon thereafter manufactured in small lots by **Källemo**—marked the apodictic end of the postwar era in Swedish design. Aside from that, Bohlin's work (see *Liv*) has almost poetic qualities. He creates design aphorisms, even with mundane objects. One of his preferred stylistic devices is the use of contrasting materials, such as in the zigzag magazine rack *Zinc* of wood and concrete. This monument to reading is at once practical—it can be used on either side—and striking, resembling a totem pole. In the design for an object called *Larv,* a leather worm that turns out to be a halogen lamp, Bohlin also goes very much his own way. All these designs are not at all "typically Swedish," as the widely traveled designer emphasizes, because "everything supposedly Swedish comes from other countries anyway."

Table *Liv,* 1996

Wooden chair with metal seat, 1990

Page 141
Halogen Lamp *Larv* for Värnamo Belysning, 1990

Jonas Bohlin's designs echo life, for example, the momentous *Concrete Chair*. He employed this rough material because he was familiar with it from his "former life," referring to the time when this designer with an engineer's diploma had worked as a bridge builder. In the mid-1980s he became a gallery owner. In the same period he also designed many pieces of furniture for Källemo and enriched the Stockholm nightlife through unusual restaurant furnishings, for example, in Rolfs' Kök or the Sturehof, the watering hole of the local design smart set.

In 1988 Jonas Bohlin was awarded the Georg Jensen Prize, the most renowned design prize in Scandinavia, and finally the radical designer was named a member of the art academy, a circle of a hundred chosen ones. The highly honored designer, however, did not let this go to his head but continues to view life from the perspective of running a frail little boat. "The boat is the small space we can control," as he has found out not only because of *Liv*. "The ocean, on the other hand, is the large space we cannot control."

1993 Exhibition *Mathsson, Chambert, Kandell, Bohlin* at the National Museum, Stockholm

1996 Aktion *Liv*

1997 Member of the Swedish Academy of Arts

Products

1980 *Concrete Chair* for Källemo

1983 Sofa *Concave*

1984 Magazine rack *Zinc*

1985 Chair *Point* (made of leather and steel)

1987 Wall map, *Espresso;* sofa *Nonting;* cabinet *Slottsbacken*

1988 Table *Triptyk*

1990 Halogen lamp *Larv*

1992 Sofa *Spring*

1997 Furniture collection *Liv*

Magazine rack *Zinc* for Källemo, 1984

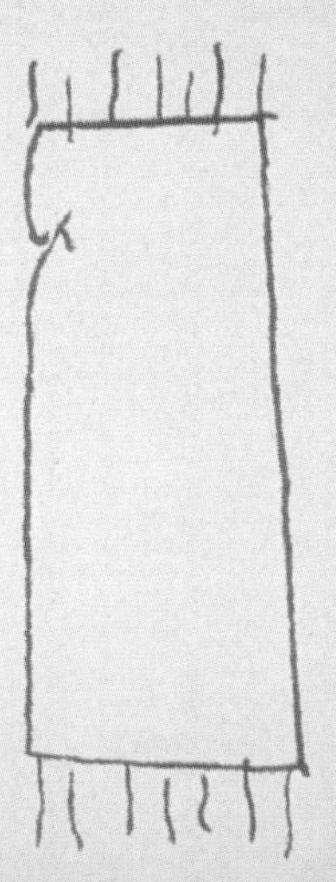

Rug *Rug on Rug* for Asplund

Kay BOJESEN

Silversmith and Product Designer / Denmark

An apprentice of **Georg Jensen,** Bojesen converted in the 1920s to a modernism whose bare but soft shapes already anticipated the Danish style of the postwar years. Bojesen realized early on that the task of the art industry was to create useful things, and he understood that simple and exquisite were necessarily opposites. This **Kaare Klint** of silver design was close to **Poul Henningsen** in his criticism of excessive ornamentation. The well-proportioned silver flatware, for which he received a prize in Milan in 1951, was considered particularly progressive. However, "Uncle" Bojesen became world-famous for a rocking horse and a whole zoo of wooden animals that gladdened the hearts of children all over the world. The connection between his areas of specialization—silver design and toy design—lies in the personality of the man himself. Bojesen's maxim was "There must be life, blood, and heart in things"—as he put it: "The lines must laugh."

1886 Born in Copenhagen
1907 Apprenticeship under **Georg Jensen**
1913 Opens own silversmithy
1931 Founds gallery Den Permanente
1951 *Grand Prix* Triennial Milan
1958 Died in Copenhagen

Products
1930 Mocha-service
1938 Silver flatware—*Casserole*
1951 Wooden spider monkey

Rocking Horse, 1930s

BOX DESIGN

Furniture Manufacturer / Sweden

Box Design AB, Stockholm

1986 Box Inredningsarkitekter (interior decorating) founded by **Ann Morsing** and **Beban Nord**

1991 Awarded Best Swedish Home Furnishings

1992 Own production as **Box Möbler,** later Box Design

1995 Distribution through **Swecode**

Products

1993 Cabinets *Frost*

1994 Wastepaper basket *Pelle*

1995 Coffee-table *Cosmo*

1998 Shelf system *Help* by Lloyd Schwan

At Box the world is still virtuous. The products offered by the architects Beban Nord and Ann Morsing (both share business as well as design activities equally) follow Sweden's iron commandments for furniture design. The two missionaries of Scandinavian style strive to be timeless, modern, and lasting. For that reason their cabinets, such as those of the series Frost, are seemingly so unobtrusive that they fit equally well in the kitchen, living room, office, store, or in a good interior design magazine. Their kitchen table model 40 is as minimalist and solid as the furniture of the good old days. But sometimes even Nord/Morsing are disloyal to their principles. The American Lloyd Schwan was the first guest designer to get a turn, and he designed shelving systems. Then lamps were added to the program, at first the multi-jointed metal lamp PJ, an object with a pedigree of its own: developed originally as a task lamp in England and later sold in Norway as Luxo lamp, it finally became an everyday icon of the century. It is now available in a refined Box version.

Chest of drawers *Frost Low Cabinet* by Ann Morsing and Beban Nord for company archive of Box Möbler

CBI

Furniture Manufacturer and Furnishing House / Sweden

In the extravagant 1980s the trend analyst **Stefan Ytterborn** noticed a backlog demand among his fellow Swedes and launched an import business to supply Sweden and the rest of Scandinavia with contemporary design products from Europe and the United States. Later he added the shop **Klara** as the first supply station for Stockholm's design clientele. The hand-picked range of beautiful and simple everyday objects was guarded by Christian Springfeldt, another key figure in the new reshuffle of Swedish design that was about to get underway. The company's newly issued collection restored long-standing and proven principles to favor. The objects were to express "humanism, respect for natural materials, comfort, function, eco-friendly simplicity, and user friendliness." Other manufacturers of more or less neo-Nordic design, such as **Asplund, Box Design,** and **David Design,** have also set sail for the same goals under the shared flag **Swecode.** In addition to the minimal furniture by **Björn Dahlström** (illustration p. 19) and **Carina Seth-Andersson's** glass cylinders, CBI products include a striking sofa-cum-folding-bed variation by the British designer James Irvine, a piece akin to the "Aalto-sofa."

CBI/Klara AB, Stockholm

1986 Founded in Stockholm as C&Bi Interior

1991 Design shop Klara opened; exhibition with Jasper Morrisson

1993 Furniture production; presentation at the furniture fair in Milan

1994 Founding of **Swecode**

1998 Participation in U.S. exhibition *New Textile Techniques*

Products

1995 Bench *BD 2* by **Björn Dahlström**

1996 Sofabed *JL 1* by James Irvine

1997 Glass cylinder *CSA 2* by **Carina Seth-Andersson**

1998 Stackable chairs *BD 6/BD 5* by Björn Dahlström

Candlesticks *BD 3* by Björn Dahlström

CLAESSON KOIVISTO RUNE

Studio for Interior Design and Furniture Design / Sweden

Claesson Koivisto Rune Arkitektkontor AB, Stockholm

1993 **Mårten Claesson, Eero Koivisto,** and **Ola Rune** found architectural firm

1995 Forsnäs Design Prize; exhibition for Svensk Form

1998 Gucci store in Stockholm

Products

1994 Experimental House *Villa Wabi*

1995 Chair *Maxply;* table A-3 with flowerholder

1996 *Polaris* lamps for **Zero**

1998 Rug *Golden Mean* for **Asplund;** wall clock *Camp* and easy chair *Bowie;* both for **David Design**

Mårten Claesson, Eero Koivisto, and Ola Rune made no secret of the fact that they took their cue from their doyen Aalto when they designed the *Bowie* bench. While the young designer trio follows his tradition consciously and deliberately, they are not paralyzed by reverence. *Bowie* has a slit in the back and is therefore more flexible and also more comfortable to sit in. In terms of production engineering, the narrow slit presented an almost insurmountable obstacle. "There are many brilliant ideas," says Koivisto, "but only very few of them are suitable for industrial production." He and his partners believe that modern Scandinavian design can be resurrected in yet more modern embodiments (illustration p. 48). The three like-minded designers, who met during their student years at Stockholm's art academy, are an unusual team—unusually productive and unusually single-minded. Before the up-and-coming designers had even graduated, they already had decorated an office in Barcelona and two restaurants in Stockholm, and one of their pieces of furniture was just going into production. The trained architects designed many objects jointly, such as the slitted *Bowie* seat, the oak bench *Minimal,* and the *Villa Wabi,* a Spartan room intended as a retreat from "visual noise." CKR combines formal asceticism with playfulness, "Nordic philosophy" with a polyglot perspective. Moreover, the three designers see their work as a response to the global "Disneyfication." Sweden's ambassador to Germany evidently also likes this: he had his new Berlin residence furnished by the three young purists.

Bench *Minimal* by Eero Koivisto and Ola Rune for Nola, 1995

Shoehorn *James* by Ola Rune

Page 147

Chair *Squerish* by Ola Rune, 1992

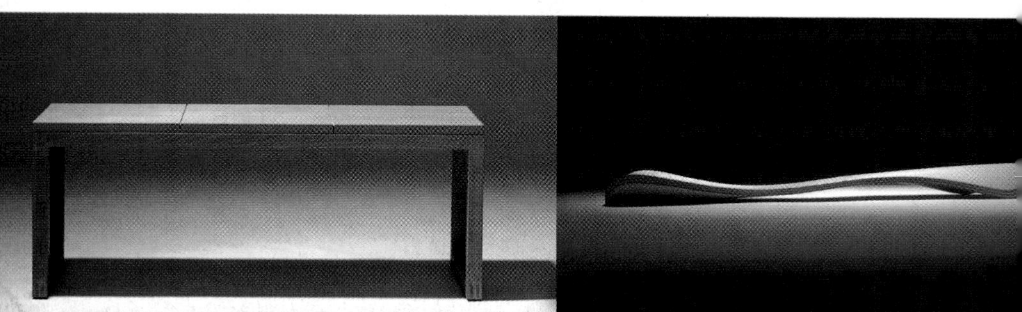

CREADESIGN

Studio for Product Design and Industrial Design / Finland

Creadesign Oy, Helsinki

1981 Founded by **Hannu Kähönen** in Helsinki, staff includes, among others, **Pasi Järvinen**

1986 *Design Product of the Year*

1992 Hannu Kähönen named industrial designer of the year (in 1995 the honor goes to Pasi Järvinen)

Creadesign's cross-country ski pole was so effective that despite complying with the relevant regulations, it was at first banned from use in competitons. Its designer **Pasi Järvinen,** carried out extensive motion studies for the sport equipment brand Exel, and finally came up with a loop that reduced air resistance and also offered an optimal use of momentum. (Over the distance of approximately thirty-one miles, this made a difference of two minutes.) Though the results of its design work are not always so spectacular, Creadesign has been one of Finland's best design laboratories has for years along with its competitors, such as **E&D,** and newcomers, such as **Muodos—Hannu Kähönen.** Creadesign's founder and president is a dyed-in-the-wool positivist who believes that to ensure good work the designer must take a backseat to his product, a postulate that was also **Kaj Franck's** motto. Kähönen developed a series of indistructable padlocks with new locking mechanism systems for **Abloy.** The padlocks' robustness is evident in their massive but

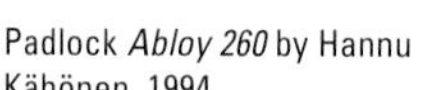

Padlock *Abloy 260* by Hannu Kähönen, 1994

Folding chair *Baby-Trice* by Hannu Kähönen, 1985

original shape. The folding chait *Trice,* light as a feather, also exemplifies Creadesign's creative pragmatism (and has been awarded several prizes). Made of fiberglass and synthetic fabric, *Trice* is a portable seat for roving city people and, like everything designed by Creadesign, suitable for mass production. Incidentally, *Trice* was not a commissioned design but grew out of one of those idée fixes Kähönen is always mulling over.

The creation of concepts is one of the main branches of his business. For example, in Kähönen's opinion, the time for parking meters has long expired. Now Helsinki has replaced those "coin coffins" with a smart card system. Another of his ideas for the future is the "chargeable" television set whose outer housing remains unchanged while the current "software" changes all the time. (**Nokia** has not yet been won over). Durability and sustained effectiveness are the key words for Kähönen who, though an active environmentalist, will by no means swear off plastic, his preffered material.

Products

1985 Chair *Trice*

1988 Official ski pole for the Olympics for Exel

1990 Locks *Ava* for Abloy

1993 Cell phones *Beta* and *Ultra* for Benefon

1994 Padlock *Abloy 260* for Abloy

1995 Ski poles *Avanti Aero* for Exel

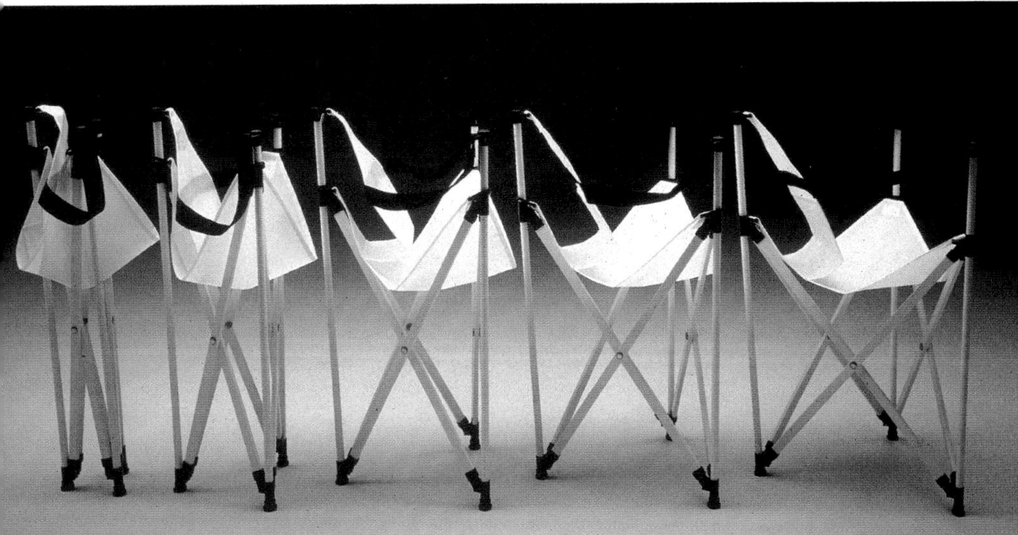

Björn DAHLSTRÖM

Graphic Artist, Furniture Designer, and Product Designer / Sweden

1957 Born in Stockholm
1978 Advertising artist
1982 Freelance graphic artist
1991 Prize for Outstanding Swedish Design (also in 1992, 1996, 1997)
1994 Presentation at the furniture fair, Milan
1998 Participation in exhibition *Puls,* Berlin and Moscow

Products
1985 *Rocking Rabbit* for Playsam
1994 Easy chair *BD 1;* benches *BD 2;* candlesticks *BD 3*
1996 Easy chair *BD 5,* all for CBI
1997 Pneumatic drill *Cobra mk 1* for Atlas Copco; pots and pans *Tools* for Hackman

A cartoon studio, an advertising agency, a design studio: Björn Dahlström's career has run a logical yet unusual course. Professionally, the graphic artist took a quantum leap when he dared the step into the third dimension. The distinctive feature of his work is that even his product designs have a two-dimensional quality. Among his early works are toys—silhouette-like "cartoons on wheels" like the streamlined *Toycar.* Even Dahlström's furniture has strong graphical features; for example, his easy chairs look like fragments of letters that somebody drew with a broad-tipped pen (illustration page 19). These reduced shapes bear witness to having been designed in the traditional method. As Dahlström explains, "If you want to make an easy chair, you have to put together a rough model of it at some point to find out if one can sit on it." Considered a virtuoso of the design industry, Björn Dahlström seems to succeed at everything he tackles, even pure, hard industrial design. For four years Dahlström worked on developing a pneumatic drill, an ambitious project in which **Atlas Copco** invested millions. The result is an extreme reduction of the vibrations, previously considered impossible by experts. In the end *Cobra mk* 1 was not only surprisingly low in noise, but also looked attractive—the Harley-Davidson among pneumatic drills, so to speak.

Pedal cars, 1980s

Page 151

Bench *BD 4*

Chair and footstool *BD 5*

Graphics program for Swecode

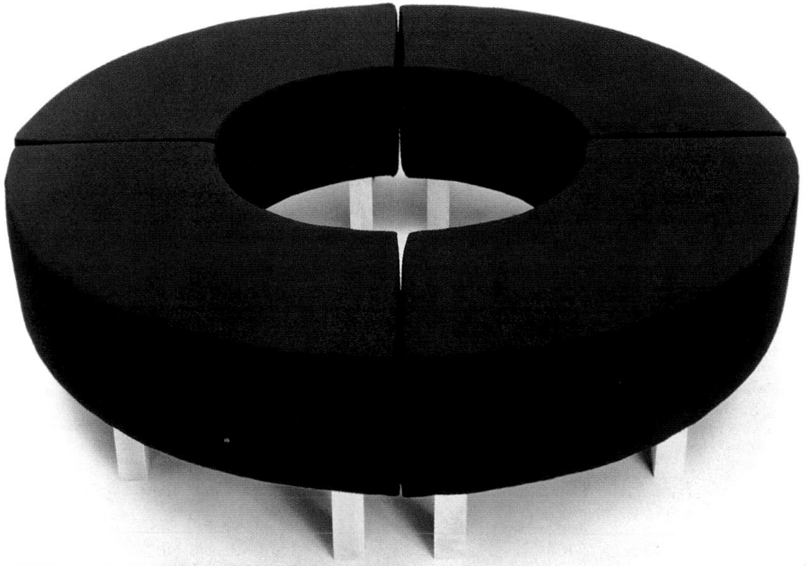

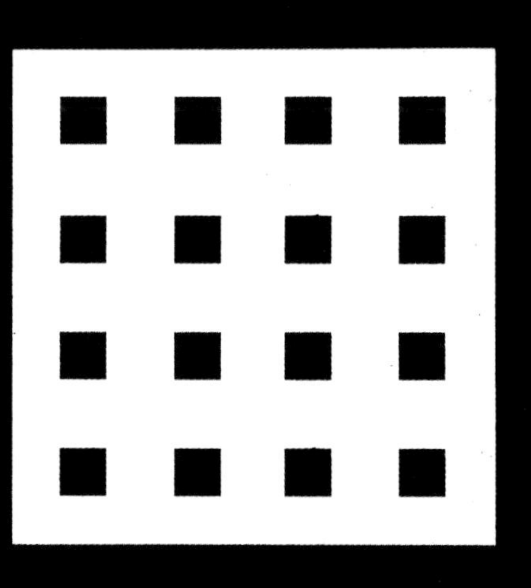

DAVID DESIGN

Furniture Manufacturer / Sweden

David Design AB, Malmö

1988 Founded by David Carlson

1995 Marketing by **Swecode**

Products

1994 Chair *Beatnik* by **Jonas Lindvall;** lamp *Taiwan* by **Helene Tiedemann**

1996 Lamps *Lowlight/Highlight* and shelves *Front de Boeuf* by **Helene Tiedemann**

1998 Bench *Bowie* by **Claesson Koivisto Rune**

The company's best-seller is called *Quasimodo* and solves dressing room problems. A lot can be hung on its rotating hooks. This dressing room utensil with chances of becoming a cult object is a showpiece for contemporary Swedish home decor. In addition to furniture and lamps, David Design's program includes housewares. "Because Sweden has been a rural country for so long, it has produced many simple, comprehensible objects," explains the company's founder David Carlson, for whom the business is named. In other words, Sweden's history offers designers a large repertory of forms. Carlson also appreciates the classical Danish design of the 1950s because it is "human" and "sensible." For him, his business is a display window offering a view of the "world of the North." Product names such as *Beatnik* **(Jonas Lindvall)** for a chair, or *Bowie* **(Claesson Koivisto Rune)** for a bench, however, point to the socialization of their creators in the era of rock and roll. Whether pop or Nordic, David Design is an important source of ideas for Sweden's design revival. In this context, even *Quasimodo* has "Nordic charm."

Bench *Bowie* by Eero Koivisto and Ola Rune

Page 153

Floor lamps *Highlight* and *Lowlight* by Helene Tiedemann

DEMOCRATIC DESIGN

1917 *Hemutställningen* (Home Show) in Stockholm
1919 Gregor Paulsson publishes *Vackrare Vardagsvara (More Beautiful Everyday Things)*
1929 Social-democratic government in Denmark
1930 *Stockholm Exhibition*
1932 Swedish welfare state through Prime Minister Per Albin Hansson
1940 Concept of "democratic living" established in Sweden
1942 **Bøge Mogensen** leading furniture designer of the Danish consumer cooperative
1949 Dinnerware set *Kilta* by **Kaj Franck**
1960 Denmark introduces "national pension" independent of earnings
1965 **Ikea** store in Stockholm; Swedish housing program "million program" launched
1995 Ikea presents its series *PS* as "democratic design"

At the 1995 furniture fair in Milan, Ikea celebrated its fiftieth anniversary and hung big banners with the slogan "Democratic Design" all over the city for the occasion. This slogan also served as the title of the company's anniversary book, which explained that democratic here means "to offer beautiful, practical furniture at a price most people can afford." Ikea sees itself as following directly in the footsteps of pioneers such as **Ellen Key,** who in 1899 was very much in the news with her book *Skönhet för alla (Beauty for All).* Appalled by the awful housing conditions of that time, Key, a socialist, called for improvements and also for an aesthetic education of the people. To this end, she organized home decor shows at the workers' institute, and in 1917 she participated in the big *Hemutställningen* (home show), where furniture and housewares were displayed.

At issue was a new functional, popular design with uncomplicated products suitable for industrial production. The "dinnerware set for workers" by **Wilhelm Kåge,** simple stoneware with rustic motifs, and Evin Oller's tinted glasses, both of which were shown at the home show are considered early examples of the new product design. However, since the 1930 Stockholm Exhibition—if not before—the democratic design reform has been driven by a rational Bauhaus-**functionalism.** Particularly following the crisis in the world economy, the reform's social component was more relevant than ever before. A prime example is **Kaj Franck's** modular combination dinnerware set that offered both a

new concept for the dining table and a successful design for ordinary folk. Contemporary Scandinavian designers also are very much aware of the social dimension of their work. To be elitist is to be design-politically incorrect. Beautiful, practical, and affordable design "for all" is also among the goals of the consumer cooperatives, an outgrowth of social democracy. For example, in Sweden they launched as late as 1978 an affordable series of basic furniture (together with Svensk Form).

However, in the meantime the working class has gotten lost in the shuffle. For half a century the social democrats have been governing the Scandinavian countries, considered the world over models for an affluent and middle-class society. Moreover, the Ikea era was already well underway, but its popular basis was not the antibourgeois movement, to which Ellen Key had still felt committed, but the new pop and leisure generation.

Ikea products are as democratic as a Volkswagen or a blouse by H&M, and the furniture supermarket found a very clever way of playing off its new collection against the chic haute-couture design at the 1995 fair in Milan. Ikea presented its novelties stylishly in a former greenhouse. For visitors who had just come from Moroso or Cappellini, where a chair could easily run into the five figures, one detail may have been particularly telling: the Ikea furniture had price tags.

"A unified taste gives a unified form to all of society. This is the deeper meaning of the slogan 'more beautiful everyday things.'"

Gregor Paulsson

From left to right:

Enameled coffeepots by Antti Nurmesniemi, 1957

Åke Huldt discusses a spindle-back chair

Table *Ted* by Nils Gammelgaard for Ikea, 1983

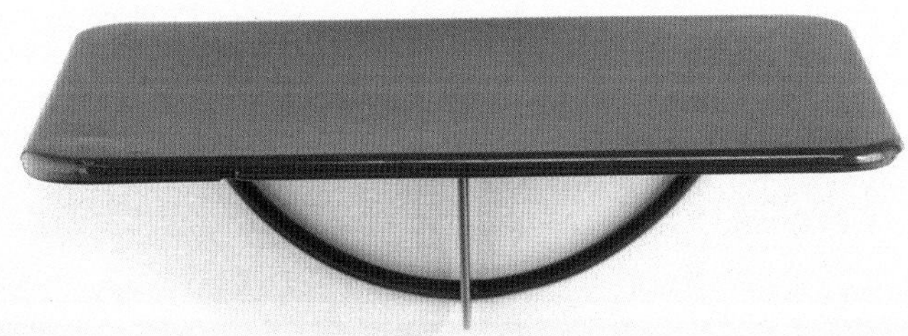

DISSING & WEITLING

Firm of Architects and Designers / Denmark

Dissing & Weitling Arkitektfirma A/S, Copenhagen

1971 Founded by **Hans Dissing** and **Otto Weitling** after the death of **Arne Jacobsen**

1980 Museum art collection, NRW, Dusseldorf

1981 ID Prize (also in 1989)

1993 iF-Industry Forum Design, Hanover

1998 Suspension bridge across the Great Belt; restoration of the IG-Farben House in Frankfurt

Products

1989 Eyeglasses *Titan*

1992 Bus shelters in Denmark

1995 Lamps for restaurant in Parliament

The warehouse in Copenhagen's Christianshavn district housing the company's offices is covered with graffiti. One of the largest architectural firms in Denmark which is also one of the most renowned in Europe is domiciled in this suburban milieu. After the death of **Arne Jacobsen,** Hans Dissing and Otto Weitling took on his clients as well as his design legacy. Their successor firm, which has already gained a quarter century of experience, employs around 100 architects, technicians, and designers and is thus prepared even for megaprojects such as the 12-mile-long connection between the islands Sjælland and Fyn, of which the largest suspension bridge in the world forms a part. Their most successful designs are smaller, however. When Hans Dissing had trouble with his reading glasses, an in-house team developed a new type of glasses, made of titanium and light as a feather, (mostly weighing less than half an ounce). The construction of the glasses in this series is unusual because they get by without any screws or soldered points. Moreover, the modular design allows an optimal order and inventory system (doing away with the usual waiting periods). In addition, the designers have worked on a great variety of products, such as medical diagnosis equipment, taxi displays, street lights, furniture, and stamps. As is typical for Denmark, public signage and an elegant, pleasing decor of towns and cities is considered important. Thus Dissing & Weitling has also contributed place-name signs, public rest rooms, and sound barriers to the tasteful decor of the urban landscape.

Suspension bridge across the Great Belt

Page 157

Titanium eyeglasses *Air,* 1990s

Nanna DITZEL

Designer of Furniture, Textile, and Jewelry / Denmark

1923 Nanna Hauberg born in Copenhagen

1945 Studied at the art academy, Copenhagen (1946 commercial arts school)

1945 Second prize at the Cabinetmakers' Guild (awarded first prize in 1950)

1946 Marriage to Jørgen Ditzel (all projects were created jointly until his death in 1961)

1954 Book *Danish Chairs;* works for **Georg Jensen**

1956 Lunning Prize

1960 Gold medal at the *Triennial,* Milan (silver medal in 1951, 1954, and 1957)

1962 One-person show in London (later also in New York, Berlin, Vienna, and Milan)

1967 Contributing editor for the magazine *Mobilia*

1968 Marriage to Kurt Heide, lives in London

1981 Chairwoman of the Design & Industries Association

1986 Return to Copenhagen

Page 159

Top: *Bench for Two,* 1989

Bottom left: Folding chair

Bottom right: chair *Tempo,* 1997

In 1944, when she was just twenty years old and still a student at the Commercial Art School, she and her future husband Jørgen Ditzel presented a completely furnished room at the traditional annual exhibition of the Copenhagen cabinetmakers. It was in every respect "furniture for modern living" commented one daily paper. Nanna Ditzel, the grande dame of Danish design, still exerts an important influence on the profession. Her concept seems to be precisely not to unnecessarily confine herself to only one thing. "When I begin to design an object," she says, "everything is possible and everything is allowed." This is both a challenge and an opportunity. "Just imagine you sit there with paper and pencil and invent something that nobody has ever seen before. That's something we did not learn when we studied with **Kaare Klint.**"

In the postwar decades, practical furniture for cramped living quarters was needed. The Ditzels, themselves at first living in a 485-square-foot apartment that also served as studio, knew those problems firsthand. After a stormy series of successes—among others at the *Triennials* in Milan—their circumstances as well as their projects changed. One of their favorite ideas was to distribute activities over several levels of a house or apartment, whether play areas for children, "legless living room furniture" that touched the floor, or meeting places at staggered heights in public parks. Back then Nanna Ditzel, who since the 1950s had also been working for **Georg Jensen's** silversmith workshop, particularly drew attention with her very successful furniture. For example, the easy chair *Ring* and the egg-shaped *Hammock Chair,* a floating wicker beach chair for crawling into (as later into **Eero Aarnio's** *Ball*), were renowned.

After the death of her husband, Nanna Ditzel's solo career began. At first influenced by the 1960s fondness for

experimentation, she became part of the avant-garde circle centering around the ambitious magazine *Mobilia* to which her young colleagues **Verner Panton** and the artist **Aagaard Andersen** also belonged. Nanna Ditzel tried her hand at foam material and fiberglass, and at the same time designed the textile series *Hallingdal,* a classic that is still in production in more than 100 color variations.

In 1968 she married for the second time and moved to London. Two decades later, after the death of her second husband, this astonishing woman returned from the British metropolis to Copenhagen to begin here her fourth career, perhaps the most amazing of all. That she now works (or could work) for all the upscale brands in the Danish furniture industry is not only due to her reputation but above all to the fact that her products sell very well. For example, **Fredericia** is said to have increased its sales by about a third merely on account of the success of the chair, *Trinidad.*

Nanna Ditzel's way of working is sensual and direct. From the first draft on paper she quickly proceeds to full-size models. "I cultivate the flowing shape," says Scandinavia's only female design star. She often takes her favorite material, plywood, to the point of splintering. One of her most exciting objects is the delicate chair *Butterfly* that rests on bent legs (illustration page 15): an asymmetrical masterpiece and also a chic antithesis to the Nordic furniture minimalism.

Products

1952 "Legless" furnishings
1955 Children's high chair
1957 Easy chair *Ring* (now **Fredericia**); *Hammock Chair*
1962 *Living Room on Several Levels;* children's chair *Trisser*
1964 Textile series *Hallingdal* for **Kvadrat**
1984 Table *Flower*
1988 Color scheme for Intercity train
1989 *Bench for Two*
1990 Chair *Butterfly* for Fredericia
1992 Chair *Fan*
1993 Chair *Trinidad;* table *Tobago* for Fredericia; wristwatch for **Georg Jensen;** office chair *In Charge* for **Claus Lundsgaard**
1997 Chair *Tempo* for Fredericia

Trevira upholstery fabric *Pisa* for Kvadrat

Hammock Chair for Bonacina, 1957

Tias ECKHOFF

Designer of Ceramics, Metal, and Furniture / Norway

Lunning prizewinner Tias Eckhoff is one of the prominent Scandinavian designers who were tremendously successful internationally in the 1950s with their lightweight, soft forms, inspired, among other things, by art nouveau. He had begun his career as a ceramist, studying with the Danish master **Nathalie Krebs** in her legendary pottery **Saxbo.** Back in Norway, while still attending classes at the university, he was hired by the porcelain factory **Porsgrund** and soon took on its artistic direction (as successor of **Nora Gulbrandsen**). His coffee and tea service *Det riflede (The Grooved Ones)* is generally considered a milestone in Norwegian design. It marks the transition from cool **functionalism** to "humane," **organic design.** In the years following, several other notable dinnerware designs had their origin on his drafting table, for example, the heat-resistant set *Glohane.* His approach was rationalist and almost scientific. As freelance product designer, Eckhoff worked for a number of renowned manufacturers, among them **Norsk Stålpress** and **Georg Jensen,** for whom he designed the award-winning silver flatware set *Cypress,* among others. Later Eckhoff also designed steel and plastic furniture in his own studio, at times even without being commissioned by a client.

1926 Born in Vestre Slidre

1945 Ceramics training at **Saxbo** (until 1949)

1953 Designer-in-chief at **Porsgrund**; Lunning Prize

1960 Design studio in Oslo

1954 Gold medals, *Triennial*

1974 Jacob Design Prize

1991 Norwegian Classics Prize

Products

1952 Dinnerware set *Det riflede* for Porsgrund; flatware Cypress for **Georg Jensen**

1961 Flatware *Maya* for **Norsk Stålpress**

1983 Plastic chair *Tomi*

1989 Flatware *Chaco* for Norsk Stålpress

Flatware *Maya* for Norsk Stålpress, 1959

Antti EKLUND

Advertising Artist, Product Designer, and Interior Decorator / Finland

1960 Born in Turku
1986 Advertising agency Daff Design
1988 Best Interior Decorator, Finland
1989 Design firm **Animal Design**
1990 Best Advertising in Finland
1992 Best Poster in Finland
1994 Design management for **Marimekko**
1996 ID Design Prize, Environment

"My name is Antti Eklund." With these words a young designer approached the Italian business owner Alberto Alessi in 1990 and pulled his presentation out of his pocket. The Italian, who had just finished giving a lecture at the University of Helsinki, had never heard of this new talent before, but since then Eklund has designed several products for the famous upscale brand (the first Finnish designer to do so since **Eliel Saarinen**). His heaviest design is the silver tray *Salamander,* his funniest the corkscrew *Funny Bunny.* Animal motifs are among Eklund's favorite themes. That is why his company is called **Animal Design.** Under this logo the communication professional, whose advertising brochures have won several awards, has been successful in such different fields as corporate identity development, interior design, and packaging design. The animals in Eklund's designs proliferate in two-dimensional as well as three-dimensional versions, for example, in an award-winning poster series for an anti-AIDS campaign, in silk ties covered with crawling, colorful lizards, in an

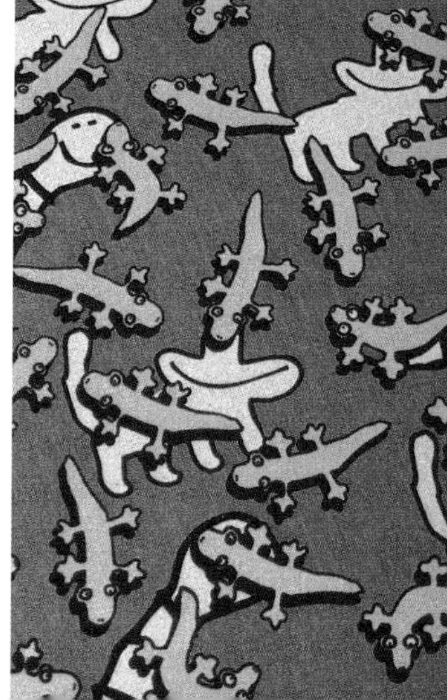

on-screen interface for an interactive TV, or in the can opener *Mouse* with Mickey Mouse ears. According to Eklund, "simply riding on the Aalto wave is a mortal sin for every Finnish designer." Nevertheless, some of his colleagues prefer to play it safe, because Finland's industry still "lacks the refinement to work with designers."

An exception to this rule is **Marimekko.** Antti Eklund played a decisive role in the revival of this Finnish legend in 1994. As outside design strategist he not only contributed a whole product group—from sunglasses to CD cases—to the company's revamped product line and reinvented its advertising image but also updated the stores of the textile chain. He had barely six weeks to furnish the first store on Helsinki's shopping mile, Pohjois Espanadi. Eklund's 2-D/3-D philosophy of graphical decor, which looks to the customers like an oversized comic, is taken to the extreme in the flat lighting elements whose height measures less than a tenth of an inch.

Products

1994 Office furniture made of recycled plastic

1995 Graphic for Telecom, Finland

1994 Tray, *Salamander* for **Alessi;** textile collection *Lisko*

1996 Corkscrew *Funny Bunny* for Alessi

1998 Can opener *Mouse* for Animal Design

From left to right:

Corkscrew *Funny Bunny* for Alessi

Fabric pattern Salamander for Marimekko
Cell phone with fur (prototype)

ELECTROLUX

Manufacturer of Household Appliances / Sweden

AB Electrolux, Stockholm

1919 Lux and Elektromekanista merge into Electrolux

1926 Vacuum cleaner factory in Germany, later in England, France (both 1927), and the United States (1931)

1928 Admission to official listing on London stock exchange

1936 One million refrigerators

1962 Refrigerator design *Future Line* (1975 *New Generation,* 1980 *Generation 80*)

1974 Largest vacuum cleaner manufacturer

1980 Bought up several companies, among them Progress, Zanussi (1984), White Consolidated (1985), Buderus (1989) and AEG (1994)

1988 Strategy *Design Families*

1992 Concept *Kitchen of the Future*

1997 Two-year reorganization, closing of 25 factories

He crossed the oceans in his luxury yacht and wherever he dropped anchor, he demonstrated the advantages of Electrolux refrigerators to his prominent guests. Axel Wenner-Gren, entrepreneur, sales genius, and rake, personifies the company's legendary success story. That story began in 1921 with the hand vacuum cleaner V. Before 1945 Electrolux had already developed into a multinational company, selling its appliances in the United States. From there the first designer was hired in 1940. None other than Raymond Loewy put in an appearance at Electrolux until the Swedish designer **Sixten Sason** took over the responsibility for streamlining the appliances. The versatile food processor *Assistant* by Alvar Lenning (illustration page 41) was one of the biggest sales successes of that time.

Back then product design was still largely the job of the engineers. Even during the 1960s—the decade so fond of innovation—a mere ten staffers handled Electrolux product design. Today about eighty employees work in four design centers scattered over the globe. Since the late 1970s Electrolux, the largest manufacturer of household appliances in the world—more than 100,000 employees produce about one million appliances per week—has been swallowing up on average two competitors per

Vacuum cleaner *Model V,* 1921

Page 165

Vacuum cleaner *Z70* by Sixten Sason

Refrigerator by Raymond Loewy

Food processor *Assistent,* 1940

ELECTROLUX
Assistent

Products

1921 Vacuum cleaner *Model V*

1925 Refrigerator *Model D* (absorption technology)

1938 Streamlined vacuum cleaner and refrigerators by Raymond Loewy

1939 National Refrigerator according to criteria of Swedish standard kitchen

1940 Food processor *Assistant,* by **Alvar Lenning**

1951 Washing machine *W 20*

1957 Vacuum Cleaner *Z 80* by **Sixten Sason**

1991 Energy-saving refrigerator (1993 free of chlorofluorocarbons CFC)

1997 Cordless vacuum cleaner *Combilite*

1998 Robot vacuum cleaner (prototype)

Page 167

Top: Vacuum cleaner *Robot* (prototype), 1998

Bottom left: Food processor *SEP 101* by Carl Gustav Frisell, 1995

Bottom right: washing machine *Zoe* by Roberto Pezzetta for Zanussi/Electrolux, 1992

month. With ninety percent of sales coming from outside Sweden, the company has established a presence in all important industrial countries. Behind this growth is a complex network of regional, national, and transcontinental brands. In spite of this confused situation, the company has designed a unified corporate identity. According to Christian Klingspor, one of the managing designers, this process is based on "the curved line," a subtle detail whose identity-creating power seems doubtful.

By means of design, product lines are tailored to particular groups of buyers and are then further subdivided according to regional tastes. For example, in Asia, where changes in design are expected to happen quickly, refrigerators are sold in bright colors and must be "technologically sophisticated," but in the United States the "cheerful" streamline-appeal dominates (e.g., Frigidaire). In its design management, Electrolux has created a hierarchy of "styling families": from conservative alpha-brands for people who want to "show off success" (e.g., Electrolux) to beta-brands appreciated for their functionality (e.g., Husquarna), inexpensive gamma-brands for starter households (e.g., Quelle) and delta-brands with pronounced "creative styling" (e.g., Zanussi). Different brands within each group differ in color and graphic design. The targeted goal is the creation of a new design for each styling family every year. Even "white goods," up to now almost design-resistant, nowadays no longer have to be white and can also be recruited into this "cyclical renewal of the company aesthetics." Electrolux wants to be seen as a leading innovator. To this end it has begun far-ranging studies—for example, of the "kitchen of the future"—and is expanding its "eco-brand" (AEG) and developing new high-tech products such as the robot vacuum cleaner or the solar-powered lawnmower that is also easy on the ears.

Electrolux
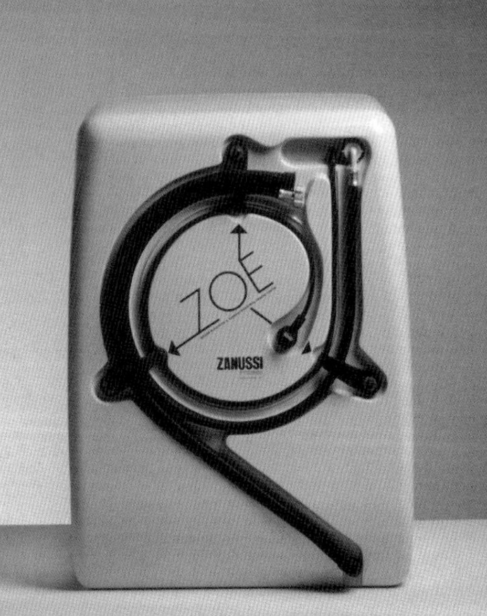
ZOE
ZANUSSI

ERGONOMI

Studio for Product Design / Sweden

Ergonomi Design Gruppen AB, Stockholm

1973 Study by **Maria Benkzton** and **Sven-Eric Juhlin** on handles for the disabled

1979 Designgruppen and Ergonomi Design merge into Ergonomi Design Gruppen (EDG)

1988 Participation in the exhibition *Design for Independent Living,* MOMA, New York

In 1988 the Museum of Modern Art in New York presented the exhibition *Design for Independent Living,* which brought a design area to the attention of the international public that had largely been hidden until then, namely, design for the sick and disabled. Two out of three exhibits came from Scandinavia. One of the most striking objects was a food slicer with a frame that worked like a saw and made it possible to slice bread with only minimal effort. It was designed by Ergonomi, a Stockholm collective which specializes in designing safe and efficient products for the disabled. Ergonomi Design Group, EDG for short, epitomizes a team-oriented approach and the ideals of the 1960s. It is one the Sweden's largest design studios, among its best known members—even outside Sweden—are **Maria Benktzon** and **Sven-Eric Juhlin,** who were the first to work on designs for the disabled. Ergonomi defines its field of activity in larger terms as "the relationship between person and machine," whether in a hospital, in a factory, or in the home. Ergonomi's designers

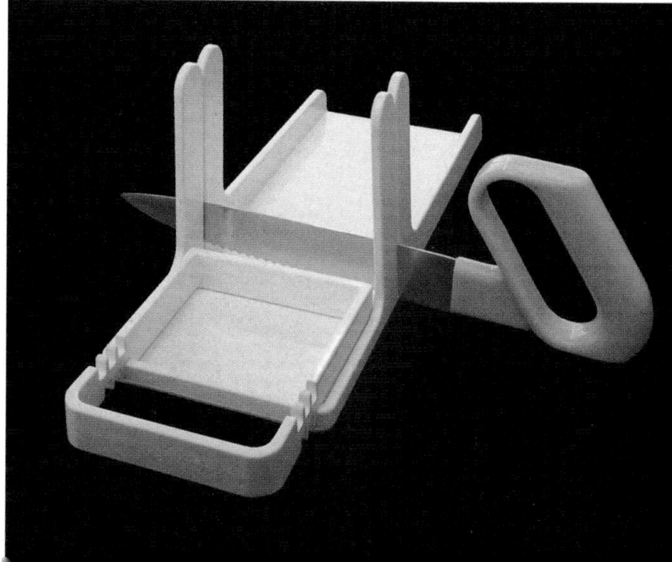

From left to right:

Food slicer *Ideal* for Hackman

Knife with ergonomic handle

Crutch with ergonomic handle

include the results of extensive interviews with end users in their decisions on a product's final design.

Every project begins with intensive research (often with videotaped motion studies). Finally the practical viability of the design is tested on life-size models. Among the first Ergonomi projects were studies on handles, first for the state institute for the disabled, later also for businesses. In collaboration with physicians and physiotherapists, EDG developed aids for the sick, such as crutches with specially designed handles designed for particular illnesses, for example, arthritis. The kitchen knife with frame was later followed by a whole collection of eating and drinking utensils for the disabled, who thanks to this collection became less dependent on their helpers for their daily needs. Ergonomi's approach follows the tradition of democratic design, supplemented here by designs for the disabled.

Products

1974 Food slicer *Ideal* with frame for **Hackman**

1979 Ball-point pen for rheumatics

1980 Flatware for the disabled

1988 Coffee service for SAS

1986 Tools *Ergo* for **Bahco**

1989 Ergonomic crutches; flatware for children with multiple disabilities

ERGONOMICS

1924 **Kaare Klint** opens furniture school in Copenhagen

1934 Chair *Eva* by *Bruno Mathsson*

1958 **Volvo** introduces the three-point seat belt

1959 Henry Dreyfuss publishes *The Measure of Man*

1967 Scissors with plastic handles by **Fiskars**

1972 Children's chair *Tripp-Trapp* by **Peter Opsvik** for **Stokke**

1974 Food slicer *Ideal* for the disabled by **Ergonomi**

1979 First *Balans* chair

1995 Computer workstation *Netsurfer* by **Teppo Asikainen** and **Ilkka Terho** for **Valvomo**

1996 **Saab** introduces "active headrests"

The exhibition *The Human Dimension,* put on by Sweden's association of industrial designers in 1994 in Bergamo, was a flop. South of the Alps people cold-shouldered forklifts, wrenches, and vacuum cleaners. The attempt to shine with ergonomic competency failed in part also because the know-how contained in the objects is usually not visible from the outside. The term "ergonomics" entered the design vocabulary during World War II when weapons had to be optimized and their operation had to be improved. In civilian life such efficient design is still a rarity. Among the pioneers of the trend to ergonomic design are **Fiskars,** which already in the 1960s gave our household scissors a more handy design, and **Kompan,** which created playground equipment properly proportioned for children. When the Swedish manufacturer **Bahco** had screwdrivers examined in the 1980s, it turned out that not one of them was suitable for two-handed use, even though workmen usually use both hands to work. As a result, the company developed the two-handed tool series *Ergo.*

Kaare Klint is generally considered the precursor of ergonomic thinking. He was one of the first to classify furniture as "tools." In designing a chair, Klint focused above all on how its proportions matched those of the human figure. His anatomical **functionalism** is paralleled by **Bruno Mathsson's** studies of seating; its modern counterpart is the work of the Norwegian **Balans**-Group, whose ingenious chair constructions unveiled completely new ways of sitting in the 1970s. The common element

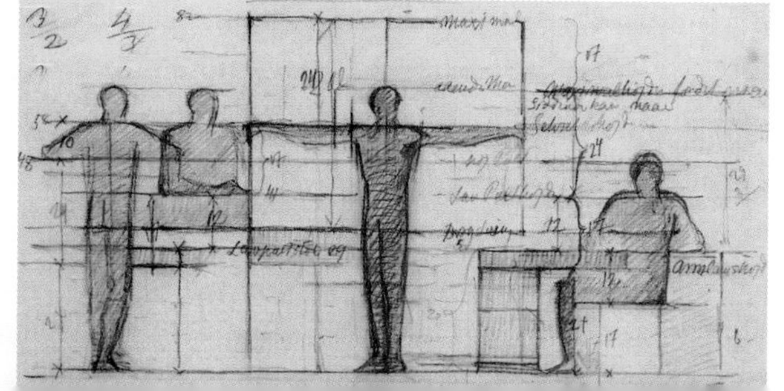

in all these designs was the focus on the interaction between chair and body. The Swedish design studio **Ergonomi** also gained recognition in this field and developed a model for the ergonomic research process. Essential elements of this process are the team approach, participation of users in the problem's definition, and finally the empirical underpinning of the design through situation analyses as well as the inclusion of disabled in the overall design program. Ergonomi became famous because of the aids it developed for the frail and infirm, everything from basic crutches to jar openers for arthritics. In most recent times the term "ergonomics" has been expanded by a cognitive component. The tactile orientation aids for the blind on public paths developed by the design studio **Knud Holscher** are a good example of this new development.

"We have to work in areas where there are unsolved problems."
Maria Benktzon

Scandinavian auto manufacturers have long since tried to set themselves off from the competition by emphasizing the "human dimension," especially in the area of safety. Innovations in this area often came from Sweden, from the three-point seat belt (**Volvo,** 1958) to the "active head rest" (**Saab,** 1996). Increasingly, Scandinavian industries have strengthened their market position through the use of ergonomic methods. An example is Oticon in Denmark, which reinvented the hearing aid. Parents also know the children's chair *Tripp-Trapp* by **Stokke** that grows along with the children. In Scandinavia, ergonomics has made its way even into the nursery.

From left to right:

Furniture studies by Kaare Klint, 1917

Firefighter's breathing apparatus by Jakob Wagner, 1998

Loppers and pruning shears by Fiskars, 1994

Oscillating chair by Søren Ulrik Petersen, 1995

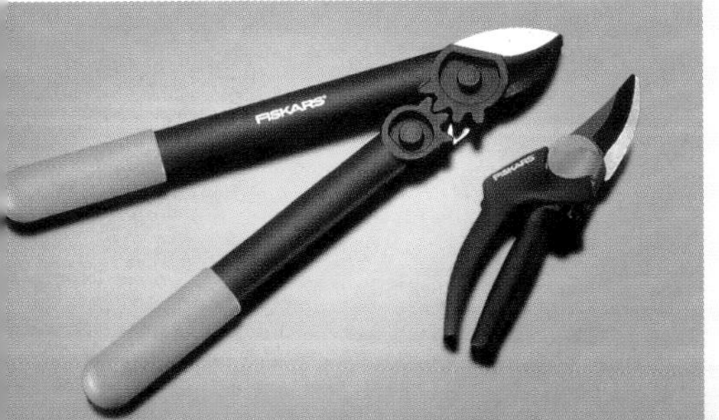

ERICSSON

Manufacturer of Telecommunications Equipment / Sweden

Cell phones are perishable items. At the end of the 1990s the half-life of new products from Sweden's largest telecommunications company was a mere twelve months. That means that every two years Ericsson develops a completely new "product portfolio"—which also serves as a job creation program for designers. By contrast, Ericsson's first telephones were long runners. The table model introduced in 1892 was not replaced until seventeen years later, but the replacement was pretty much on the cutting edge and set the standard for Europe for the coming years. For the first time an artist was consulted in the development of this new product. The Norwegian painter and modernist **Jean Heiberg** gave the new compact model a functional form with clear edges and angles. The apparatus was rational through and through. The Bakelite housing had definite advantages; it was not only easier to mold but also saved on weight and, even more important in terms of production engineering, it did away with the several coats of paint that had been necessary before, thus shrinking production time

Telefonaktiebolaget LM Ericsson, Stockholm

1876 Lars Magnus Ericsson founds workshop for telegraph equipment

1885 First Ericsson telephone

1932 Losses due to economic crisis; ITT takes over thirty-four percent of shares (bought back by Wallenberg in 1960)

1942 Radar for defense industry

1950 First automated exchange in the world, Stockholm-Copenhagen

1981 Division information systems established

1983 Participation in *Gripen-Jet*

1989 Division mobile communications established

1996 Strategic study *2005*

dramatically from days to only minutes. The new phone, introduced in Sweden in 1931 and then exported to England, conquered the British Empire. In the mid-1950s Ericsson put the *Ericofon* on the market, signaling another telephone revolution (illustration page 25). An in-house design team had worked on this model for fifteen years. This new phone caught the eye immediately because of its soft, candy-colored shapes; with its convenience it anticipated later telephone generations. It was the first phone made in one piece, that is, the receiver and dial were no longer separate. Ericsson, today a high-tech company with around 90,000 employees (almost a quarter of them work in development) intensively advertises its line of pocket telephones. Products such as the five-ounce mini cell phone *GF 788,* which can be operated with one hand, and the cordless telephone *DT 120,* a flat, slightly curved disc that stands out clearly from the popular biomorphous design, are top products from the late 1990s—and yet will be on the scrap heap tomorrow.

Products

1892 First table telephone

1923 Introduction of the dial

1931 Bakelite telephone by **Jean Heiberg**

1956 *Ericofon*

1966 Telephone with key pad

1991 First digital cell phone system

1997 Cordless telephone *DT 120* by Richard Lindahl; cell phone *GF 788* by Lawton & Yeo

Bakelite telephone by Jean Heiberg, 1931

Cell phones, 1980s and 1990s

Thomas ERIKSSON

Architect and Furniture Designer/Sweden

1959 Born in Örnsköldsvik (northern Sweden)

1981 Studies architecture in Stockholm (until 1985)

1988 Freelance architect

1992 Furniture exhibitions in Milan, New York, and Cologne for Cappellini

1995 Swedish Design Prize for product program

Products

1993 Medicine cabinet for Cappellini

1994 Sofa table *TE 1*

1995 Candlestick *PS* and TV-table for **Ikea**

1998 SAS *Euroclass Lounge*, Milan and London; interiors for **Absolut**

Absolut, Cappellini, H&M, **Ikea, SAS,** Virgin: this partial client list shows the architect Thomas Eriksson to be very much in demand, his preference for the understatement notwithstanding. Cappellini's catalog *progetto ogetto* offers, in addition to bathroom fittings of pronounced simplicity and a ladder-shaped coatrack, objects of almost symbolic significance, such as the traffic-light red medicine cabinet in red-cross design and racks whose E-shape alludes unequivocally to their creator. Eriksson's contributions to Ikea's furniture series *PS,* for whose presentation he was responsible, are similarly minimalist. One of the designers around **Swecode,** Eriksson is also represented in the collections of **Asplund** and **CBI.** He has designed the interiors of renowned companies. For many years he worked on the lounges of SAS, which offers its passengers not only in Stockholm and Copenhagen but also in Heathrow and Newark neo-Nordic flair and an open fire in the grate. At SAS one is always surrounded by blond wood whether in the bar or in the lavatory.

Occasional tables *Progetto 9304* for Cappellini

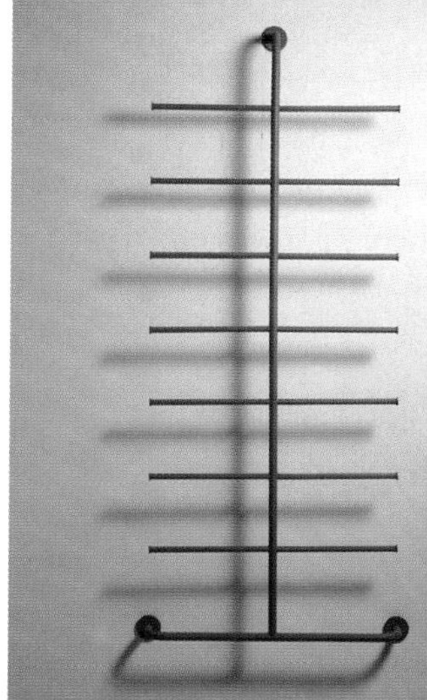

Wall coatrack for Cappellini

FISKARS

Tool Manufacturer / Finland

When Finns abroad see orange-colored scissors, they are seized by a feeling of national pride and check discretely whether it is indeed an original—Fiskars scissors made in Finland. In 1967 Fiskars introduced scissors whose ergonomically designed, shining orange plastic handles caught the eye. The cutting tool with the handy grips was the first of its kind worldwide and soon became the best known industrial product of the country—indeed, something of a cult object (*Classic* scissors, illustration page 46). Since then Fiskars has become a flagship of Finnish design. In a country where designers are honored like gold-medal winners, this is a notable feat, particularly for a company whose designers remain largely in the background. Encouraged by the Finnish design boom of the 1950s, Fiskars had worked back then with the silversmith **Bertel Gardberg.** But the company's breakthrough came only with the trendy scissors. In the meantime it is in its fifth generation and is offered in eighteen different versions. "The **ergonomics** can always be improved,"

Fiskars Oy, Helsinki

1649 Founded as ironworks

1837 First machine room in Finland

1918 Bought up tool manufacturer Billnäs

1988 ION Prize, Netherlands

1990 *High Design Quality NRW* (also in 1996); the old factory becomes a designer and artisan colony (see Guide)

1994 *Good Industrial Design,* IFD, Hanover (also in 1996)

1997 Good Design Award, Chicago; European Design Prize

Ax *Handy* by Olavi Lindén

Products

1957 Flatware *Triennial* by Bertel Gardberg

1967 Scissors with plastic handle by Olof Bäckström (now *Classic*)

1990 Ergonomic shovels and pitchforks

1994 Collapsible pocket scissors

1995 Ax *Handy*

1996 Garden tools *Planters;* garden loppers *Clippers*

says Olavi Lindén, the head of development. He has additional catchphrases handy, such as "Design is the art to make the consumers' wishes coincide with the possibilities of industrial production." Or, "Good industrial design must improve the products and lower the costs." The company philosophy is based on pure ergonomics and pure positivism, which accepts only facts as criteria. Therefore, the six staff members of the design and development department can often be seen working in gloves and rubber boots.

All products are tested again and again under actual working conditions, and the results speak for themselves. The company's collection of international design prizes is awe-inspiring. At the same time Fiskars has also caught on in building supply stores, its most important sales channel. Though its largest export market is the United States, the company is especially proud that its ergonomic shovels, introduced in the 1990s, became the best-selling product of their kind in the gardening paradise Great Britain. Now Fiskars has reinvented the ax. Ever since axes were made of metal, the handle has been connected to the blade through an eye in the blade. By contrast, in the *Handy* ax the plastic handle grasps the blade, a much more stable constellation. A similarly pioneering development is the mechanism in the *Clippers* loppers, which has won several awards and noticeably increases cutting power. For the sake of greater distinctiveness, the company here also deviated from the path of simplicity and gave the loppers a stylish, biomorphous form.

Fiskars employs about 4,000 people in four plants. Since its historical factory was given up, artisans, artists, and designer studios have settled there and breathed new life into Finland's oldest iron foundry with their well-attended exhibitions.

Page 177

Loppers *Clippers* by Olavi Lindén, 1996

FISKARS

Brita FLANDER

Glass Designer and Artist / Finland

1957 Born in Vasa

1994 *Master* for Industrial Design in Helsinki

1988 Freelance designer, teaches glass design at the Design School in Helsinki

Products

1989 Glass object *Retretti 91*

1991 Candlestick *Runko* for **Marimekko**

1992 Ceiling light *Bemböe*

1993 Glasses *Kvinnor* (women) for Marimekko

1996 Bowls *Enträgna Nippor* for **Hackman**

In the past Finland's brightest sources of light were sticks of resinous fir called *Päre.* They burned with a clear, bright flame and a farmer might use thousands of them per year. Brita Flander's *Päre* is made of plywood, light textile fibers, and polished crystal glass. The 16-foot-high creation, hangs from the ceiling, bends easily under its own weight and also pays homage to an extinct culture.

The very special relationship of the Finns to light and darkness is one of Brita Flander's great themes to which she has devoted many an installation. She is considered the new hope of Finnish glass design, which threatened to stagnate in the 1990s. The novice learned the traditional glass art under Unto Suominen, one of the last glassblowers of the old school from the legendary **Nuutajärvi** factory.

She became known through the furnishing house **Skanno's** 1993 "Pro Luce" competition for lighting that would help against *kaamos,* the time in which the days hardly get light at all. Brita Flander's contribution was *Räppänä* (hole in the wall), a flat, window-shaped wall light that can brighten breakfast tables and lift darkened spirits. An idea as simple as this was magical, and this design was followed by a series of lamps with glass shades. Flander, now living in France, sets new trends, particularly with her work for manufacturers such as Skanno, **Artek,** and the textile company, **Marimekko,** for which she has designed drinking glasses.

Ceiling light, Sammonlathi Church

Floor lamp *Light Cube,* 1996

Ceiling Lamp *Luoti* for Skanno, 1993

Page 179

Wall lamp *Räppänä* for Skanno, 1993

Kaj FRANCK

Ceramics and Glass Designer / Finland

1911 Born in Viipuri

1932 Completes studies of commercial arts in Helsinki, works as illustrator, interior decorator, and textile designer

1946 Artistic director at **Arabia** (until 1961); art glass for **Iittala**

1950 Artistic director of the glass factory **Nuutajärvi** (until 1976)

1951 Design Prize *Triennial*, Milan (also in 1954 and 1957)

1955 Lunning Prize

1956 Trip to the United States

1957 Compasso d'oro

1960 Directs design school in Helsinki and reforms curriculum (until 1968)

1973 Professor of art

1989 Dies

1992 Retrospective at the MOMA, New York

In a recently published monograph about Franck, the Swedish design consultant Stefan Ytterborn apologizes for once having been "against Franck's ideas" and promptly rehabilitates him as "extremely relevant." Since the exhibition of his work at the Museum of Modern Art in New York, Franck's relevance has been common knowledge among experts. More importantly: after Franck's classics had been taken out of production in the 1970s, they are now again best-sellers at **Arabia** and at **Iittala.** For example, the glass series Kartio made a comeback in the beginning of the 1990s. It is exemplary for Franck's design principles: clear colors, simple forms, mix-and-match possibilities, and multifunctionality (illustration p. 28).

Kaj Franck, who is from a German-Swedish family, learned Finnish from his nanny and at first studied interior decorating. This master of ceramics for daily use triggered a "revolution on the dining table," as a Danish daily paper wrote back then, and became an influential teacher, especially when he joined Helsinki's faculty of design, whose curriculum he reformed. His career began after World War II, at first at Iittala, then as design director at Arabia and **Nuutajärvi.** As is so often the case, at first Franck had great difficulties gaining acceptance for his ideas.

Glass pitchers *2744* for Arabia, 1955

Page 181

Plate, mug, and bowl *Teema* for Arabia, 1977

Service *Teema* for Arabia

Products

1946 Bowls *DA* for Arabia (as all subsequent ceramic products)

1947 Vase *3239* with bubbles for Iittala

1949 Dinnerware set *Aurora;* service *Kilta* (1977 *Teema*); cocktail glasses *2744 (Kartio)*

1951 Teapot *KF*

1954 Glass vases *1541* for Nuutajärvi (as all subsequent glass products); Glass plate *5268*

1955 Dinnerware set *Snowball*

1957 Carafe *1502*

1958 Shaker *KA*

1959 Heat-resistant teapot *LA*

1960 Carafe *505*

1968 Goblet *KF 486*

1976 Glass pitchers *Art Rosso*

1977 Striped glass tumblers (individual pieces)

Moreover, because he preferred the Bauhaus-oriented "geometric spirit" to the prevailing trend of soft curves, he was considered an angry young designer. His credo was "to be radical and social" and that in deliberate contrast to the "Scandinavian idyll."

Franck's goal was a new material culture for ordinary folk. His plates, bowls, and glasses were as practical as stackable chairs. He wanted to "design things that are so obvious that they are hardly noticeable." He found his models in the simple and robust everyday articles of indigenous ethnic groups and in the typical "folk items" in manufacturers' pattern catalogs. His breakthrough came with Kilta (now Teema, a revised microwave-safe version), an anti-service against the prevailing European table etiquette. Franck's dinnerware set, by the way, was fired in the same kiln as Arabia's wash basins and toilet bowls. The novelty: the service was no longer intended for completion but consisted of more than thirty pieces that could be mixed and matched at will. "Mix-and-match" became a popular sport, first in Europe and then also in Finland. Some of the more than 25 million pieces sold ended up in illustrious locales, such as the cafeteria of the Picasso Museum in Paris. Franck's extensive glass production (for Iittala and Nuutajärvi) is also noteworthy; there he distinguished strictly between art and utilitarian objects. Among his colleagues are well-known contemporary Finnish glass designers, including **Oiva Toikka, Heikki Orvola,** and **Kerttu Nurminen.** It almost goes without saying that Franck strictly refused to have his name used in advertising—for that, so he reasoned, would only distract from the objects.

Josef FRANK

Architect and Furniture Designer / Sweden

The Austrian architect Josef Frank had to swallow some criticism for the duplex house he contributed in 1927 to the Stuttgart housing development, Weissenhof. It reminded one journalist of a brothel. In contrast to the angular **functionalism** of architecture, the interior consisted largely of soft, upholstered furniture strewn with cushions. In 1933 Frank, one of the renowned architects of the young Austrian Republic, emigrated to Sweden, where he was soon part of the inner circle of European modern design. But unlike his contemporary Le Corbusier, he did not want to completely rationalize living. For him a house was not a machine. It was part of his approach to design never compile his design principles into an imperative form.

As a cultivated humanist and connoisseur of historical furniture styles, Frank considered personal taste and the desire for comfort the basis of home decor. Among other things, he alluded to quantum physics, especially to Heisenberg's principles of uncertainty and randomness, and accordingly designed rooms

1885 Born in Baden near Vienna
1903 Architect in Vienna
1911 Marries the Swede Anna Sebenius
1925 Founds the company *Haus & Garten*
1927 House for Weissenhof housing development in Stuttgart
1932 House for Werkbund housing development in Vienna
1934 Emigrates to Sweden (Swedish citizen in 1939) works for Estrid Ericson, owner of **Svenskt Tenn**
1937 Design of the Swedish pavilion at the World's Fair in Paris and 1939 in New York, popularizes "Swedish Modern"
1952 Exhibition *Josef Frank: 20 Years at Svenkst Tenn*, National Museum, Stockholm
1967 Dies in Stockholm
1996 Retrospective, Bard Graduate Center, New York

Serving Trolley *691* for Svenkst Tenn, 1930s

Products

1925 Easy chair *No. 300* in walnut and leather; linen fabric *Primavera*

1930 Cabinet with *Mirakel*-pattern; iron plant stand

1934 Large sofa for Svenskt Tenn (as all subsequent products)

1936 Easy chair *No. 542*

1938 Three-armed candlestick

1939 Three-armed floor lamp

1940 Rattan chair

1944 Patterns *Gröna Fåglar, Manhattan,* and *Terrazzo*

1946 Display cabinet on cherry-wood base; table *No. 1057*

1950 Glass jewelry box; wooden candlestick

Page 185

Sofa with flowers, 1934

Fabric *Terrazzo,* 1944

Chair *300* (walnut), 1948

all for Svenskt Tenn

as though "chance has played the biggest role" in the decor. To him, an overly pure style seemed "bloodless," one reason why he picked a fight with Sweden's progressive Bauhaus-oriented designers.

Nevertheless, Frank later claimed the credit as inventor of "the Scandinavian style." He found his sphere of activity thanks to his patroness and comrade-in-arms, the entrepreneur Estrid Ericson. She made the outsider designer-in-chief of the furnishing house **Svenskt Tenn,** known for its modern, simple products. The eclectic Frank, however, approached his task quite differently. His designs were colorful, ingenious, and surprising. Instead of birch and elm he used walnut and mahogany. The extravagant curved lines of the oversized sofa he introduced in 1934 contrasted sharply with his lightweight, Viennese living room chairs and represented an open affront to the functionalist faction.

Frank preferred light, natural materials such as cane and rattan. Their selection was often based on East Asian models. One of his preferred models was the English Windsor chair. By constructing his furniture as lightweight and breezy as possible, Frank intended to make rooms appear open, spacious, and accessible. During his career the hard worker designed an astonishing 2,000 plus pieces of furniture, which comes out to one per week on average, not including his countless textile designs. Under his direction Svenskt Tenn developed a previously nonexistent variety of furniture types and materials, all in keeping with Frank's motto: "Whatever style we use, whether Baroque or tubular steel, is unimportant. What modern design has given us is freedom."

FREDERICIA

Furniture Manufacturer / Denmark

Fredericia Stolefabrik AS, Fredericia

1911 Founded in Fredericia

1955 Taken over and headed by Andreas Graversen (since 1995 by his son Thomas)

1971 Danish Furniture Prize

1995 ID Prize (for *Trinidad chair*)

Fredericia is one of the players in the top league of the Danish furniture industry. But that was not always the case. In the uncertain times after World War II, the chair factory in the town of the same name was close to bankruptcy. Andreas Graversen, owner of a furniture workshop in the same town, then took over the ailing competitor for a token sum and in short order made it into one of the top companies in the industry. The essential prerequisites for this development were already in place, namely, the beginning boom of Danish design and Graversen's contact to one of the most sought after furnituremakers.

Graversen persuaded **Børge Mogensen** to work for the salvaged company. The cabinetmaker designed a new collection at short notice. His furniture was practical and unpretentious, the incarnation of well-built Danish furniture then being exported all over the world. To this day Mogensen's *Spanish chair* is Fredericia's best known product. The creative artist and the businessman had met at the right moment. A similar stroke of

good fortune was to occur four decades later, when in 1990 the company began working with **Nanna Ditzel,** who had just returned from England. Thanks to her chair *Trinidad,* a prizewinner in the United States (and reminiscent of the wooden architecture of the colonial era or of an extended stay on the sunny Caribbean island), the company's sales shot way up.

With Ditzel, Fredericia—usually known for its decidedly Danish solidity—dared to step into the avant-garde realm. The designer's red and black *Butterfly* chair (illustration page 15) and the *Bench for Two,* as unusual as convincing, shattered the complacency of the industry. With this courageous artist the company now tried out new paths in technology. Ditzel's most recent chair, *Tempo,* has neither screws nor soldered points. The shell-like chair is held together by a newly developed super-adhesive tape, a highly efficient process that also reduces production time considerably, as its name indicates.

Products

1958 *Spanish Chair*

1962 Chairs 2212 and 2213

1965 *Shaker* table

1971 Sofa 2333, all by **Børge Mogensen**

1989 *Bench for Two*

1990 Chair *Butterfly*

1993 Chair *Trinidad* and table *Tobago,* all by **Nanna Ditzel**

1995 Sofa *Max* by **Pelikan**

1998 Chair *Tempo* by Nanna Ditzel

From left to right:

Chair *Trinidad* by Nanna Ditzel

Spanish Chair by Børge Mogensen

Spanish Chair (detail)

FRITZ HANSEN

Furniture Manufacturer/Denmark

Fritz Hansen A/S, Allerød

1872 Started as cabinetmaker's workshop by Fritz Hansen in Copenhagen

1898 Production in Allerød

1936 Seating for the royal theater

1979 Taken over by Skandinavisk Holding

1982 Bought up furniture manufacturer Kold Christensen (and in 1987 Munch Möbler, a manufacturer of office furniture)

1997 Anniversary exhibition

Products

1931 *Dan-Stol* in bentwood; first Danish tubular steel chair

1935 Work chairs with tubular steel

1950 Chair series *AX*

1952 Chair *Myren* (Ant)

1955 Chair *3107,* both by **Arne Jacobsen**

Page 189

Top: Chair *Myren (Ant)* by Arne Jacobsen, 1952

Bottom left: Chair *PK 0* by Poul Kjaerholm, 1952

Bottom right: Easy chair *Svanen* by Arne Jacobsen, 1958

"Objects are not born on the drafting table. They are the result of a close collaboration between designer and manufacturer," explains Vico Magistretti. For that reason the Italian regularly spends time in rural Denmark. The chairs he designed for Fritz Hansen are a deliberate continuation of the line that began with Arne Jacobsen. Curved tubular steel is among the designs elements. In the relationship with his client, however, Magistretti seems to stand apart from his predecessor. With the latter "There was actually no direct cooperation," remembers a former colleague. "I only heard from **Arne Jacobsen** when he didn't like something, and that happened often."

When the architect Jacobsen in the early 1950s submitted a chair design to Fritz Hansen that he had just completed for the cafeteria of the pharmaceutical factory **Novo Nordisk,** he was turned away. Back then the design seemed too daring to the Hansens, the risk too high. Since then, however, the three-legged chair *Myren* and its successors in the "series of sevens" have become the company's most successful products and are among the best-selling design objects. With the chair *3007,* Hansen GmbH aroused its competitors' envy and achieved sales in the millions. The company, which employs around three hundred people, is Denmark's top-selling furniture manufacturer with a sales volume of around sixty-six million dollars (1996).

Fritz Hansen, a Copenhagen master cabinetmaker, had started the company in his backyard workshop at the end of the nineteenth century. He supplied frames and turned legs for solid middle-class furniture. His first experiment was a bentwood chair built in the Thonet method. In the early 1930s he began adding tubular steel furniture to his product line, back then a novelty in Denmark that his customers found hard to accept. In those days the company made good money by installing seating in movie houses. One of its

1958 Polystyrene easy chair *Aegget* (egg) and Svanen (swan) by A. Jacobsen

1974 System chair *123* by **Verner Panton**

1982 Deck chair *PK 24* by **Poul Kjaerholm** (design 1965)

1984 Table with wing flaps by **Niels J. Haugesen**

1994 Chairs *Vico;* chairs and tables *Vicoduo* (1997) by Vico Magistretti; conference table *Click* by **Erik Magnussen**

1996 Office chair series *Spin* by Burkhard Vogtherr; room divider *Viper* by **Hans Sandgren Jacobsen**

Page 191

Top left: Window blind *Viper* by Hans Sandgren Jacobsen (detail)

Top right: Window blind *Viper*

Office chairs *Spin* by Burkhard Vogtherr

successful postwar products is the chair AX, intended for export and shipped disassembled in a box. This was only a prelude to the break with the past the Jacobsen chairs were to cause later on. More than fifty different models have resulted from the profitable business contacts with the reckless architect. Initially, the manufacture of extremely thin tubular steel legs presented a technical challenge. At the end of the 1950s another innovation followed, shell chairs made of foamed polystyrene; they too became best-sellers. Jacobsen's bold lines symbolized the break with tradition, above all that of the furniture trade.

The veneers for the shell seats are pressed just like sheet metal for automobiles. In the assembly process, the successful model *3107* is welded together at sixteen points, a procedure that takes only one second. In the 1970s a drop in sales plunged the company into a crisis, and even the sale of real estate did not save the family-owned business from being taken over by a tobacco concern. But now it is turning a profit again. Fritz Hansen has not only acquired a new corporate identity but also a considerable collection of classics, among them the table *Superellipsis* by **Piet Hein** and **Bruno Mathsson** as well as **Poul Kjaerholm's** very convincing work (illustration p. 17). Currently only a quarter of the company's sales revenue comes from within Denmark. Collaboration with designers such as Vico Magistretti and Burkhard Vogtherr in Germany is part of Fritz Hansen's image as an international company. The house recipe has remained the same, however, and furniture, especially office furniture, must be economical and practical. Like the earlier Jacobsen designs, the idea behind Fritz Hansen's furniture is often an astonishingly simple one, as in the award-winning room divider *Viper,* which is lighter than it looks because it is made of papier-mâché.

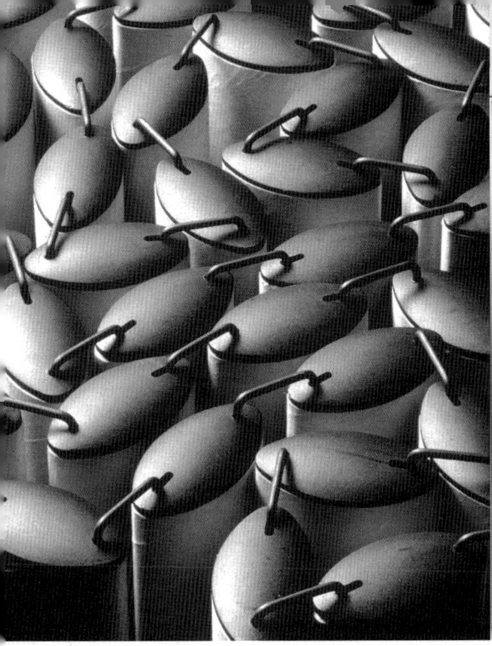

FUNCTIONALISM

1917 Founding of De Stijl; **Kaare Klint** studies furniture types
1919 Founding of the Bauhaus
1926 Lamps *PH* by **Poul Henningsen**
1927 Weissenhof housing development in Stuttgart; Sanomat building by **Alvar Aalto**
1930 *Stockholm Exhibition*
1932 Exhibition *International Style* at the MOMA, New York
1949 Dinnerware set *Kilta* by **Kaj Franck** for **Arabia**
1952 Chair *Myren* by **Arne Jacobsen** for **Fritz Hansen**
1965 Portable radio *Beolit 600* by **Jacob Jensen**
1972 Product series *d-line* by **Knud Holscher**
1975 Thermos by **Erik Magnussen** for **Stelton**
1995 Folding stool *Stockholm* by **A&E**
1997 Easy chair *Airbag* by **Ilkka Suppanen** for **Valvomo**

Toward the end of the 1950s Finland experienced an extensive migration to the cities. Hundreds of thousands of abandoned houses in the country were secured with padlocks bearing the label **Abloy.** Abloy is now one of the largest manufacturers of padlocks worldwide. Together with **Creadesign** it developed models that combine robustness, new cylinder systems, and innovative shapes. Abloy's padlocks are even included in the collection of the Museum of Modern Art in New York. Abloy epitomizes an application of design where functionality is of prime importance and design as such has traditionally played only a very minor role, if any. The padlocks are a typical case for Scandinavia, where the call for "more beautiful things" was heeded and where functionalism now seems to permeate everyday life completely. This has not always been the case.

Though designers like **Alvar Aalto** and **Poul Henningsen** did pioneering work in their fields, functional product design was long a stepchild of the profession, even after the 1930 *Stockholm Exhibition,* which demonstrated functionalism but could not gain acceptance for it. It was not until the 1940s that conditions became favorable. In postwar Sweden (and everywhere else in Scandinavia at just about the same time) the principles developed by the Bauhaus became a matter of general consensus. The left-wing government of Tage Erlander saw functionalism as the appropriate aesthetic for the realization of its commitment to progress. Together with the consumer cooperative, which owned

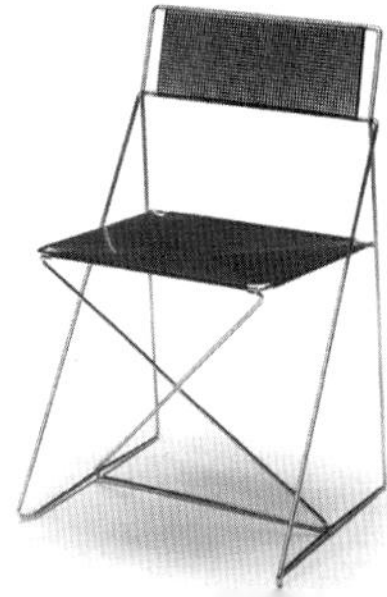

the ceramics factory **Gustavsberg,** among others, the government developed a design policy on a grand scale, financed extensive research programs, and established standard specifications.

In Denmark the artist **Børge Mogensen,** a member of the cooperative who lived in a tiny apartment in Copenhagen, developed one of the first modular wall units. Born of necessity, his modular furniture marked the beginning of a more flexible decor style that gained ground in the 1950s. The term *functionalism* had already arrived in the furniture advertisements of the time. Just as Mogensen cleared out the parlor, so **Kaj Franck** uncluttered the dining table. His multifunctional dinnerware set, such as the evergreen hit *Kilta,* survived even the postmodern 1980s unscathed.

In addition to its other remarkable achievements, Scandinavian product design seems to have stopped the natural aging process of several products, for example, **Jacob Jensen's** minimalist hi-fi systems. Jensen was one of the first to apply the flawless straight lines and the rejection of all frills to technical consumer products. To this day his approach, which turns the pieces of equipment into timeless monoliths, has found numerous followers. The young Finnish designers around **Snowcrash** chose another approach, however. They have taken up Victor Papanek's concept of "nomadic furniture" and see their work as a response to the predictable functionalism of a completely digitalized, hypermobile future.

"A design object should not reflect its time. It should point to the future."

Antti Nurmesniemi

From left to right:

Flatware by Kay Bojesen, 1930s

Stacking chair *X-line* by Niels Jørgen Haugesen, 1977

Lamp with shade by Timo Salli, 1996

Carpenter's level by Erik Magnussen, 1988

GÄRSNÄS

Manufacturer of Furniture and Lights / Sweden

The small town Gärsnäs in the Schonen district is the headquarters of the eponymous company consisting of approximately 120 employees. It would be a typical medium-sized furniture factory if it were not for its decidedly design-conscious management, which has incorporated product design for the last several decades (and won prizes for its work). In the first half of its existence the company specialized in "period furniture" for high-end tastes, but in the 1960s it discovered design as a viable survival strategy. In 1967 a chair in blond beech kicked off the new trend, which was later expanded and given functional form by designers like **Åke Axelsson** and Ralf Lindberg. In addition to solid wooden chairs, lighting classics are part of the company's program, for example, the balloon lamp *Napoleon.* Thanks to its reliability, Gärsnäs has managed to land showpiece contracts, such as furnishing **Volvo's** headquarters and the Australian Parliament. It is thus not surprising that for the company's 100th anniversary even the royal couple put in an appearance at Gärsnäs.

Gärsnäs AB, Gärsnäs

1893 Founded in Gärsnäs as Andersson's Möbelverkstäder
1912 Sold furniture to Stockholm
1933 "Period furniture" in Baroque
1964 New name and new design concept
1984 Chairs for **Volvo** headquarters
1990 Design Management Prize

Products

1954 Laminated *Formstol*
1963 Chair *S217* by **Åke Axelsson**
1976 Floor lamp *Napoleon* by Tore Ahlsén (design 1940)
1978 Chair *Vaxholmaren* by Åke Axelsson
1988 Chair *Upptäcktes* by Ralf Lindberg
1990 Ceiling Lamp *AV* by **Gunnar Asplund** (design 1926)
1991 Chair *Sitting Bull* by Björn Hultén

Chair *Sar* by Åke Axelsson

Floor lamp *Napoleon* by Vid Nilen

GEORG JENSEN

Silver Manufacturer / Denmark

When a name was needed for a new design prize at the end of the 1980s, the choice soon fell on Georg Jensen, whose name stands for a unique career in the early twentieth century. Originally he had planned a career as an artist but then became famous as a smith. Jensen, who grew up in the northern part of Copenhagen as the son of a worker, completed his studies at the art academy with honors. In between he ran a small but successful art pottery, and to supplement his income, the academic sculptor took on a second job in a silversmith's workshop.

In 1904 Georg Jensen opened his own studio and already before World War I his first foreign branch in Berlin, which was followed by others throughout Europe's major cities. The number of his employees rose to several hundred. The company was awarded prizes at international exhibitions. While other Danish silver workshops still worked in the ornamental style of the "Skønvirke," Jensen was influenced by art nouveau. He

Georg Jensen, Copenhagen

1904 Georg Jensen opens a silversmith workshop in Copenhagen

1909 First branch in Berlin

1926 Georg Jensen retires from the company

1988 Georg Jensen Design Prize awarded

1997 Merger with **Royal Copenhagen,** later Royal Scandinavia

Silver pitcher by Henning Koppel, 1952

Grape bowl by Georg Jensen, 1918

accepted no dogma on how to use silver. In his flatware design *Antique,* for example, he took his cue from the shape of Denmark's traditional wooden spoons. The combination of a restrained decor—by the standards of the time—and a dull, finely hammered surface produced a subtle charm previously unheard of. From the beginning Jensen worked with artist friends, such as **Johan Rohde** and Harald Nielsen. After World War II a new generation of designers took on the task of developing up-to-date forms, among them were **Nanna Ditzel** and **Henning Koppel.** The latter founded the new tradition of reduced, "timeless" clocks and watches, which is now continued by in-house designers such as **Allan Scharff** and **Jørgen Møller.** In the meantime the company has been merged into **Royal Scandinavia** and currently employs a staff of twenty-five silversmiths. They still get along without software, but they are equipped with great patience and an unusually instinctive skill.

Products

1906 Sterling silver flatware *Antique*

1908 Pin with amber and green agate

1919 Grape bowl *No. 543*

1922 *Teapot No. 1017* with ebony handle

1932 Teapot *Pyramid* with ebony handle all by **Georg Jensen**

1954 Serving bowl for fish

1966 Flatware *New York*

1977 Wristwatch *321A*, all by **Henning Koppel**

1990 Wristwatch *359* by **Ole Kortzau**

1993 Series *Complet* by **Jørgen Møller**

1995 Bowls *Hand-Me-Please* by **Allan Scharff**

Wristwatch *Steel* by Jørgen Møller

Bowls *Hand-Me-Please* by Allan Scharff, 1985

HACKMAN

Manufacturer of Housewares / Finland

"What does the optimal saucepan look like?" Scandinavia's leading manufacturer of housewares was of course ready with an answer, namely, its new series, *Tools,* "functional, innovative, and simple." While the design is simple, the company is complicated. The Finnish Hackman Group is a diversified enterprise (sales in 1997 in excess of $465 million) that was founded about two centuries ago by the immigrant Johan Friedrich Hackman. It sells kitchen furniture and fittings for the pros as well as flatware but also milk coolers, cartridge shells, and plasticwares—and owns more than 62 square miles of forest. In the early 1990s Hackman became Finland's foremost design house after taking over **Arabia** and **Iittala.** With *Tools* the parent company now also goes in for high design, relying on the advice of **Stefan Ytterborn.** Among the designers hired, in addition to the superstar Renzo Piano, are young Scandinavians such as **Björn Dahlström, Stefan Lindfors,** and **Carina Seth-Andersson.**

Hackman Designer Oy, Helsinki

1790 Johan F. Hackman starts trading company in Viipuri

1809 Purchase of a sawmill

1876 First flatware factory

1976 Branch for kitchen furniture and fittings

1990 Takes over **Arabia** (together with **Rörstrand**) and **Iittala**

Products

1962 Flatware set *Carelia* by **Bertel Gardberg**

1974 Food slicer *Ideal* with frame by **Ergonomi**

1994 Cooking pots and pans *All Steel*

1996 Pan series *Hot Pan*

1997 Flatware set *Artik;* kitchen utensils *Tools;* among others by **Björn Dahlström, Stefan Lindfors**

Flatware by Antonio Cittero and Glen Oliver Löw, 1998

Casserole by Björn Dahlström

HADELAND

Glass Manufacturer / Norway

Production began in the eighteenth century under Christian VI, king of Denmark, and back then consisted mostly of everyday glass. The turning point came only when Sverre Peterson joined the company in 1929 as the first artist with a full-time contract. Now it nearly has a glass monopoly in Norway. Hadeland moved to the forefront of the Scandinavian glass avant-garde with its clear, Bauhaus-inspired series. The new glass models fit in very well with the white dinnerware sets produced at that time by **Porsgrund.** In the 1950s the intrepid management fostered young designers, some of them hired directly from college. Two of those creative talents were **Arne Jon Jutrem** and **Benny Motzfeldt.** Jutrem achieved international acclaim with his art glass. Motzfeldt left her mark on the Norwegian glass design of the 1960s with free-form works. In addition to new objects, for example by Markéta Burianová, a Norwegian by choice, Jutrem's modern glass classics are still Hadeland's best-sellers.

Hadeland Glassverk, Jevnaker

1762 Founded under Danish rule (1765 beginning of bottle production)

1852 Production of clear glass

1929 **Sverre Petterson** first artistic director

1933 Success at the *Triennial,* Milan

1950 **Arne Jon Jutrem** hired (until 1962; from 1988 on artistic director)

1992 Artist wineglass series

1998 Artist champagne glass series

Products

19th century Goblet Monarch

1986 *Objects in Blue* by Arne Jon Jutrem

1927 Functionalist glass series by Sverre Pettersen

1992 Plates *10814* by Arne Jon Jutrem

1997 Pitchers *Confetti* by Markéta Burianová

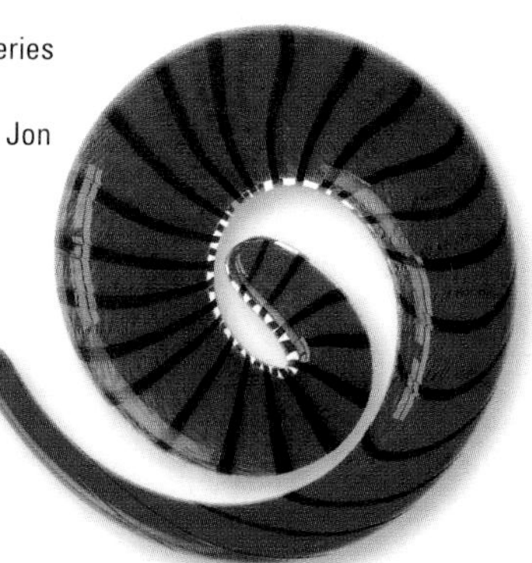

left: *Reptile*

right: *Objects in Blue*

both by Arne Jon Jutrem

Kristofer HANSÉN

Product Designer / Sweden

Before settling down to product design, Kristofer Hansén toured Europe as a jazz musician and worked for a time as a graphic artist. He is among the new designers who perceive changes in technical paradigms as a challenge. The multi-talented artist, who has worked on such varied projects as automated teller machines and sundials, must use a magnifying glass for his design specialty: miniature medical equipment that is worn on the body. Examples of these intricate instruments are a device for continuous blood tests and a minidialysis pump. This market niche offers a promising future for Sweden's manufacturing and technology companies, but has so far been pretty much a dead loss for design firms. But Hansén has broken new ground. He is the first designer to be awarded a prize for one of these mini-instruments. The most recent prize-winning object, a container for a micromembrane that promotes tooth growth, is the size of a thumbnail. One of Hansén's preeminent tasks is to create a visual presence for this totally new high-tech product.

1959 Born in Stockholm

1978 Freelance graphic artist

1990 Works for **Ergonomi** Design Gruppen; founds studio **Monitor Industrial Designers**

1991 Teaches at the Design University, Umeá

1995 Prize for Outstanding Swedish Design (also in 1997)

1997 President of the Association of Swedish Industrial Designers (SID)

Products

1991 Taxi shelter for Stockholm airport; portable blood analysis instrument *Minipump 106* for microdialysis; sundial for Nola Industrier

1994 Container for dental micromembrane for Guidor

1996 Mobile crane navigator for Scanreco El

1997 Respiration frequency gauge for Otovent

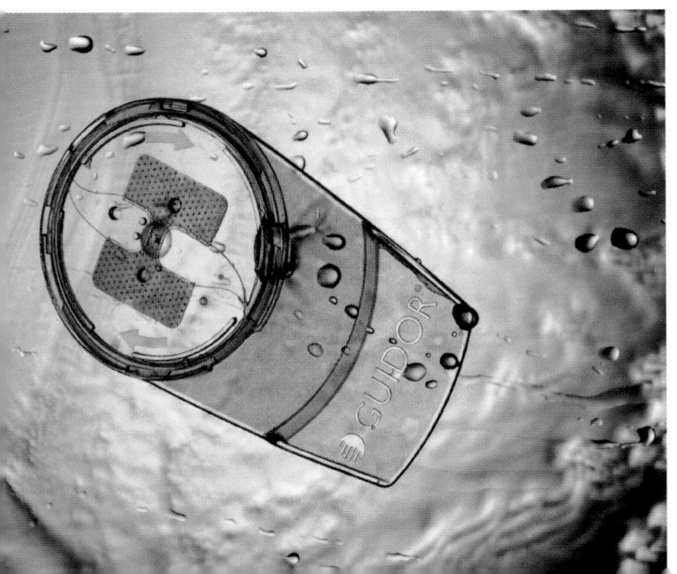

Case for micromembrane for Guidor, 1997

HASSELBLAD

Camera Manufacturer / Sweden

Victor Hasselblad AB, Göteborg

1935 Victor Hasselblad publishes the book *Flyttfågelstråk (Paths of Migrating Birds)*

1941 Develops reconnaissance camera *HK 7* (until 1945)

1948 Founding of company; new camera launched in New York

1962 Hasselblad camera in space

1990 Sets up electronic imaging division

1998 50th anniversary of the company

Products

1948 Hasselblad *1600 F* by **Sixten Sason**

1969 *Lunar Camera*

1954 *Supreme Wide Angle*

1996 Model *503 CW*

During his many trips the amateur photographer and hobby-ornithologist Victor Hasselblad dreamed again and again of the perfect camera. Upon returning home from one, he described in an article what this ideal camera would look like and promptly received an order from the Swedish Air Force to construct such a camera for reconnaissance purposes. The result was the model *HK7,* the first single-lens reflex camera in 6 x 6 format with exchangeable replacement cartridges, designed during World War II. Still during the war, Hasselblad developed a civilian model, the *1600 F;* it was launched in 1948 in New York and set the standard for studio photography all over the world. From the beginning Hasselblad included a designer in the project, a great exception back then. His choice fell on **Sixten Sason,** a silversmith by training, who came recommended by **Electrolux** and **Saab.** The camera (which was initially called *Rossex*) had to be as compact as possible. Sason reduced the housing to the shape of a block and designed an uncluttered arrangement of the operating buttons, a masterpiece of ergometrics (illustration page 44). He put an elegant black-silver coating on the streamlined housing. Sason created—if the word is appropriate anywhere, then here—a classic. This camera continued to be fine-tuned over the next half century and yet remained remarkably unchanged. To this day "the Hasselblad" is an icon of predigital photography, a welcome anachronism in an era when new styles of cameras appear on the shelves every day.

Videocamera *203 FE*

NASA astronaut with Hasselblad *Super Wide Cad,* 1966

Page 201

Hasselblad *1600 F* by Sixten Sason, 1948

HASSELBLAD
Kodak
Co.
ET11176

Niels Jørgen HAUGESEN

Furniture Designer / Denmark

1936 Born in Copenhagen
1961 Graduated from Commercial Arts School
1966 Works for **Arne Jacobsen**
1971 Freelance designer
1986 ID Prize (also in 1987)

Products
1977 Stacking chair *X-line*
1984 Folding table *Haugesen* for **Fritz Hansen**
1988 Furniture series *Nimbus* for **Bent Krogh**
1989 Modular cabinets *Folder*
1994 Chair *No. 4* for Tranekaer
1996 Outdoor furniture *Xylofon* for **Bent Krogh**

Niels Jørgen Haugesen, despite having relatively few polished designs, has achieved considerable success. Often the staunch minimalist allows projects to mature for years. His preferred material is metal, often in combination with wood. When a U.S. department store chain advertised a design competition for new furniture, his design received second prize and the most attention. The jury was fascinated with the *Haugesen* folding table that could be set up in next to no time. The table top sections disappear underneath the table, a principle Haugesen invented. A cabinetmaker by training, Haugesen worked for several years in architectural firms, eventually also for **Arne Jacobsen,** whose imaginative designs and work ethic greatly influenced the younger artist. For Niels Jørgen Haugesen furniture design is a constructive task whose internal logic must be carefully thought through. For example, the design of his steel stacking chairs *X-line* both illustrates the underlying principle and depicts the forces at work in it.

Folding table *Haugesen,* 1984

Poul HENNINGSEN

Architect, Writer, and Lighting Designer / Denmark

A urinal as advertising space for beer and liquor: the small drawing Poul Henningsen showed at the 1925 *Exhibition des Arts Décoratifs* in Paris merely confirmed his reputation as a master of provocation. Yet it was also a serious suggestion for the design of a modern city, as were his most important exhibits, including the lights *PH* (illustration page 26). Surrounded by mostly classicist designs, these six highly innovative lights in the Danish pavilion were probably a shock to visitors.

Henningsen, a man of significant accomplishments as architect, writer, songwriter, director, and designer, was also a careful observer of the urban milieu. He was particularly interested in the up-and-coming electric light. The lamp designs—which were named after him—were reflection machines whose cleverly interlocking shades directed the light to the precise area where it was needed and yet kept it from blinding the eyes. Henningsen experimented with different materials, such as glass and copper, and varied his principle

1894 Born in Copenhagen

1917 Breaks off architecture studies; writes for art magazines

1924 Light experiments with multishade lamps; housing development project

1925 Gold medal at the *Exhibition des Arts Décoratifs,* Paris, for his lamps

Ceiling Lamp *PH 5 Pendant* for Louis Poulsen, 1958

1926 **Louis Poulsen** produces *PH* lamps; magazine *Kritisk Revy* launched (until 1928)

1929 Review *Paa Ho'det (Upside Down)*

1930 New generation of *PH* lamps; builds villa in Gentofte

1935 Documentary about Denmark

1941 Editor of *Nyt,* magazine of Louis Poulsen (until 1967)

1951 Poetry and song anthology, *Springende Vers*

1955 Aphorism collection published, later other books, among others *Erotik for Millioner*

1959 *Traffic Flow Light*

1964 Publishes first Danish consumer magazine

1967 Dies in Copenhagen

Page 205

Ceiling light *PH Kogelen* (cone) for Louis Poulsen, 1957

again and again, gearing it to specific situations and fine-tuning it. The result was the impressive *Kogelen* from the 1950s, a complicated structure of overlapping blades that sheds light on an area of the maximum possible size, and because of its dull copper-colored surface the light is warm and inviting. Henningsen's constructions were almost without exception striking and aesthetically impressive, and sometimes irritating, objects. His *PH* lamps, which are still in production at **Louis Poulsen,** were Denmark's most important modern industrial design prior to 1945 and the first to be exported all over Europe. At the same time, the lamps complied in all points with the catechism of functionalist design.

Henningsen's lamp designs were based on scientific analysis and were painstakingly derived from light diffusion graphs and reflection sketches. They were constructed for mass production, designed as a product family, and therefore suitable for all conceivable applications, from dance bars to indoor tennis courts, from churches to amusement parks. During the war Henningsen invented blackout lights for the Copenhagen amusement park Tivoli. Ultimately the *PH* lamps promoted technological as well as social progress because they contributed to improving living conditions through improved lighting and were also affordable for everybody—they were popular sources of light, so to speak, at least in Denmark.

In the early 1930s Henningsen designed tubular steel furniture, for example, the *Snake Chair,* which consisted of a single curved tube. A paragon of functionalism, he presented his often unpopular views in numerous magazines, among them the *Kritisk Revy,* which he also edited. Conceived as a cultural magazine, in the late 1920s *Kritisk Revy* also served Henningsen as a forum for his design concepts. Poul Henningsen—PH to his

friends and enemies—was a left-wing radical and chain-smoker who spoke Danish with a hard Copenhagen slang and had become Denmark's intellectual voice. He loved nothing more than to hold a mirror up to his society, whether in the 1920s with a hymn of praise for Josephine Baker's naked dances; or after World War II when he denounced Nazis, namely Danish ones; or in the 1950s when Danish design was at the peak of its popularity and he promptly warned against too much complacency. At the 1959 Stockholm exhibition *Dansk Form og Milljø (Danish Form and Milieu)* he found only "expensive, handmade upper-class items that have no place in any Danish milieu of significance." As the personified conscience of design, he later published the first magazine for consumer protection and always tried to fire his young colleagues' resistance, in line with one of his primary principles: "Disagreement makes us strong!"

Products

1919 Crystal chandelier for **Carlsberg**

1921 Street light *Slotsholm*

1926 Lamp *PH* for Louis Poulsen (as all subsequent lamps)

1928 Lamp *Duo*

1931 Lamp *Circular;* Lamp *Septima;* colored glass shades; dentist lamps

1932 Celluloid piano; surgery lights

1936 Lamp *Globe*

1941 Light *Black-Out* and table lamps for Tivoli, Copenhagen; neon lamps; paper lamps

1943 Hanging lamp *Spiral*

1949 *Tivoli Lamp;* ball lamps

1957 Hanging lamp *Louvre;* floor lamp with 3/2 shade

1958 Hanging lamp *PH 5;* hanging lamp *Kogelen;* lamp *Plate*

1961 Table lamp *PH 5;* Wall lamp *PH 18*

Snake Chair, 1932

Ceiling lamp *PH Louvre* for Louis Poulsen, 1924

HOLMEGAARD

Glass Manufacturer / Denmark

When the kingdom of Denmark lost its Norwegian province in 1814, it also lost its glass production. This led the entrepreneurial Count Danneskiold-Samsö to establish a glassworks in the marshes south of Copenhagen, which provided sufficient peat for fuel. But in the early twentieth century the Swedish competition outstripped Holmegaard's glassblowers. Holmegaard's response was to establish the position of artistic director at the end of the 1920s and hire the architect and sculptor Jacob E. Bang to fill it. His designs, for example, *Primula,* were critically acclaimed but enjoyed no popular success. Ultimately, management was more interested in beer glasses for the average consumer. Bang's successor was **Per Lütken,** and his light, flowing, and also very expressive forms were typical of the 1950s. Lütken, who continued to direct the company's design department even after two mergers and who offered younger talents like **Anja Kjaer** a chance, preserved over more than half a century the maximum "lip-friendly" continuity.

Holmegaard Glasvaerk, Copenhagen

1825 Glassworks founded in Holmegaard Marsh

1926 Jacob E. Bang artistic director

1937 Exhibition *Ten Years Danish Art Glass*

1942 **Per Lütken** artistic director (until 1998)

1962 **Arne Jon Jutrem** hired (until 1966)

1965 Merger with Kastrup glassworks

1975 Integrated into **Royal Copenhagen**

Products

1926 *Primula* and *Viola*

1928 Beer glass *Hogla* all by Jacob E. Bang

1955 Bowls *Prevence*

1966 Glass series *Perle* 1992; drinking glasses *Living Glass* all by Per Lütken; Wineglasses *Attica* by **Anja Kjaer**

1996 Glass series *Harlekin* by Anja Kjaer

Bowl with Waves by Per Lütken

Knud HOLSCHER

Architect and Product Designer / Denmark

1930 Born in Rødby

1957 Completed architecture studies in Copenhagen

1959 Works for **Arne Jacobsen**

1965 British Design Award (also in 1966 and 1970)

1974 Consultant for **Georg Jensen**

1986 Airport terminal, Copenhagen

1989 First prize in the EG competition for energy-saving office design

1995 Knud Holscher founds Industrial Design

Products

1972 Stainless steel products *d-line* for C. F. Petersen

1983 Housewares for **Georg Jensen**

1984 Flatware set *Club Manhattan*

1992 Lights Quinta for Erco

1994 Coffeepot for Royal Copenhagen

1997 Orientation system for the blind

His company portfolio is as thick as a medium-sized catalog and features such diverse items as task lighting, bathroom fittings, office furniture, orientation aids for the blind (illustration page 30), sound barrier walls, and corporate identity for a design museum. Sometimes Knud Holscher wonders whether he has perhaps spread himself too thin. The tireless designer began his career as an architect and is now among Scandinavia's most sought after product designers. And unlike the majority of Danish designers, he often works for international clients. Holscher studied under **Arne Jacobsen** and learned from him "which red wine to drink," but, more importantly, he adopted his teacher's puritan work ethic and his principle that quality prevails, even at the cash register. Among the designs expressing his principles, Holscher can point to the *d-line,* strikingly simple stainless steel fixtures. Almost thirty years after its introduction, the series, which includes the well-known door handles and also bottle openers and soap dispensers, was successfully established in Japan. In Knud Holscher's glassed-in 6,455-square-foot office in an industrial district, ornamentation and frills get the maximum penalty, but occasionally even the master of the timeless allows himself to go beyond the purely utilitarian. The high-tech task lighting he designed (in the best spirit of a **Poul Henningsen**) for the German manufacturer Erco shows decorative lines and the base of the floodlight *Zenith* reveals a touch of Nordically restrained expressiveness.

Ceiling-mounted spotlights *Quinta* for Erco

Page 209

Door handle *d-line*

Bottle opener *d-line*

TUBORG
LEVERANDØR TIL DET KGL

Johan HULDT

Furniture Designer / Sweden

1942 Born in Stockholm
1964 Studied at the Konstfackskolen, Stockholm (until 1968)
1968 Starts furniture company **Innovator Design**
1978 Store system *Basic Design*
1994 Director of Svensk Form

Products
1972 Serving trolley *Tech-Trolley*
1973 Easy chair *Woodstock*
1974 Sofa *Balluff*
1982 Easy chair *Slim*
1988 Rack *Satellite* on casters

In the 1960s young Johan Huldt launched the brand **Innovator.** Under the catchy slogan, "Design you can afford" he designed (initially with his partner Jan Dranger) a furniture program for alternative times, merging rustic and industrial styles. Many of the ideas of that era still appear up-to-date today, for example, the lightweight tubular steel furniture, the removable covers on easy chairs, and the shelf units on wheels. However, the Swedish furniture industry turned a cold shoulder to the reformer and his "un-Scandinavian" concepts, and his first products were sold to Terence Conrad in England. The success there was unstoppable. Soon even **Ikea** took up Huldt's designs. Ultimately Innovator had production facilities in four countries and exported all over the world. The polyglot designer (who speaks five languages) also worked on other aspects of design, working as UN consultant, as director of Svensk Form, and—here the much-copied artist could contribute valuable expertise—as head of a commission on furniture plagiarism.

Serving trolley *Tech-Midi*, 1981

Easy chair with removable cover, 1982

both for Innovator Design

Niels HVASS

Furniture Designer and Artist / Denmark

Among organizers of fairs and shows he has an outstanding reputation, because for the media, eye-catchers such as his *Stacking Chair* are always worth a photo. He has no objections against the fuss even though the attention and publicity are not what his work is all about. For Niels Hvass what constitutes true design is intangible, namely, "the idea behind it." This sounds very unusual in a profession where chairs are designed "for one reason only, namely to make money with them."

Hvass was one of the cofounders of the group **Octo**. In the late 1980s these young designers staged unusual exhibitions, often in abandoned warehouses: happenings between design and art, staged events at which a spiritual atmosphere could arise and call forth new ways of seeing and thinking. Consequently, Hvass-chairs are statements, multilayered, often ironic objects, as for example, his wicker chair (illustration page 31) or the stacking chair that fascinates experts and the lay public alike even though its underlying idea is so simple. Hvass simply

1958 Born in Copenhagen
1987 Studies design
1988 Best Danish Furniture award
1989 Group **Octo** founded
1992 Professor at the Design School, Copenhagen
1997 Participated in exhibition *Design with a Future*, Bremen and Cologne

Easy chair *Yesterday's Paper*, 1995

glued together daily newspapers and then piled them hip-high before sawing a cube out of the mass. The outer contour is determined by the newspaper format. The geometric block has an archaic "flavor"; it looks like a parody of Le Corbusier's 1928 design *Fauteuil Grand Confort* while also projecting into present-day reality. In this chair one sits on yesterday's headlines. Hvass abrogates everyday logic and questions the seemingly incontrovertible. For him paper is not just flat, metal not inflexible. His bent aluminum easy chair made in one piece seems to violate physical laws but nevertheless obeys an amazingly simple principle. A concept designer, Hvass experiments with elementary determinants, such as statics, material, and light. But he also does not withhold personal commentary, as for example, in the bench design where birch branches split by an ax form the legs. Like "all other Danish boys," Niels Hvass had to split firewood during his boyhood.

Products

1994 *Wicker Chair*, limited edition; chair *Nissa* for Atlantis, Italy

1995 *Easy chair Yesterday's Paper*, limited edition

1996 Easy chair *Flight* for Källemo (made of a single aluminum plate)

1997 Chaise lounge Wave for Källemo (made of two aluminum plates)

Easy chair *Loopchair*, 1995

Cardboard chair with handle, around 1990

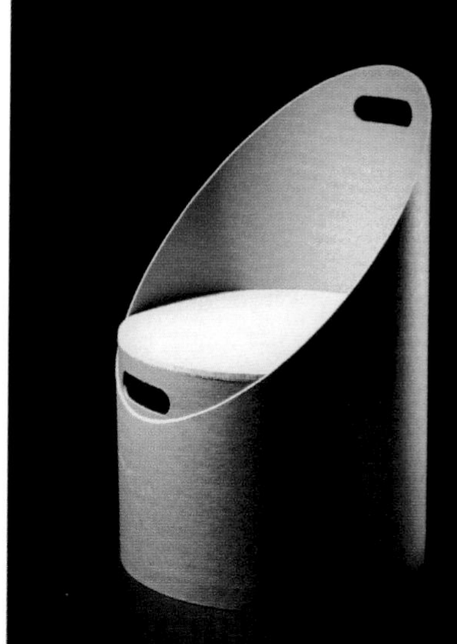

IITTALA

Glass manufacturer / Finland

When **Timo Sarpaneva** designed a new glass collection in 1956, he also supplied the logo. The white I in the red circle became Iittala's company logo. The new glasses were unlike anything he had made until then. Sarpaneva had been very successful with extravagant art glass, that could be admired only at exhibitions. The *i-Line* was the opposite; the utility glass collection avoided any eccentricity. It marked the beginning of modern product design in Finland's glass industry and a turning point in the history of the company. Iittala, founded by Swedish glassblowers, for decades had produced only banal, everyday glass. During World War I, it acquired the Karhula concern, which brought the plant up to date. Since the 1930s several artistic competitions were advertised (by Karhula) in which the couple **Alvar** and **Aino Aalto** frequently participated. Their designs, above all the vase *Savoy* (illustration p. 43), have almost mythic significance now, but they didn't experience a comeback until the 1980s. A selection of Aino Aalto's famous pressed glass (original

Iittala-Nuutajärvi Oy, Iittala

1881 Founded by Swedish glassblowers

1917 Part of the Ahlström concern

1946 **Tapio Wirkkala** and **Kaj Franck hired**

1950 **Timo Sarpaneva** hired

1951 Success at the *Triennial,* Milan (also in 1954 and 1957)

1990 IIttala-Nuutajärvi Oy is taken over by **Hackman** concern

Glasses and pitcher *Bölgeblick* by Aino Aalto, 1932

Tealight holder *Ballo,* by Annaleena Hakatie, 1995

Products

1948 Glass series *Aarne* by Göran Hongell

1956 *i-line* by Timo Sarpaneva

1958 Glass series Kartio by Kaj Franck

1964 Art glass collection *Finlandia* by Timo Sarpaneva

1968 Glasses *Ultima Thule* by Tapio Wirkkala

1972 Glass series *Aurora* by Heikki Orvola

1983 *Claritas* by T. Sarpaneva

1986 Vase *Savoy* by Alvar Aalto (design 1936); pressed glass series *Bölgeblick* by Aino Aalto (1932)

1993 Glass series *Majesteetti* by Timo Sarpaneva

1995 Tealight holders *Ballo* by Annaleena Hakatie

1997 Vases/bowls *Rondo* by Kerttu Nurminen

name *Bölgeblick*) was not reissued until 1994. Iittala's golden age began after World War II when in 1946 two young artists, **Tapio Wirkkala** and **Kaj Franck** were hired. Their work deviated sharply from what had been the usual designs until then. Later Wirkkala took over the artistic direction, and Timo Sarpaneva began to work for Iittala.

Sarpaneva and Wirkkala were the first star designers whose names every Scandinavian child recognizes, even today. With the series *Finlandia,* which was blown into wooden molds, Sarpaneva started a new trend that lasted until the 1970s, a decade of decline in whose aftermath Finland's independent glassworks were merged into the **Hackman** group. For some time now efforts have been underway to create an up-to-date product line. Together with famous name artists, such as the glass poet **Oiva Toikka** and the Franck prizewinner Kerttu Nurminen, young designers like **Annaleena Hakatie** are rejuvenating the current collection, which is gaining an international flavor through its collaboration with foreign glass designers, as for example in the project "Relations."

Pages 214/215

Vases *Aalto-Flower* by Alvar Aalto, 1939

Glass bird *Fasaani* by Oiva Toikka, 1994

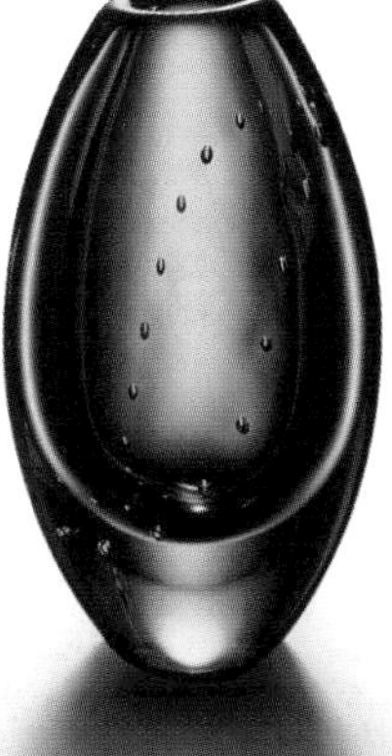

Vase with enclosed air bubbles by Timo Sarpaneva, 1953

IKEA

Furniture Manufacturer and Furnishing House / Sweden

Whether or not do-it-yourself assembly does indeed "reduce the alienation between user and producer"—as the design theoretician Viktor Papanek assumes—is best decided by those who have tried it. Undeniably, though, making the customers work is a brilliant idea. Swedish companies have been developing such modular furniture systems since the 1940s. One example is Ikea which has grown into the largest furniture chain in the world. The company now employs around 36,000 people and has nearly doubled the number of its stores since the mid-1980s to the current high of 144. In that same time period Ikea almost quadrupled its sales to more than seven billion dollars by the late 1990s. The founder of the company, Ingvar Kamprad, as the firm legend has it, wrote his name into the commercial register at the early age of seventeen. He started out selling low-priced goods by mail order before specializing in furniture. He shipped his furniture in flat packages that fit exactly onto the new Euro-pallets. From the outset the company's secret lay in rationalization. Ikea consistently applied this principle not only in its production but also in marketing and sales, thus extending the assembly line into its customers' living rooms. In the early years, developing new products mostly meant cribbing ideas. However, the affected

Ikea International A/S, Humlebaek

1943 Founded by Ingvar Kamprad in Älmhult as mail order business

1953 First furniture exhibition in Älmhult

1965 First furniture store in Stockholm

1974 Furniture store in Munich, the first outside of Sweden

1975 Design consultant **Niels Gammelgaard** hired (since 1994 **Studio Copenhagen**)

1995 Acquisition of the furniture store chain Habitat

Sofa bed *Tajt* by Gillis Lundgren, 1973

Products

1958 Easy Chair *Ägget* by Gillis Lundgren

1963 Lamp *Viisi* by **Tapio Wirkkala**

1970 Floor lamp *Telegano* by Vico Magistretti

1974 Easy chair *Rapid* by **Jan Dranger** and **Johan Huldt**

1977 Swing chair *Poem* by Noboru Nakamura

1983 Chair *Ted* by Niels Gammelgaard

Page 219

Occasional table *PS* by Thomas Eriksson, 1995

Ikea warehouse

companies, among them the furniture house **Dux**, could rarely enforce their claims in court, and Ikea meanwhile fared well, despite its tattered reputation. It was not until the early 1980s, after the advertising agency **Hans Brindfors** designed a new, sassy corporate identity and openly disclosed the sources that inspired the imitations, that the era of mattresses and wooden shelves was finally checked off. A cut-rate store selling simple pieces of furniture by the millions—among them the wobbly folding chair *Ted* (current price $8.50)—Ikea's products suit everyone's lifestyle at affordable prices. This Swedish institution has influenced the taste of the masses. Constantly introducing new product lines and product families such as complete textile and lamp collections, the blue-yellow giant has advanced from the foyer and nursery into the living room and bedroom. At the same time, the quality of the merchandise improved, and outside designers were hired. One of the first, **Niels Gammelgaard** from Denmark, had already been hired as a consultant in 1975. He supplied a considerable number of designs, and in the second half of the 1980s he set up "Studio Copenhagen," Ikea's first outsource design supplier. Ikea's move from provincial conventionality to an international modern style is epitomized by Gammelgaard's sofa

Sofa *PS* by Thomas Sandell, 1995

Chair *Nevil* by Niels Gammelgaard, 1994

1985 Sofa *Moment* by Niels Gammelgaard

1986 Halogen lamp *Pianino* by Peter Röing (won prize for Outstanding Swedish Design)

1994 Chair *Nevil* by Niels Gammelgaard

1995 Product series *PS* by **Thomas Eriksson, Thomas Sandell, Pia Vallén,** and others

1997 Product series *365+* by Magnus Lundström, Susan Pryke, and Ani Spets (won prize for Outstanding Swedish Design)

Moment and by "homemade" products, such as Tomas Jelinek's glass showcase *Stockholm* and the halogen lamp *Pianino.* This transition turned Ikea into a genuine alternative for people who, as the advertising has it, have "more taste than money." The company's impetuous globalization in the 1990s went hand in hand with a return to its uniquely Swedish virtues. To date, reeditions of "Gustavian" furniture from the eighteenth century represent the peak of this "Swedish revival."

The company's new self-confidence finds contemporary expression in product programs such as *365+* and especially in the series *PS.* The latter, launched by Stefan Ytterborn, Thomas Eriksson, and Thomas Sandell, was introduced to the wide-eyed international design in-crowd in a spectacular presentation at the Milan furniture fair as epitome of democratic design (illustration page 39). As the saying goes in Sweden, "the social democrats built 'national housing,' and Ingvar Kamprad has furnished it."

Candlestick *PS,* 1995

Grandfather clock *PS,* 1995 both by Thomas Eriksson

INNO

Furniture Manufacturer / Finland

As company philosophy has it, Inno offers things that are beautiful and useful but don't try to hog the limelight. For more than two decades Harri Korhonen has been the soul of the company—he is businessman, art director, and designer all in one. Inno specializes in furnishing public buildings; it is an ambitious outsider and half of its contracts come from outside Finland. Among recent prominent project sites are the Strasbourg EU-Parliament and a palace in Kuwait. It almost goes without saying that INNO has also furnished Helsinki's new Kiasma art museum. The company's most extensive furniture series is called *C.D.* and consists of unobtrusive designs for all occasions in a choice of beech, birch, or metal (also for patio or porch). The company's bestseller is *Oscar,* an anthropomorphic object with a soft seat cushion and a hard backrest. In addition to furniture, the company manufactures lamps—for example, a model called *Loom* that wears Viking horns—and some innovative items, for example *Cruiser,* a system for separating office trash that comes complete with wheels.

Inno Interior Oy, Espoo

1976 Founded by **Harri Korhonen** in Espoo

1997 Furniture for the EU-Parliament, Strasbourg

Products

1990 Easy chair *Oscar*

1992 Furniture series C.D.

1997 Easy chair *Cricket*

1998 Easy chair *Hippo* all by Harri Korhonen; table lamp *In-Tensive* by Soini & Leino; clotheshorse *Cocoon* by Jari Lundgren

Chair *Wood A1* and easy chair *Oscar A1* by Harri Korhonen

Fujiwo ISHIMOTO

Textile Designer / Finland

1941 Born in Japan
1964 Works as advertising artist
1970 Emigrates to Finland
1974 Textile graphics for **Marimekko**
1991 Finnish National Design Prize
1994 Kaj Franck Design Prize

Products
1977 Fabric *Jama* (all designs for Marimekko)
1982 Fabric *Maisema*
1991 Fabric *Lepo*
1994 Tablecloth/sheet *Ukonhattu*
1996 Fabric *Paratiisi*
1997 Tablecloth/sheet *Myksi;* curtains *Vire* and *Lehmus*

"It doesn't matter to me how they are used," Fujiwo Ishimoto said. At the award ceremony for the Kaj Franck Prize, Finland's highest design honor, he could hardly have thought of something more suitable to say. At times a curtain, a dress, a wrap, a tablecloth, a sheet: in the eyes of experts the versatility of Ishimoto's designs shares the Franckian spirit that predestines him (illustration p. 24).

For the past twenty-five years Ishimoto has been in-house designer at **Marimekko,** still Finland's most renowned textile brand. Some Finns think Ishimoto, a Finn by choice, is even more Finnish than they. When Ishimoto studied graphic arts in Tokyo, he regularly visited a Finnish furniture store. In particular, the large-patterned textiles by **Maija Isolas** made quite an impression on him. Later, when he wanted to leave Japan—he had worked several years in the kimono department of a department store—Finland was the only country he considered. After an interlude in an advertising agency, Ishimoto got the chance to design a complete collection for Marimekko. Since then he has created several hundred pattern designs. Whether the company was in the red or in the black, his fabrics were always among the most prominent items Marimekko had to offer, and they have shaped the company's image decisively. Simple and ingenuous, aesthetic and decorative, Ishimoto's designs are never banal. For inspiration he has always drawn upon nature as well as the photocopier.

Fabric *Big Bear Collection* for Marimekko, 1983

Page 223

Fabric *Lepo* for Marimekko, 1991

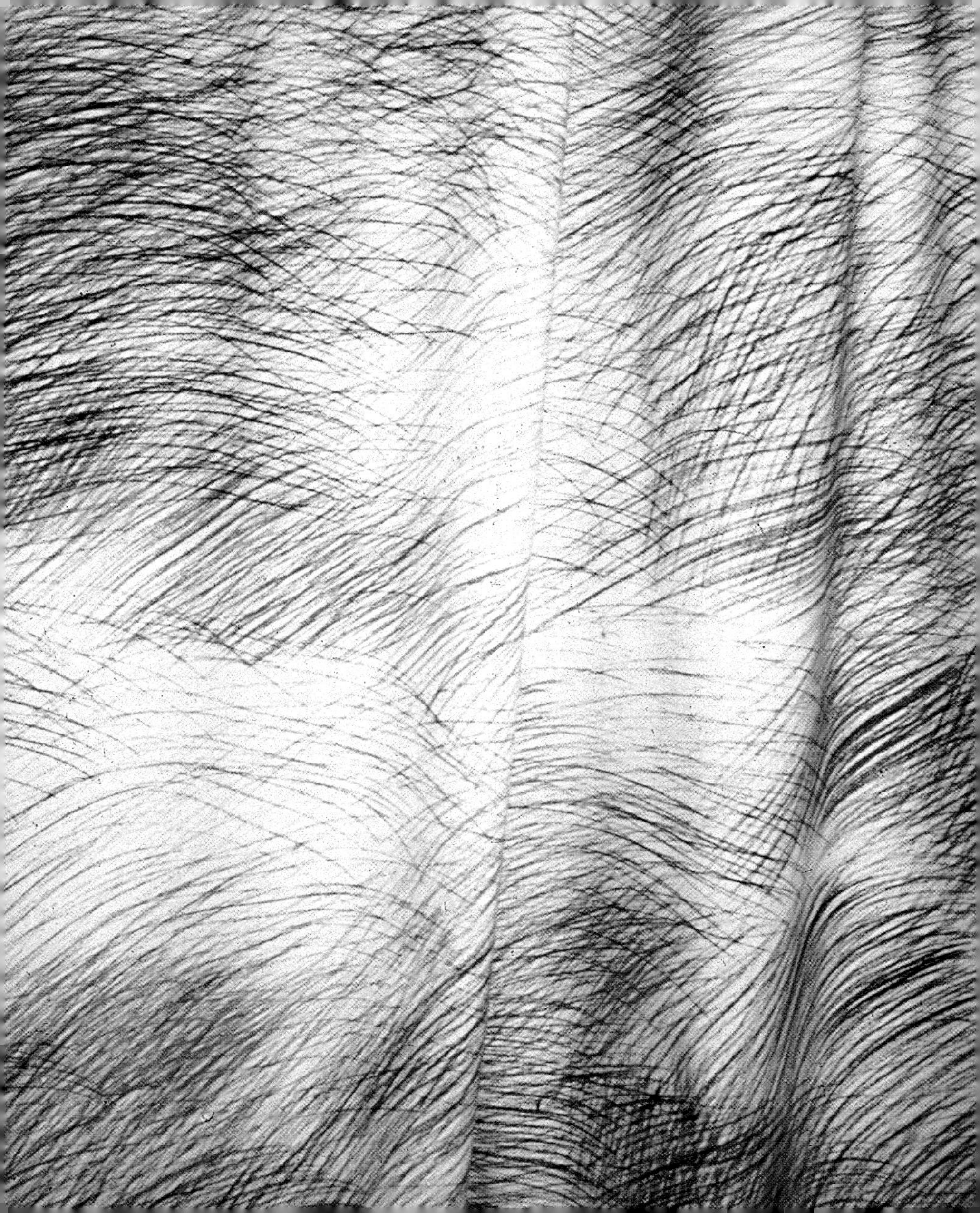

Arne JACOBSEN

Architect, Furniture Designer, and Product Designer / Denmark

1902 Born in Copenhagen
1927 Completed study of architecture in Copenhagen
1925 Prize for chair design at the *Exposition des Arts Décoratifs,* Paris
1927 Freelance architect, trip to Germany
1929 *House of the Future* at the building trade show in Copenhagen
1930 Rothenborg House in Ordrup
1932 Apartment house Bellavista (until 1935)
1935 Novo factory
1937 Texaco gas station in Copenhagen
1946 Row houses in Søholm (until 1951)
1949 Munkegård School (until 1957)
1954 Rødovre city hall (until 1956)

When the twenty-three-year-old Arne Jacobsen was told by his father in no uncertain terms that he could not become an artist, his son painted the expensive, flowered wallpaper in his room white—a modernist demonstration, like his "house of the future" several years later. He furnished his visionary dwelling machine, whose roof also served as heliport, with tubular steel chairs, the first of their kind in Denmark. In the meantime, Jacobsen had visited Germany and had encountered there the "new building art." Arne Jacobsen, a champion of progress and a passionate driver (who already in those days demonstrated a predilection for streamlining with his choice of BMW sports car) infiltrated the country with modern design, starting with the residences for rich, progressive-minded citizens. In the late 1930s, larger projects followed, among them the Bellavista residential development and factory buildings for Novo, a manufacturer of pharmaceutical products. The young trendsetter soon became a sought-after architect and usually had several projects going at the same time. Only a few years after World War II, Jacobsen designed a development of row houses in Søholm which epitomized the casual modernism considered typically Scandinavian in the 1950s. It brought Jacobsen his first international recognition.

During that time period, Jacobsen also worked on a plywood chair, a material he had used before the war for movie theater seating. A few years earlier, the Americans Charles and Ray Eames had introduced the first chair with a double-bent plywood shell, a method originally used by the U.S. Air Force to line airplanes. Jacobsen procured an Eames chair for himself to make sure his model would not be a more or less close copy of the Eames original. Jacobsen's *Myren (Ant)* was a stroke of genius and a turning point in his design career (illustration page 29). The spindly chair was an unequivocal rejection of the craft-based Danish

Page 225

Chair *3107* for Fritz Hansen, 1955

1956 Royal Hotel Copenhagen (until 1961)

1960 St. Catherine's College, Oxford (until 1963)

1961 National Bank, Copenhagen (until 1978)

1970 City hall, Mainz (until 1973)

1971 Died in Copenhagen

furniture tradition. It was also the designer's final farewell to the strict **functionalism** of the prewar era. In 1952 *Myren* was one of the first truly industry-compatible chairs. It had only two parts, a seat and legs, that were connected. Its construction was thus very economical, in terms of the minimal use of materials.

Ultimately *Myren* ended up with only three legs and a narrow "ant" waist. The design appeared so avant-garde that the manufacturer Fritz Hansen at first did not believe it could be mass produced. Since then more than one million *Myren* chairs have been sold. The chair is available in many different colors, something Jacobsen, a purist, would never have consented to. In the mid-1950s Jacobsen repeated the successful principle with the somewhat more robust model *3107* and since then has taken his basic design through more than fifty different variations. His lightweight stacking chairs are standard equipment for classrooms, seminar rooms, lecture halls, and cafeterias all over the world. Their advantages are obvious: practical, beautiful to

look at, and comfortable to sit on because of their soft shapes, which offset the hardness of the material.

In the late 1950s Jacobsen worked on his largest project, the Royal Hotel of the airline SAS in the center of Copenhagen. He designed the building down to the smallest detail; even the wineglasses, the teaspoons, and the curtains were all genuine Jacobsen designs. Unfortunately, this unique work of art was later renovated to death. The greatest sensation of the project were the arm chairs *Aegget (Egg), Svanen (Swan), Dråben (Drop),* and *Gryden (Bowl)* that populated the twenty-story building from top to bottom. These seats were unusual not only because of their exciting, curved shapes but also because they were not upholstered. Jacobsen used a new invention from chemistry, polystyrene granules, which could be sprayed as a foam and then stretched.

As always, he was on the cutting edge of progress and since 1955 behind the wheel of a Citroen *DS 19,* one of the most

From left to right

Classroom furniture with chair *Tungen,* 1957

Flatware set *AJ* for Georg Jensen, 1957

Easy chair *Aegget (Egg)* for Fritz Hansen

Pitchers *Cylinda-Line* for Stelton

Products

1952 Chair *Myren (Ant)* for **Fritz Hansen**

1955 Chair *3107* (Series of Sevens) for Fritz Hansen

1956 Easy chair series *3300,* door handle *AJ* for Fritz Hansen

1957 Classroom furniture with *Tungen* chair (tongue); flatware set *AJ* for **Georg Jensen**

Page 229

Easy chair *Svanen* for Fritz Hansen

Furniture Royal Hotel Copenhagen with sofa *Svanen,* circa 1960

technologically advanced cars available in those days—like Jacobsen's chairs, the car was also a symbol of the times. *Svanen* and *Aegget* are perhaps the most copied easy chairs in the history of furniture. How did Arne Jacobsen come up with his designs? His furniture designs were developed down to a fraction of an inch using full-scale plaster models. Jacobsen did not get his hands dirty during this process, however; he supplied the idea and supervised its realization. He "designed chairs the way Matisse painted pictures, in a free, playful way," says **Knud Holscher,** a former colleague. Jacobsen's introduction of abstract forms into furniture design is reminiscent of **Alvar Aalto,** and there are other parallels between the two great designers: both developed most of their designs in connection with larger building projects and for the most part during a short productive phase. For Jacobsen that phase occurred in the 1950s, between the City Hall in Rødovre and St. Catherine's College in Oxford, his favorite project. Though modern, Jacobsen was also a man of the

1958 Easy chair *Aegget (Egg)* and *Svanen (Swan)*

1959 Easy chair *Dråben (Drop)* and *Gryden (Pot)*; lamps *AJ* for **Louis Poulsen**

1962 Chair *Oxford*

1965 Chair series *Oxford*

1967 Series *Cylinda* for **Stelton**

1969 Bathroom fittings (ID Prize) for Vola

1970 Series *3600* for Fritz Hansen

old school, with a classical education, a weakness for antiques, expensive cigars, and for what one calls good taste. "He would comment on an object simply 'it is ugly' or 'it isn't so ugly at all!,' and the latter was tantamount to unconditional praise," recalls Niels Jørgen Haugesen, another colleague.

Of course, Arne Jacobsen was controversial. A conservative public responded to this Henry Moore of furniture design with the same irritation it brought to abstract art. After the Royal Hotel opened, journalists jokingly and derisively called the designer an "egg-tekt." Perfectionists like his colleague **Poul Kjaerholm** rejected Jacobsen's intuitive method as too superficial. However, more important than design theory was the fact that Jacobsen's designs sold well, and therefore he was commissioned for more and more projects in the 1960s. For example, his series *Cylinda* originated from a **Stelton** proposal. Although postmodernism has caught up with Jacobsen's architecture, his designs have hardly lost any of their magic.

Easy Chair *3300* for Fritz Hansen

Ceiling Lamp *AJ* for Louis Poulsen

Jacob JENSEN

Product Designer/Denmark

The tuning button could be operated effortlessly at the touch of a fingertip; it was a silvery disc, about the size of a saucer, and completely flush with the housing, as were all the other buttons. Nothing stood out above the housing of the flat, oblong set. The *Beomaster 2000* design of 1974 was an ideal cuboid with absolutely clean lines. The radios, record players, and stereo systems (illustration p. 20) Jacob Jensen has designed for **Bang & Olufsen** since the 1960s bear none of the typical traits of electric appliances; yet their flawless, smooth surface conveys the impression of total perfection. Jensen developed a new species of hi-fi equipment and changed once and for all our notion of what such equipment should look like. His amplifiers could be hung on the wall or placed on a stand, like a shrine to the pop era. As a youth, Jensen had worked in his father's small upholstery workshop and occasionally designed this or that chair for the family's own use. After studying at the Copenhagen Commercial Arts School, he went to work in for the design firm

1926 Born in Vesterbro

1951 Works at **Bernadotte & Bjørn** (headed the studio starting in 1954)

1958 Opens own studio

1963 Works for **Bang & Olufsen,** product and design strategy (until 1991)

1978 Exhibition *Bang & Olufsen: Design for Sound by Jacob Jensen* in the Museum of Modern Art, New York; son Timothy Jacob Jensen joins the company (heads it since 1991)

Oven *EB 984* for Gaggenau, 1990s

Record player *Beogram 4000* for Bang & Olufsen, 1972

Bernadotte & Bjørn. He did not realize who **Sigvard Bernadotte** was until one day Queen Ingrid came by to visit her brother at work. This basic training in industrial design, the pinstriped clientele, as well as a stay in the United States turned the small-town boy into a designer with a promising future. In the late 1970s the Museum of Modern Art exhibited twenty-eight of his sleek appliances, and they must have hit Americans like a culture shock. These sound- and status-generating objects looked as though they had been flown in by a spaceship.

Now Jacob Jensen's design firm is a family business directed by his son, Timothy. More than one hundred international design prizes have accumulated as the impressive results of an unparalleled career spanning five decades. Jensen's casual synthesis of functionalism and elegance works as well as ever, whether in a vacuum cleaner for **Nilfisk,** an extractor hood for Gaggenau, or a towering windmill on Denmark's coast.

Products

1963 Microphone *Beomic 2000*

1965 Portable radio *Beolit 600*

1967 Loudspeaker *Beovox*

1970 Receiver *Beomaster 1200*

1972 Record player Beogram *4000*

1974 *Beomaster 2000,* all for Bang & Olufsen

1979 Telephone *Comet* for Alcatel

1986 Hi-fi system *Beocenter 9000*

1988 Wristwatch for Georg Jensen

1992 Glasses *Quintessence* for Rodenstock; vacuum cleaner *GM 200* for **Nilfisk**

1993 Oven and microwave oven *EB 900/EM 900* for Gaggenau

1997 Indoor thermometer for Georg Jensen

Windmill *Nec Micon* for Nordtank, 1990s

KÄLLEMO

Furniture Manufacturer / Sweden

Småland is one of Sweden's most barren regions. Its inhabitants, so the stereotype goes, are therefore shrewd and stingy. Fact is that this region is the cradle of Sweden's furniture industry. Here **Ikea** had its start and from here comes its opposite: Källemo, one of the most unconventional furniture manufacturers. For Källemo's owner, Sven Lundh, pieces of furniture are not primarily practical and useful but are above all works of art. This view alone—at which many manufacturers would only shake their head—is considered sacrilegious in this country of **functionalism.**

Lundh, a connoisseur of art and by training a business manager, is a gallery owner in his second job. In the midst of the harsh climate of the furniture market he carved out a space for unorthodox design. Under his aegis objects were created in small editions that, says Lundh, represent the opposite "of everything that is mass produced, without contours and impersonal." Each of his designs knocked, so to speak, the yardstick out of the

Källemo AB, Värnamo

1965 Founded by Sven Lundh in Värnamo

1998 Plans for Museum Arena in Värnamo (architect, Renzo Piano)

Products

1982 *Concrete Chair* by **Jonas Bohlin**

1983 Chaise lounge *Concave* by Jonas Bohlin

1988 Tubular steel easy chair *GA-1* and *GA-2* by **Gunnar Asplund**

Cabinet *National Geographic Magazine* by Mats Theselius, 1990

1989 Shelves *Pilaster* by John Kandell

1990 Easy Chair *Theselius* by **Mats Theselius**

1992 Aluminum chair *...and so it goes* by Fredrik Wretman

1994 *Laminated Iron Easy Chair* by Mats Theselius

1995 *Källemo Bicycle* by Sögreni; iron table *Board* by Alf Linder

1996 Sofa *Dynamo* by Dan Ihreborn; chair *Puma* by **Komplot Design**

1997 TV-cart *Keaton* by Frank Kallin

hands of the furniture institute's standard-setters. A new era dawned for the furniture industry. After the unveiling of **Jonas Bohlin's** concrete chair (admittedly the utter consternation at the sight of this almost delicate-looking piece of furniture is hard to understand nowadays) nothing was as it had been before.

Källemo's furniture collection is designed like an art collection. Thanks to collaboration with many original designers—among them **Mats Theselius,** one of the most original—one tour de force follows the other. Bohlin's lamps *Espresso* and *Larv* are metaphors of light. On **John Kandell's** shelf *Pilaster* books lie sideways. The sculpture chairs by Bjørn Nørgaard sit in silent contemplation. The couch by Mats Theselius glows in Ferrari-red. Irritations are, of course, intentional, for if Svend Lundh is absolutely sure of anything, it is that "what is truly important is always first met with incomprehension by the present." Soon Lundh will exhibit the truly important in a museum of his own.

Chaise lounge
by Mats Theselius, 1992

Page 235

Sculpture chairs by
Bjørn Norgaard, 1995

Chair *Cobra* by
Mattias Ljunggren, 1990

Poul KJAERHOLM

Furniture Designer / Denmark

1929 Born in Öster Vra

1949 Apprenticeship as cabinetmaker

1952 Completed studies at Commercial Art School in Copenhagen

1953 Married Hanna Dam, an architect

1955 Works for the furniture manufacturer E. Kold Christensen; teacher at the Royal Art Academy (1976 professor)

1957 Grand Prize *Triennial*, Milan (also in 1960)

1958 Exhibition design *Formes Scandinaves*, Paris; Lunning Prize

1960 Exhibition design *The Arts of Denmark*, United States

1973 ID Prize

1980 Dies in Hillerod

1982 Kjaerholm furniture at **Fritz Hansen**

Among the great Danish furniture designers, Poul Kjaerholm is considered the one with the most flawless conception. As a representative of the younger, second generation of designers, he has contributed a number of uncompromising designs that have helped solidify the good reputation of Danish furniture. Since the mid-1950s he has worked exclusively for Kold Christensen, an inspired design dealer who shared Kjaerholm's ideas and for whom Kjaerholm developed an extensive furniture program (now sold by **Fritz Hansen**). The duo Kjaerholm-Christensen epitomizes the close and successful cooperation between businessman and designer, a relatively frequent phenomenon in the heyday of "Danish Modern."

In only twenty years of creative work, Poul Kjaerholm designed a huge number of chairs, sofas, and tables, including several classics such as the folding stool dating from 1961 and the daybed of the same year. Unlike the furniture of his colleagues, Kjaerholm's furniture, almost without exception, was designed for mass production—even though he was a cabinetmaker himself. Like his contemporary **Arne Jacobsen,** Kjaerholm broke with the Danish tradition of using solid wood. In other respects, however, Kjaerholm and Jacobsen do not have much in common even though both were strongly influenced by the classic European modern style. In contrast to Jacobsen, who loved to improvise, Kjaerholm methodically followed a plan. His designs were well thought-out and harmonious down to the last screw. They were based on experiments and distinguished by their clarity of idea and honesty of construction (illustration page 17).

Page 237

Lounge *PK 24* for Fritz Hansen, 1965

Table *PK 61* for Fritz Hansen, 1955

Already very early on the perfectionist tried his hand at unusual materials, such as aluminum and wire and frequently combined a steel frame with a seat covered in a natural material, such as leather, wicker, or cloth. An example is his lounge *PK 24*

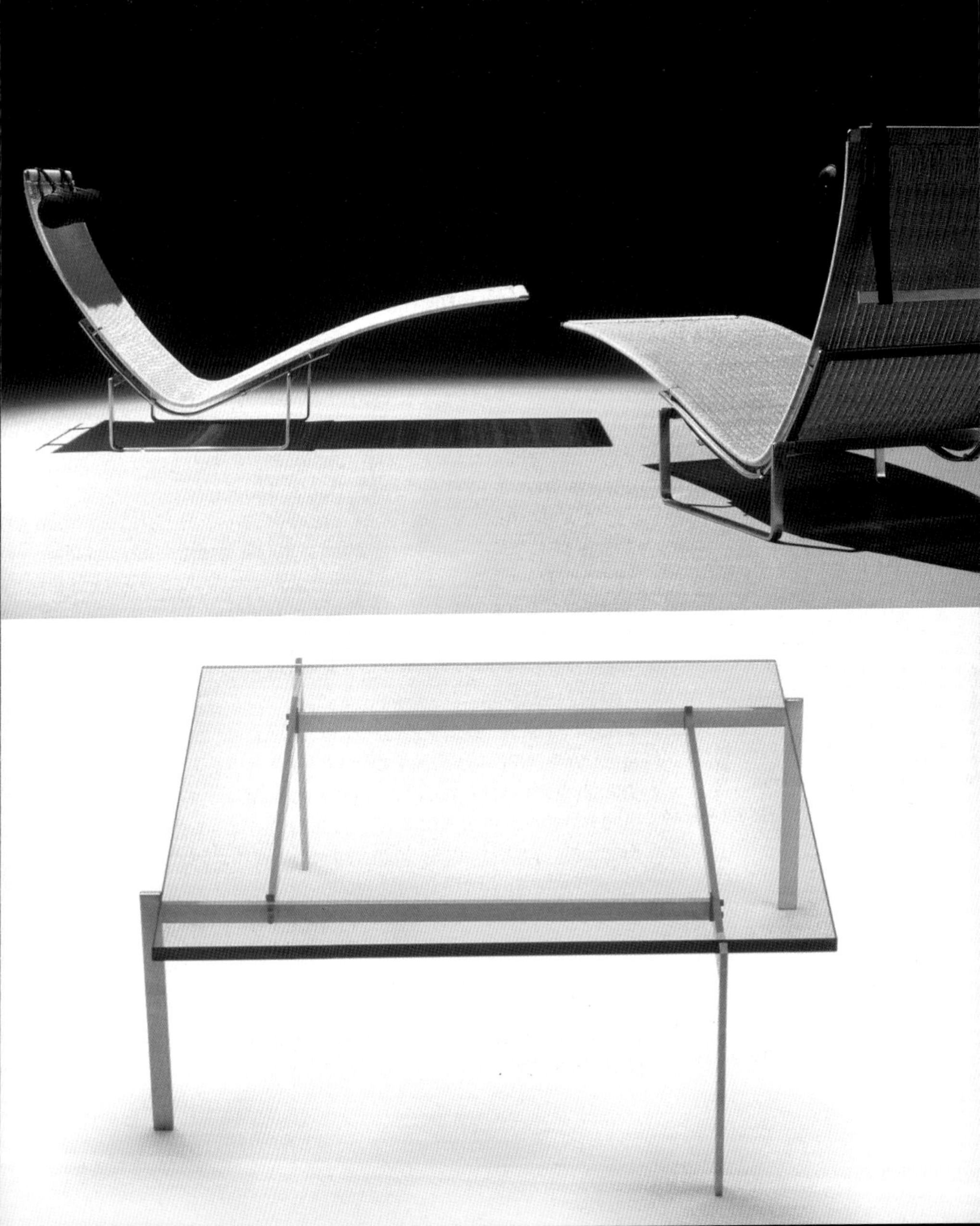

Products

1951 Armchair *PK 25*

1952 Chair *PK 0* (1997 at Fritz Hansen)

1955 Table *PK61*

1957 Lounge *PK 80;* table *PK 71*

1959 Stool *PK 91*

1965 Lounge *PK 24*

1967 Easy chair *PK 20*

1976 Chair for concert hall in the Louisiana Museum

1980 Table *PK 40*

page 238

Chair *PK 22,* 1956

Easy chair *PK 20,* 1967

Page 239

Upper left: Shell chair, 1960

Upper right: Armchair *PK,* 1964

Bottom: Lounge *PK 80,* 1957; stool *PK 91,* 1959; folding stool *PK 31,* 1961

dating from 1965, which combines an inconspicuous frame of steel strips, woven cane, and a continuously adjustable mechanism. The lightweight construction is reminiscent of Le Corbusier's famous chaise longue and, with its silhouette shrinking down to a line, describes a V-outline. Kjaerholm used the same combination of materials in his 1967 cantilever chair, whose good overall impression stands up to close scrutiny: seat and frame are not soldered together but screwed or clamped.

His coffee table *PK 61* is similarly succinct while also slightly jarring. The staggered legs of the frame are visible through the glass top; their captivating constructive severity appears original and unusual. One of Kjaerholm's early works, the plywood chair *No. 0* dating from 1952 expresses the dynamism of those optimistic postwar years, as does the **Saab** bodywork dating from the same period. The plywood chair consists merely of two chair shells screwed together; it embodies Kjaerholm's virtuoso reductionism, the deliberate abstention from any touch of supposedly typically Danish coziness.

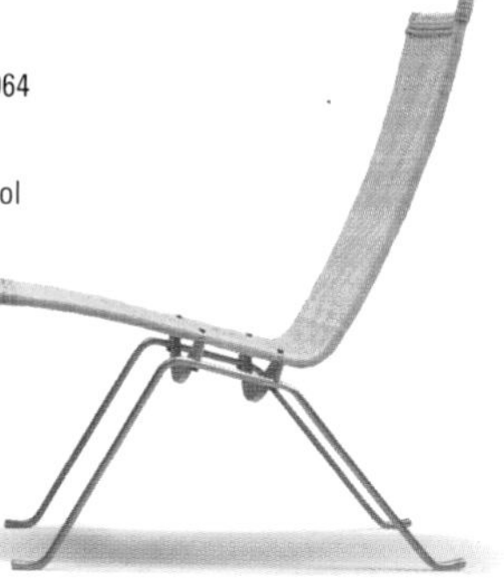

KLÄSSBOLS

Textile Manufacturer / Sweden

Klässbols Linneväveri AB
Klässbol

1920 Founded in Klässbol

1981 Tablecloths for Swedish embassies

1994 Tablecloths for the royal family

Products

1965 Dishcloths *Kijstrivsel* by **Astrid Sampe**

1991 Tablecloth and napkins *Nobel* by **Ingrid Dessau**

1992 Set of bed linens *Bolster* by Lena Rohoult

1997 Tablecloths *Cactus* by Ingela Berntsson

1998 Tablecloths *In Light and Shadow* by Pasi Välimaa

Textile designer Lena Rohoult has a collection of old duvet covers she uses for her research. Many of the old fabrics come from Dalarna, a region of Sweden where national costumes and traditions have survived longer than anywhere else and where **Carl Larsson** chose to settle. In fact, many of Rohoult's fabrics look as though they have been taken from a Larsson picture, for example, the striped set *Bolster,* for which she won a prize. Weaving mill Klässbols specializes in linen fabrics and in the contemporary interpretation of great-grandmother's simple apron designs. The natural charm of the fabrics and patterns is, depending on one's point of view, pure nostalgia or "part of the Nordic cultural heritage." In addition to dishtowels and napkins in red, white, and blue, tablecloths make up the bulk of the product line. They have long since become a matter of prestige and are among the standard contents of the royal chest of drawers. When a Swedish ambassador sits down to dinner anywhere in the world, the table is most likely set with cloths from Klässbols.

Tablecloths *Linus* by Peter Condu

Kaare KLINT

Furniture Designer / Denmark

He launched the modern era in Danish furniture design but was conservative nonetheless. Klint's approach combined craftsmanship with empirical and historical considerations. He drew upon historical models, for example, Shaker design. Eighteenth-century English furniture design proved to him that functionalism can produce satisfying aesthetics. In 1917 Klint was one of the first designers to do proportion studies on the interplay between person and furniture. For example, he meticulously documented sizes and number of pieces in dinnerware sets in order to calculate the ideal cupboard dimensions. A strict teacher, he used the results as the foundation of his classes at the art academy and backed up his arguments with design models like his famous chair *Safari.* Klint also worked in graphic design and product design, and his clients included a Danish car manufacturer. But it was his 1940s invention that made him truly popular: his folded paper lamps became best-sellers.

1888 Born in Copenhagen

1917 First ergonomic furniture studies

1920 Freelance architect

1924 Furniture faculty at the Art Academy, among his students were **Børge Mogensen** and **Nanna Ditzel**

1929 Gold medal at the World's Fair in Barcelona (1935 in Brussels)

1944 Professor at the Art Academy in Copenhagen

1954 Died in Copenhagen

Products

1914 Furniture for the Fåborg Museum

1924 Model designs and corporate identity (CI) for the car manufacturer Triangel

1927 Chair *Safari*

1933 Deck chair

1944 Folded paper lamps for **Le Klint**

Deck chair, 1933

Church chair for Fritz Hansen, 1936

KOMPAN

Toy Manufacturer / Denmark

Kompan A/S, Ringe

1970 Founded in Ringe

1994 European Design Prize

Products

1970 Model *M 100/Classic* (animal on spring)

1982 Slide *M 320;* playground system *Legeby*

1990 Equipment for sandboxes, for example, *Pirate ship,* series *Play Town*

The basic model is familiar to all, even to grown-ups. Throughout Scandinavia and many other countries, the famous metal spiral with a wooden seat is a fixture in pedestrian malls (illustration page 7). Kompan introduced the space-saving seesaw in the early 1970s and later was the first manufacturer to design child-appropriate outdoor playground equipment proportioned specifically for safety, a design that gained worldwide acceptance. The original spiral is now also available in motorcycle (with side-car) and surfboard versions. In addition, the company developed an ingenious system of play components made of varnished laminated wood; the components can be combined in various ways, depending on the size of the playground and children's age group. Organic forms and primary colors impervious to fashion combine in this simplified equipment to create a play atmosphere with high recognition value and a language of simplicity understood by children the world over. Kompan's playful designs contrast as sharply with the playground equipment of ages past as with the bleak cityscape surrounding them.

Slide *Little Clown,* 1990s

Henning KOPPEL

Artist, Silversmith, and Product Designer / Denmark

The serving bowl for fish designed in 1954 (illustration page 40) has been exhibited all over the world and by now is probably the best known Scandinavian metal design. But does that also make it typically Scandinavian? First of all it is Danish, rooted in a rich tradition of luxury items. Henning Koppel, the first artist to be hired at **Georg Jensen** after World War II, brought the traditional smithy up to date with his powerful, expressive style, becoming an innovator of silver design. Trained as a sculptor, he turned his ability to forming three-dimensional objects out of precious metal. His designs gave a plastic-sculptural and sensuous quality to the material. He designed his objects as pure form, using the reflective characteristics of the material and flowing, asymmetrical lines with an obvious affinity to contemporary art. Eventually Koppel developed from a specialist into an all-rounder and designed stamps, flatware, glass, and dinnerware sets as well as "timeless" wristwatches without numerals.

1918 Born in Ostenvold, Copenhagen

1937 Art Academy, Copenhagen

1939 Académie Ranson, Paris

1945 Works for **Georg Jensen**

1951 Gold medal at the *Triennial,* Milan (also in 1954 and 1957)

1953 Lunning Prize

1966 ID Prize, Denmark

1971 Works for **Orrefors**

1981 Dies in Copenhagen

Products

1954 Silver serving bowl for fish for Georg Jensen

1957 Flatware series *Caravel* for Georg Jensen

1963 Dinnerware set *Koppel White* for **Bing & Grøndahl**

1964 Flatware series *New York* for World's Fair in New York

1977 Wristwatch *321 A* for Georg Jensen

Silver bowl for Georg Jensen, 1950

KOSTA BODA

Glass Manufacturer / Sweden

Orrefors-Kosta Boda AB

1742 Kosta Glassworks founded by Anders Koskull and Georg B. Staël von Holstein

1864 Boda Glassworks (founded by Kosta glassblowers)

1876 Åfors Glassworks founded as a smithy

1898 **Gunnar Wennerberg** first artist at Kosta

1929 Elis Bergh first artistic director at Kosta (until 1950)

1946 Merger of Kosta and Boda

1950 **Vicke Lindstrand** artistic director at Kosta (until 1973)

1970 Boda Nova founded (sold in 1982)

1971 Merged with Kosta and Boda into the Åfors Group

1990 **Orrefors** takes over Kosta Boda

1998 Taken over by **Royal Copenhagen**

Behind the world-famous double name stands three small glassworks: Åfors, Boda, and Kosta. Throughout their history they have often changed name and ownership. Although long since merged with their former big competitor **Orrefors** (and now part of **Royal Scandinavia**), the three neighbors nevertheless have retained a certain independence. Around the turn of the century Kosta gave the artists **Gunnar Wennerberg** and **Alf Wallander** the first opportunity to realize their own designs. They followed the decorative style fashionable in Europe at the end of the nineteenth century, a style called **Jugendstil** (art nouveau) in Sweden and epitomized in Wennerberg's turn-of-the-century colorful vases decorated with flower and foliage motifs. During the First World War the company experienced a short burst of progressive design, thanks to the painter Edvin Ollers who had come to Kosta on Svenska Slöjdföreningen's initiative in 1917. That same year he designed a collection for the *Hemutställningen* (Home Show) in Stockholm that blatantly contrasted with everything Kosta had produced before. His delicately tinted glasses with simple, slightly curved shapes were far ahead of their time. In part due to the overwhelming success of its competitor **Orrefors,** Kosta experienced a phase of stylistic disorientation during the 1920s. When **Elis Bergh** was hired as artistic director in 1929—the company's first full-time designer—the situation began to turn around. His work was authentic, light, and simple. And Bergh is without a doubt the record-holder among Sweden's designers of utilitarian glassware, since this genre makes up the largest part of the more than 2,500 designs he left behind.

The 1950s were a very creative period for Kosta, particularly because of designers like the versatile **Vicke Lindstr**and, who loved to experiment, and Mona Morales-Schildt, who had studied

Page 245

Blue urn, around 1800

Bottle with engraving, 1836

Bowl by Elis Bergh, 1933

KOSTA

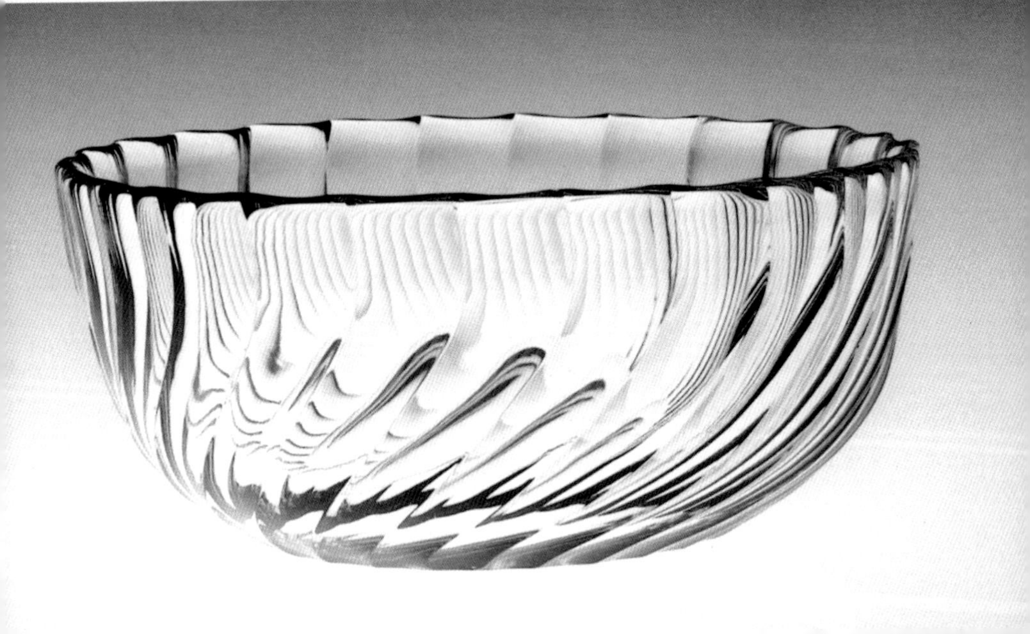

1896 Glass series *Odelberg*
1899 Vase with black orchids by G. Wennerberg
1929 Glasses *Koh-i-noor*
1934 Glasses *Moiré,* both by Elis Bergh
1955 Glasses *Mambo*
1963 Glass sculptures *Homa sum,* both by Vicke Lindstrand
1973 Vase *Grass* by Lisa Bauer and **Sigurd Persson**
1980 Vase *Utopia* by **Goran Wärff**
1992 Pitchers *Amazon* by Gunnel Sahlin (until 1998)
1996 Glass series *Kaboka* by **Ulrica Hydman-Vallien**
1998 Bowls and plates *Tonga* by Monica Beckström

under Paolo Venini. With these talented young designers a fresh, international wind blew through Swedish glass design. In the 1960s, the decade of liberalization, design finally attained its status as a decisive marketing instrument. Back then many first-rate design artists moved to Sweden's glass district, for example, Monica Bäckström, **Bertil Vallien** (illustration page 14), and **Goran Wärff.**

A key figure in the subsequent, increasingly difficult period was the businessman Eric Rosén. He had joined Boda in 1947, and by 1976 he was managing no less than six glassworks. After the 1970s wave of mergers and after the boom of art glass in the 1980s, **Gunnel Sahlin** and **Ann Wåhlström** were hired, two young designers from the American studio glass movement. Since then the old technique of glass-staining has had a revival, artistically as well as in sales figures, with **Ulrica Hydman-Vallien's** work being particularly in demand.

Sculpture by Goran Wärff, 1988

Page 247

Top left: Stained glass *Cat Lady* by Ulrica Hydman-Vallien, 1986

Top right: Vase *Trees in Fog* by Vicke Lindstrand, 1953

Bottom: Glass series by Erik Höglund, 1950s

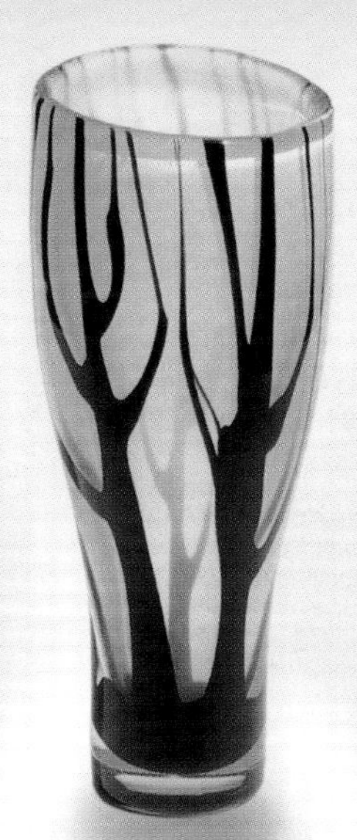

Yrjö KUKKAPURO

Interior Decorator and Furniture Designer / Finland

1933 Born in Viipuri
1959 Freelance designer
1962 Works for furniture manufacturer Haimi
1963 Stores for **Marimekko**
1972 Interior design for Rank-Xerox headquarters, Helsinki
1973 Subway stations, Helsinki (until 1982)
1978 Rector of the University for Art and Design, Helsinki
1980 Works for **Avarte**
1995 Kaj Franck Design Prize; exhibition *Classic Makers*

Products

1964 Easy chair *Ateljee* at Avarte (all products)
1965 Easy chair *Karuselli*
1970 Easy chair *Remmi*
1976 Office chair *Fysio*
1982 Office chair *Sirkus*
1983 Easy chair *Experiment*
1995 Plywood chair *S-Chair*

Yrjö Kukkapuro lives in a Helsinki suburb in a 1960s dream house, surrounded by trees, under whose cambered roof there are neither walls nor rooms. Kukkapuro, who as a boy lived with his parents, grandparents, and four siblings in a three-bedroom apartment, places a high value on empty space, closeness to nature, and team spirit. His success, he says, is not the result of "solitary work," but entirely due to "designer, businessman, and marketing people pursuing the same goals." Apart from **Antti Nurmesniemi,** Kukkapuro played the greatest role in giving Finnish furniture design an international character. For twenty years now the uncompromising modernist has been designer-in-chief at furniture manufacturer **Avarte,** a company that has never subscribed to the usual separation of "salable," utilitarian design from avant-garde, "fun" products. Kukkapuro, who shares **Poul Kjaerholm's** fondness for steel and leather, produced his masterpiece in 1964: the easy chair *Ateljee,* which was immediately recruited for the MOMA collection. Yrjö Kukkapuro achieved fame with his bold revolving armchair *Karuselli* and his skeleton-like chairs constructed of metal rods that were screwed together. Later in his career, however, the purist moved to plastic and plywood—and finally even to solid Finnish birch.

Chair A-509

Chair A-502

Page 249

Easy chair *Karuselli 412,* all for Avarte

LAMMHULTS

Furniture Manufacturer / Sweden

Lammhults Möbel AB, Lammhult

1945 Founded in Lammhult as Mekanista Verkstad (LMV)

1996 Georg Jensen Prize

Products

1968 Bar stool *S 70*

1983 Easy chair *Duet,* both by **Börge Lindau** and **Bo Lindekrantz**

1996 Easy chair *Cinema* by **Gunilla Allard**

1998 Easy chair *Casino* by Gunilla Allard; easy chairs *Stockholm* and *Paris* by **Jonas Bohlin**

A provincial workshop grows into an international company with a distinctive design image—a typically Swedish fairy-tale, but with a different twist in this case, setting Lammhults apart from its neighbors **Ikea** and **Källemo.** Lammhults made a name for itself in the 1960s through its collaboration with **Börge Lindau** and **Bo Lindekrantz.** The two designers staged a furniture revolution with designs like the chair S 70, which often triggered an uproar when unveiled at fairs. Meanwhile, Lammhults has acquired an image of innovative solidity and awarded more design prizes than ever. In 1996 **Gunilla Allard** was awarded the Jensen Prize. Allard, a set designer, convinced the jury with her "minimalist and elegant design expression." She contributed fashionable retro furniture to Lammhults' collection. **Johannes Foersom** and **Peter Hiort-Lorenzen** were awarded the Bruno Mathsson Prize; both are regulars in the Lammhults catalog. Other designers in the current program are **Jonas Bohlin** and **Love Arbèn,** two representatives of the new "Swedishism."

Easy chair *Casino* by Gunilla Allard

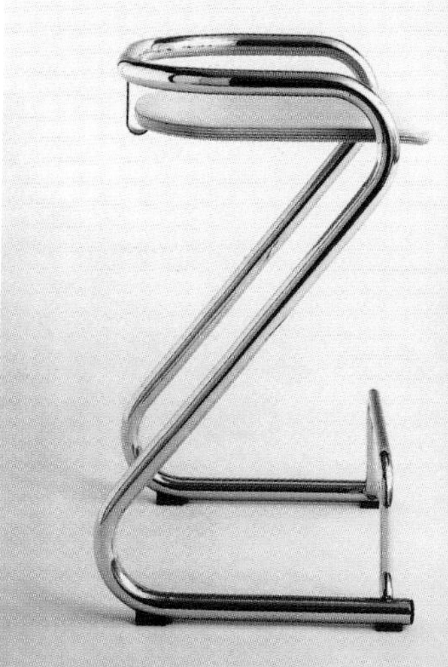

Bar stool *S 70* by Lindau & Lindekrantz

LEGO

Toy Manufacturer / Denmark

When the master cabinetmaker Ole Kirk Christiansen, a maker of wooden toys, included an English manufacturer's plastic building bricks in his product line in 1949, his international career was launched. Soon developed into the "Lego System," these were initially traditional building bricks, suitable only for building towers. Only the addition of tubes in the hollow underside of the bricks—allowing them to be assembled in many different combinations—turned the toys into a patentable invention. Numerical proof is not really needed to define the magic of this toy and its infinite potential. Nevertheless, Lego has done the arithmetic and calculated that two bricks with eight studs can be combined in 24 different ways; four bricks yield 1,060 combinations; and six bricks more than 100 million.

Lego owes its pedagogical **functionalism** to the fundamental simplicity of the bricks, which allow children's imagination maximum freedom. This freedom is based on different ways of assembling (and taking apart) the pieces, that is, on the modular principle.

Lego Gruppen, Billund

1932 Founded as workshop for ladders and wooden toys by Ole Kirk Christiansen in Billund

1934 "Lego" (leg godt = play well) becomes the company's name

1947 First plastic toys

1954 *Lego System* developed

1956 Marketing abroad, first in Germany

1968 *Legoland* opened in Billund

1980 Department for learning aids

1987 Development of programmable bricks in collaboration with the Massachusetts Institute of Technology ("MIT Programmable Brick Research")

1994 "Legoland Windsor" opened near London

Robot system *Mindstorm*, 1998

Products

1949 *Automatic Binding Bricks*

1958 Classic *Lego* brick with inner tubes

1969 Brick *Duplo*

1974 Lego figures

1977 Lego program *Technic*

1995 *Primo* for toddlers

1997 CD-ROM game *Adventures on Lego Island*

1998 Programmable *RCX* brick (Lego *Mindstorm*) introduced

Page 253

Primo bricks

Freedom is fun. And the pleasure in playful freedom has a strong symbol in the distinctive, simple design of the bricks themselves: their rectangular shape, their studs, their clear, bright colors, and their lightweight yet sturdy material. Lego's elementary design has become a part of childhood and growing up all over the globe—in other words, a mini-icon of the twentieth century. The colorful, chaotic pile of building bricks in the nursery is a strong signal evoking fond memories in children of all ages (illustration page 16).

Lego protects its homemade iconography, which is backed up by an ingenious graphic CI, by rigorously combating plagiarism. The company signs cooperative deals only with other multinational concerns, such as Kellogg's or McDonald's, that already have at least as much of a cult status among children as Lego itself. Today six hundred Lego sets (with more than two thousand different elements) are on the market, and the company continuously adds new ones. All themes suitable for children are covered, from the dollhouse set to the robot with assembly instructions on CD-ROM, and the company now offers appropriate toys for every age group. The product family *Primo,* introduced in the 1990s, is a starter set for toddlers (with extra large bricks for baby hands and simplified faces) with a successful, consistent design. In particular, the dome-shaped studs lend the extra-large bricks a distinctive silhouette and predestine them to become toy classics.

A wide range of marketing activities, among them competitions such as the ongoing one for new records in tower building, have created a Lego culture of global and multicultural dimensions. The company's most recent innovation represents a step into the next millennium. The "intelligent" brick developed together with American scientists will allow electronic controls and is designed to prepare both Lego and those who play with it for the digital future.

Jouni LEINO

Furniture Designer and Interior Decorator / Finland

Jouni Leino's freestanding bathroom tissue holder *Frog* was a witty contribution to an all-too-human situation. And he offers other contemporary answers to problems thought long resolved. His unobtrusive, highly functional *CD Tower,* made of wood scraps, can be stacked (and put away) easily. For the business school in Helsinki, which he furnished, Leino designed variable and computer-compatible classroom furniture, for example a clever system of oval tables that can be positioned to allow on-screen work either in groups or solo. Triangular wall tables offer ideal seats for brief laptop sessions. In collaboration with his colleagues Milla Björk and **Sari Anttonen,** Leino has developed the brand eMotion, furniture that says the world must not be taken too seriously. This irreverent statement comes loud and clear, for example, from the shelf unit *Jotso,* whose door pivots on its own axis, and from the pendant lamp *Planet,* literally an object with a different slant.

1961 Born in Turku

1992 Design studio

1993 Lecturer at the West-Finnish Design Center, Vaasa; exhibition design *Finnhits* (Finnish chair classics)

1997 Launches the brand *eMotion* for experimental furniture, together with **Sari Anttonen** and Milla Björk

1998 Interior design for **Nokia** Research Center

Products

1991 Coffeehouse furniture *Kaffet* for **Avarte**

1995 Bathroom tissue holder *Frog* for Formverk

1996 Café table *Boris* for **Vivero**

1997 Pendant lamp *Planet* for eMotion; café chair *Doris* for Vivero

CD Tower

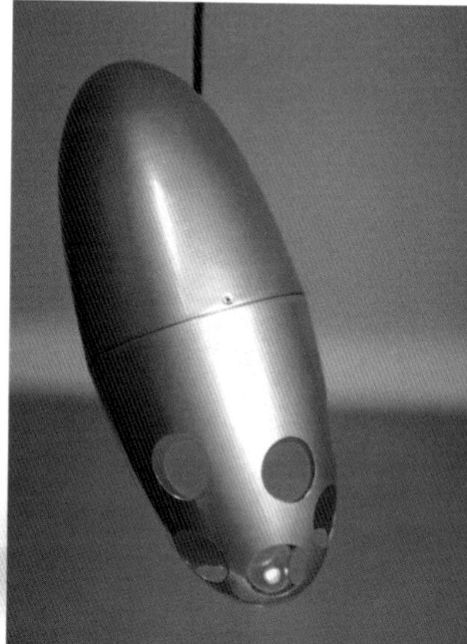

Pendant lamp *Planet* by Jouni Leino, Sari Anttonen, and Milla Björk

LINDE, HAGERUP & PETERSEN

Studio for Product Design / Denmark

When Copenhagen's city council announced a design competition for new park benches in 1996, almost 200 architects and designers participated, including the big names. However, the prize was awarded to a team hardly anybody had heard of before. Linde, Hagerup & Petersen are three young fathers, all born in Copenhagen, who know the social environment of the municipal parks firsthand, and, as they put it, they simply "talked about the project for weeks." The result is true innovation: a knee-high chair on runners. Its low silhouette fits nicely into the urban greenscape; its proximity to the turf promotes communication. And because the chair can hardly be used for anything else, it is less likely that somebody will walk off with it.

The three designers have set up their office in Nørrebro, an old district with a high percentage of foreigners, scene cafés, and an anarcho-creative flair. Linde, Hagerup & Petersen bring their own life experience and their respective areas of specialization to their work. Like all Danes, Leif Hagerup, a former

1996 Studio set up by **Morten Linde, Leif Hagerup,** and **Søren Ulrik Petersen** in Copenhagen; chair design for Copenhagen parks wins a competition.

Park chair *København* by Linde, Hagerup & Petersen, 1996

Bicycle trailer *Dolphin* by Leif Hagerup for Winther, 1995

colleague of **Knud Holscher** and an ardent cyclist, turns ordinary bicycles into serious means of transportation. The trick here is to juggle the contradictory demands of stability and lightness. Hagerup seems to have achieved this balance with his trailer *Dolphin* (for Winther). The multipurpose vehicle can be used as a baby carriage or shopping cart and meets high safety standards. Søren Petersen, a cabinetmaker by training, designed a transportable bookshelf that leans against the wall. His contribution to ergonomic seat design is a chair based on the self-righting principle that is easy on the back. Still only a prototype, the design is now in production on a smaller scale as a saltshaker. Morten Linde worked formerly in the studio of **David Lewis,** designing, among other things, hi-fi equipment for **Bang & Olufsen.** Since then he has developed a digital cordless telephone (for Kirk Telecom) with many useful features but minus all aesthetic frills. Of the three designers, Linde is the one known for typically Danish no-nonsense design.

Products

1992 *Beosound 9000* by **Morten Linde** with **David Lewis** for Bang & Olufsen

1993 Chaise lounge *Chip* by L. Hagerup and S. U. Petersen

1995 Bicycle trailer *Dolphin* by L. Hagerup for Winther (ID Prize); cordless telephone *Dect-Z* by M. Linde for Kirk

1996 Chair *København* for the city of Copenhagen and café table for Eilersen, both by Linde, Hagerup & Petersen

1997 Pillow chair by L. Hagerup

1998 Saltshaker for **Royal Copenhagen** by S. U. Petersen

Chair *Eddi* by Leif Hagerup, 1994

Stefan LINDFORS

Artist, Product Designer, and Interior Decorator / Finland

"I am conservative," explains Stefan Lindfors. And: "Design functionaries have way too much control." And: "Finland has never been a design country." Lindfors only reluctantly passes up an affront. Wherever he appears, he is either loudly booed or enthusiastically applauded. This "Saarinen of the 1990s" (in the words of the jury of the Väinö Tanner Trailblazer Awards, Scandinavia's highest cultural award) made a name for himself in the 1980s. Soon he was considered by some a great talent of Finnish design and branded by others its enfant terrible. The halogen lamp *Scaragoo* was his first product to be sold outside of Finland and got him included at once in the *International Design Yearbook.* Success like this is typical of Lindfors. He was one of the first in the country of Aalto who managed to escape the great man's shadow. Lindfors, who has a slight Swedish accent when he speaks Finnish, lists both Helsinki and New York as his address. When an all-star design team is assembled for a project anywhere in the world, it can be safely assumed that his name is

1962 Born in Mariehamm

1988 Completed study of interior decorating and furniture in Helsinki

1990 Väinö Tanner Trailblazer Award

1992 Georg Jensen Prize

1993 Professor at the Kansas City Art Institute; SIO Design Prize for best Finnish interior design

1995 Exhibition *Freedom of Speech* in Washington, D.C.

Salad servers *Tools* for Hackman

Children's chair *Angel* for the Kiasma museum

1995 Clock tower sculpture *Winged Victory* for Swatch; Good Design Prize, Athenaeum, Chicago

1997 Interior design for the restaurant Piégon, Helsinki

Products

1987 Table lamp *Scaragoo* for Ingo Maurer GmbH

1995 Chair for the Kemper Museum, Kansas City

1996 Chair *Lindfors 1* for Korhonen; oil container for Neste

1997 Coffee service *EgO* for **Arabia;** salad bowl with servers *Lindfors 98;* tools for Hackman; raincoat and bag *Alaris* for **Marimekko**

1998 Children's chair for the Kiasma museum, Helsinki

Page 259

Table lamp *Scaragoo,* 1987

on the list of chosen candidates. At the Museum of Modern Art's 1995 "Mutant Materials" exhibition in New York the whiz kid was represented with two products, the *Kemper Chair* and the biomorphic oilcans made of transparent plastic, which Finland's giant chemical firm Neste sells at its gas stations. The chair has a seat shell of fiberglass; its organic lines contrast with the constructive aluminum legs, clearly recalling **Antti Nurmesniemi's** *Triennial chair.*

Visitors at the New York exhibition encountered a disciplined Stefan Lindfors, but visitors at another exhibition on the other side of the continent experienced a very different side of the artist. The installation artist Lindfors had turned a Los Angeles gallery into a labyrinth of monumental insects and larvae. Environments of steel, fiberglass, resin, and light combined to create a veritable Hades bursting with mysticism and metaphors. Lindfors had already given his lamp *Scaragoo* zoomorphic features; it stands on rod-like legs and looks like an unknown, new species of scorpion.

Bold expressiveness is an important dimension of Finland's design tradition, but just as important is the understatement or, as the Finns say, the "silence." Stefan Lindfors, more than anyone else, embodies this dichotomy, as is evident from two of his interiors in Helsinki: the café in the Design Museum and the restaurant Piégon, both very calm rooms for relaxing. In 1998 Lindfors went to work for **Hackman,** Finland's greatest design company , and for its upscale brand **Arabia.** He designed bowls and salad servers for Hackman's series *Tools* and also a "growing" coffee service in plain white by the name of *EgO.*

LOUIS POULSEN

Lighting Manufacturer / Denmark

1874 Loudvig R. Poulsen opens wine business

1906 Move to Nyhavn 11, still the company's headquarters today

1918 Production of electric appliances

1924 Collaboration with **Poul Henningsen** (1926 lamp production)

1927 British and French catalog (1928 German *PH*-lamp company, Karlsruhe)

1933 Discount models because of economic crisis

1941 Company newsletter *Nyt* edited by Poul Henningsen (until 1967)

1962 Foreign branch in Germany (1964 in France, 1975 in Sweden, 1985 in United States, 1991 in Japan)

1964 Purchase of a wholesale business and other acquisitions

From left to right:

Outdoor lights *Homann* and *Nyhavn* by Alfred Homann as well as bollard lamp *Peter Plan* by Peter Bysted

Page 261

Ceiling light *Airport* by Louis Poulsen

When Copenhagen's first power station was built in 1892, Louis Poulsen supplied the equipment, thus turning from a wine merchant into an electrical wholesaler. Later he was to become a lamp manufacturer and a paragon of minimalist Danish design. As a result of his collaboration with the light constructivist **Poul Henningsen,** Poulsen added lamp production in the 1920s; meanwhile lamps account for about a third of the company's sales.

Poulsen and Henningsen are one of those inspired, highly functional dyads of manufacturer and designer that have been such a blessing for modern Danish design history. Henningsen's lamps *PH* (illustration page 26) virtually catapulted the company to the rank of a national institution. Louis Poulsen was one of the first Danish design companies to take his business to international markets. And it certainly did not hurt the company's chances for international success when in 1927 Henningsen's new lamps were chosen for the Stuttgart Weissenhof project—a model housing development initiated by the German crafts association (Werkbund) which attracted avant-garde architects across Europe. Subsequently the PH lamps became the favorite objects of progressive architects like Hannes Meyer, Ludwig Mies van der Rohe, and Alvar Aalto; the latter used the lamps in 1928 in a theater in Turku.

In 1930 Louis Poulsen's catalogs appeared in ten different languages, including German, English, Dutch, Czech, and

1977 Listing on the stock exchange

1994 Book *Light-years Ahead* on the history of PH

1995 Divisions communications and data lines set up

1997 Acquisition of British Outdoor Lighting Ltd.

Products

1926 Lamps *PH*

1959 Lamps *AJ* by **Arne Jacobsen**

1970 Floor lamp *Pantella* by **Verner Panton**

1973 Lights *Albertslund* by **Jens Møller-Jensen**

1992 Bollard lamp *Columbus* by Louis Poulsen

1993 Ceiling light *Pulsar* by Alfred Homann

1995 Lamp series *Beret* by Marianne Tuxen

1996 Bollard lamp *Borealis* by King-Miranda, Milan

1998 Light for line scan camera applications *Plate* by Vesa Honkonen and Julle Oksanen

Page 263

Left: Floor lamp *Royal* by Arne Jacobsen

Right: Bollard lamp *Borealis* by King-Miranda

Hungarian. Back then the export business was transacted largely through license agreements. It was only in the 1960s that Louis Poulsen opened its own branches outside of Denmark.

The company has remained true to its design concept throughout the decades and refrained from any eccentricity. Louis Poulsen produces lights for indoor as well as outdoor use, and the catalog featuring the full product line has grown to impressive proportions. All the lights are developed by renowned architects, among them **Arne Jacobsen** and the Italian studio, King-Miranda. But Poul Henningsen's original lights are still the company's showpieces, from the functionalist chandelier variation Kogelen (*Cone*), an impressive slat structure, to the multishade table lamp *PH 5.*

In the 1950s and 1960s new classics elbowed their way into the product line, among them Arne Jacobsen's perennial series *Royal,* **Henning Koppel's** kerosene lamp in an organic design, **Verner Panton's** pop shades *Panthella,* and the lamp *Albertslund* designed by the architect **Jens Møller-Jensen.** The latter consistently applied Poul Henningsen's principle of nonglaring design, and to keep the costs low, he used only mass-produced standard components for his lamps. Poul Henningsen was so pleased with the result that he chose Møller-Jensen's lamps to light up his garden.

In the company's current catalog a neutral white, the signature color of functionalism, predominates. The optical restraint is underscored by absolute geometric discipline, particularly in Louis Poulsen's own designs, for example, the classic task light *IT* with hinged arm and the ceiling light *Skagen.* One of the latest products, however, goes against the product line's overall asceticism: the bollard lamp *Borealis,* though white, has an expressive, bud-shaped head.

Erik MAGNUSSEN

Product and Furniture Designer / Denmark

1940 Born in Copenhagen
1960 Completes training as ceramist in Copenhagen; freelance designer of ceramics, furniture, and glass
1961 Works for **Bing & Grøndahl**
1967 Lunning Prize
1970 Teacher at the Art Academy in Copenhagen (until 1973)
1972 ID Prize (also in 1977 and 1987)
1976 Works for **Stelton**
1978 Works for **Georg Jensen**
1983 Designer of the Year
1996 Bindesbøll Medal

"I have never spent less than a year on a product," explains Erik Magnussen. Even though this may not be true for every teapot he designed, it is clear that this is a perfectionist speaking. The design for the thermos *Model 2000* (for **Stelton**) took a full six years. "Every little detail was a problem," recalls Magnussen. And details are important to him. The new thermos consists of only two components, a cylindrical stainless steel container and an ingenious top that can be operated with one hand. The trick is that the metal bail, which the thumb presses down to pour, is also used to remove the top. One of the most challenging problems was posed by the combination of steel and plastics, which react very differently to heat. For that reason alone the design development required close consultation between designer and producer.

From an early age (Magnussen's father was an art dealer) Magnussen was drawn to art. In the 1960s he produced series of free-form ceramic sculptures that met with considerable positive response. However, he was more interested in "real things," which in his view took place in factories. He designed his first dinnerware set in 1965 for the porcelain manufacturer **Bing & Grøndahl.** This service stirred things up in the industry because it represented an attack on the bourgeois Danish parlor table. Magnussen, then just twenty-five years old, subjected the traditional dinnerware to a radical revision (as **Kaj Franck** had done before him in Finland). The name of his design was provokingly functional: *Form 679* was its production number. The teapots, bowls, and cups were all stackable; the saucers also served as lids and vice versa.

In the 1970s Erik Magnussen succeeded **Arne Jacobsen** at Stelton, a connectionthat continues to this day. His first product, a thermos intended to complement Jacobsen's famous line

Page 265

Tubular steel chairs for Kevi

Thermos for Stelton

Pewter teakettle for Selangor

Cylinda, became a best-seller right off the bat. Magnussen designed a T-shaped lid that opens and closes automatically when the thermos is tilted (illustration page 13). This thermos exemplifies Magnussen's design principles. His goal was the design of a product that was new, durable, cost-effective to produce, easy to use, and simple in form. The same also applies to his furniture. Magnussen has a preference for tubular steel because it can be bent in any direction. In the late 1960s he introduced a canvas-covered folding chair consisting of two identical pieces of tubular steel that were connected at only one point; the chair was stabilized by the weight of the person sitting on it. Similarly astonishing was the chair he designed in those days for the Copenhagen Bernadotte School. It consisted of only one bent piece of tubular steel and was reminiscent of **Poul Henningsen's** *Snake Chair.*

In the late 1980s Magnussen applied the same principle several more times. The small chair for **Paustian,** for example, is constructed of one tubular steel piece and a steel plate that are connected at only one point. The work tables in the series *Click* (for **Fritz Hansen**) are also big on tubular steel. They are lightweight (sandwich-board top) and can be clamped together; they approach the limits of design.

Magnussen's scientific approach has also been an advantage in other areas. He designed several technical instruments, for example a portable navigation instrument that combines the latest satellite-supported technology with digital data processing. Magnussen's approach proves that the principle "form follows function" still holds, even on the threshold to the next century. His designs provide the evidence. They bear hardly any traces of fashion.

Products

1965 Dinnerware series *Termo* for Bing & Grøndahl

1968 Chair Z

1971 Dinnerware series *Hank*

1975 Thermos for Stelton

1986 Series of bowls for Stelton

1988 Dinnerware series *Servizz;* kerosene lamp *301* for Harlang and Dreyer; china collection *Erik Magnussen* for Selangor Pewter, Malaysia

1989 Chair and table for **Paustian**

1994 Table system *Click* for **Fritz Hansen**

1998 Thermos *2000* for Stelton

Page 267

Wall clocks for Georg Christensen

Table *Click* for Fritz Hansen

Tubular steel chair for Paustian, 1989

970
980
990
1000
1010
1020
1030
1040
1050
mb

MARIMEKKO

Manufacturer of Textiles and Accessories / Finland

Marimekko Oy, Helsinki

1951 Founded by Armi and Viljö Ratia in Helsinki

1953 **Vuokko Nurmesniemi** artistic director (until 1960)

1956 First fashion show in Stockholm

1959 Annika Rimala hired (until 1981)

1960 Fifth store in Finland

1961 Fashion show in the United States

1966 Pilot house for *Mari Village*

1968 Exhibition To *Finland With Love,* New York

Operation rescue began in 1991. It only took six months for the former advertising manager, Kirsti Paakanen, to make the ailing company profitable again. Since she has succeeded in giving the legendary Marimekko a new future, Paakanen has become star of Finland's design business and the shining example of what marketing can accomplish even in times of crisis. Kirsti Paakanen is by no means the first charismatic woman in Marimekko's history. That role is occupied by Armi Ratia, who began manufacturing printed cotton in a small, 215-square-foot workshop. The young entrepreneur then took a decisive step when she followed the advice of her friend **Arttu Brummer,** a professor, and hired some of his most talented students, among them **Vuokko Nurmesniemi,** Marimekko's first designer-in-chief, who reinvented Finnish fashion. Other designers came on board later, for example **Maija Isola,** Ristomatti Ratia, **Annika Rimala,** and Marja Suna. On the whole, Marimekko was Finland's first textile company to have its own design department. It updated its

collection so rigorously that its abstract patterns soon became inside tips in jazz cellars and other hot spots. If one believes company lore, the financial upturn began with a modern-day fairy-tale. A Marimekko fan in Massachusetts ordered dresses in 1960 and displayed them in a Cape Cod store. Coincidentally, the Kennedys lived nearby, and Jacqueline bought no less than seven models. Coincidentally, it was also a year of presidential elections, and the first lady, who had been criticized for her expensive Parisian wardrobe, presented herself to the press in her new, saucy Finnish frocks. That was the beginning of the Marimekko wave.

By the end of the 1960s the company had more than 400 employees, two new production facilities, and about 100 branches worldwide. The driving forces behind this success were the ideas of Armi Ratia and her vision of "total design." The word "fashion" was taboo. The byword was "dress," and it meant antifashion: casual unisex style, simple cuts, leisure-wear for

1974 **Fujiwo Ishimoto** hired

1979 Armi Ratia died; **Marja Suna** hired

1985 Sold to the Amer-Concern

1991 Kirsti Paakanen new owner, subsequently restoration of profitability and new stores by **Stefan Lindfors** and **Antti Eklund**

1999 Store center in the Hotel Kämp, Helsinki

From left to right:

Magazine *Mobilia,* Denmark, 1964

Magazine *Elle,* France, 1965

Fabric *Melon* by Maija Isola, 1963

Dress *Kikapuu* by Liisa Suvantu, 1974

Products

1955 All-purpose dress made of fabric *Rimini* by V. Nurmesniemi

1956 Fabric *Little Stones* by **Maija Isola**

1957 Shirt *Jokapoika (Every Boy)*

1959 Dress Rowan, both by V. Nurmesniemi

1961 Fabric Lokki by Maija Isola

1969 Leotard with long stripes by Annika Rimala

1972 Marimekko bags

1982 Fabric *Landscape* by Fujiwo Ishimoto

1992 Glass series *Women* by **Brita Flander**

1994 Collection *Lisko* by Antti Eklund

1997 Handbag *Triangle;* backpack *Black Sack*

Page 271

Bathing collection, 1997

Umbrella by Annika Rimala, c. 1975

Candlestick *Runko* by Brita Flander, 1991

Fabric *Jonah* by Maija Isola, 1961

dancing. The collection was augmented by new types of clothing, such as T-shirts and all-purpose jackets, and by towels, tablecloths, curtains, and duvet covers—offering complete immersion in the world of Marimekko. Almost all designs were striped, dotted, or checked, often in cheerful, contrasting colors. Excursions into art were also quite common; for example, Vuokko Nurmesniemi designed free patterns in the manner of the American artist Jackson Pollock.

In the company's advertising the public encountered the "Marimekko Girl." Advertising campaigns were geared to young, independent people, and back then that was what everybody wanted to be. One of Marimekko's most successful products was the shirt *Jokapoika (Every Boy),* which is still being produced. Marimekko provided the uniform for the horizontally striped rebellion against convention and an early lifestyle concept of which the projected "Marimekko Village" was to be an exemplary realization. However, Armi Ratia's dream of a modern commune in which her staff would also be living did not come true. Only one pilot house had been completed when financial problems reared their head in the early 1970s, problems that had been masked by the hectic pace of expansion. Uncertain times followed, and the company proved itself unable to develop a new concept. By the end of the 1980s huge debts had accumulated.

"I started with the assumption that everything had to change," explains Kirsti Paakanen. Customers first noticed the change in the stores, which were newly designed by **Stefan Lindfors** and **Antti Eklund,** among others. New discoveries, like the glass designer **Brita Flander,** have helped expand the product line. But design veterans continue to play a role, for example, **Fujiwo Ishimoto** and **Annika Rimala,** a woman of the first hour whose dresses were featured in the 1960s on the pages of *Vogue* and *Elle.*

Bruno MATHSSON

Furniture Designer / Sweden

1907 Born in Värnamo

1936 Exhibition in the Röhsska-Museum, Göteborg

1937 Participated in the World's Fair, Paris (1939 in New York)

1948 Study trip to the United States (until 1949)

1950 Glass house with furniture exhibition in Värnamo

1957 Participated in Interbau, Berlin

1964 Founds Mathsson International AB (MIAB)

Bruno Mathsson grew up in the small town of Värnamo. A fifth-generation cabinetmaker, he was an apprentice in his father's cabinetmaking shop and worked there all his life. When he began to design his own furniture in the early 1930s, the trade was just entering a state of turmoil triggered by the 1930 Stockholm Exhibition, which had unleashed a veritable battle between conservatives and modernists. The young Bruno Mathsson, enthusiastic about the new school, started to experiment with progressive furniture concepts. In 1933 he introduced his first chair frame made of bent, glued wood laminate and covered with woven leather strips. In his design, seat and backrest merged into a curved unit. In 1936 he displayed the results of his experiments, among them the work chair *Eva*, in the Göteborg Röhsska-Museum, where his furniture drew a lot of attention because the likes of it had never been seen before.

It turned out to be trendsetting in anticipating the **organic design** that was to gain acceptance in the following decades,

Lounge *Pernilla*, 1944

and in that regard, Mathsson's work is on a par with **Alvar Aalto's** designs of the same period. The design principles underlying the furniture he presented in Göteborg remained constant factors in his designs for the rest of his career. And there is another parallel between the two designers: like Aalto, the energetic Mathsson also took the production and marketing of his furniture into his own hands. The critics were highly enthusiastic about his designs, but as so often happens, the industry shied away from the risk of production. Therefore, the cabinetmaker's son decided to produce his furniture in his parents' workshop, which gave him the additional advantage of complete control over quality. Moreover, direct selling by mail order turned out to be a lucrative alternative.In this regard also Mathsson was a pioneer. It wasn't until the 1970s that Mathsson started working with other furniture manufacturers, in particularly with **Dux.**

Mathsson's chairs are striking above all because of their seeming lightness, an impression conveyed by their simple

1966 Prince Eugen Prize

1978 Distribution through **Dux** (to this day his classic collection)

1983 Mathsson Foundation for the Support of Scandinavian Designers established

1988 Died in Värnamo

1993 Retrospective in the National Museum

Table *Superellipsis* for Fritz Hansen (together with Piet Hein)

Products

1931 Easy chair *Gräshoppan* (grasshopper)

1934 Chair *Eva*

1936 Table *Annika*

1944 Lounge *Pernilla*

1964 Table *Superellipsis* together with **Piet Hein** for **Fritz Hansen**

1966 Office chair *Jetson*

1969 Easy chair on casters *Karin*

1973 Tubular steel bed *Ulla* for Dux

1983 Computer workstation

1987 Easy chair *Minister*

Page 275

Chair *Eva,* 1934

structure. Originally he preferred materials such as bent beech and woven canvas or leather for the seats. His chairs have obvious sculptural characteristics and often seem almost animated; for example, the early chair he called *Gräshoppan* (grasshopper). The legs of his design *Pernilla* look as though they are ready to pounce, and the lounge of the same name looks like a body in resting position. From the outset the dynamic tension inherent in his seating furniture was not an aesthetic end in itself; the shapes of the furniture were molded to fit the human body. Mathsson strove for the optimal combination of support and comfort. To achieve this he based his designs on anatomical studies—following Denmark's **Kaare Klint** in this respect. His scientific analyses of seating comfort made him one of the pioneers of **ergonomics.**

After WW II he expanded his collection into an astonishingly extensive œuvre. For more than a half a century, Bruno Mathsson was Sweden's best-known furniture designer. A number of his designs set new standards for combining craftsmanship and attention to detail, and in this they resembled the work of **Hans J. Wegner.** At the same time Mathsson's designs also had the innovative quality exemplified by **Poul Kjaerholm,** among others. In the 1960s Bruno Mathsson also worked with tubular steel frames. His famous table design *Superellipsis*, a form somewhere between a rectangle and an ellipsis, was the result of Mathsson's collaboration with its inventor, **Piet Hein.** In his later years Mathsson, a restless innovator, designed ergonomic computer workstations. For some time prior to that he had worked on the possibility of heating glass houses with a combination of heat from the earth's interior and solar energy—in this regard he was once again ahead of his time.

Grethe MEYER

Architect, Ceramic Designer, and Product Designer / Denmark

1918 Born in Svendborg

1947 Completed study of architecture in Copenhagen

1955 Works for Building Research Institute, among other things on *Bau-Buch (Book on Building)*

1960 Freelance designer

1965 ID Prize (also in 1976)

1982 Bindesbøll Medal

1997 Design Prize of the Danish Design Council

Products

1952 Modular wall unit *Boligens Byggeskabe*

1957 Table and chair, both with **Børge Mogensen**

1965 Dinnerware service *Blåkant* for **Royal Copenhagen**

1976 Porcelain *Ildpot*

1982 Porcelain *Picnic* with **Ole Kortzau**

When awarding her its annual prize in the late 1990s, the Danish Design Council couldn't help admitting that this woman's ideals had temporarily "sunk into oblivion." Among these ideals was an unshakable demand for quality and the habit to always look at objects from their user's perspective. After 1945 the young architect worked for more than ten years on the multivolume book *Bau-Buch (Book on Building),* which focused on interior design. During that period she worked closely with **Børge Mogensen** in developing standardized, modular consumer products. The modular wall unit *Boligens Byggeskabe* that they designed for the Danish Consumer Cooperative became highly popular and now fetches high prices as an antique. Grethe Meyer played an important role at **Royal Copenhagen** where she gave fresh impetus to the design with her simplified, sometimes rustic shapes (illustration page 45). Many of her designs are still in production, such as the vase *Ocean* and the faience dinnerware service *Blåkant.*

Flatware *Copenhagen* for Royal Copenhagen

Børge MOGENSEN

Furniture Designer / Denmark

The simpler the better—this credo of Børge Mogensen's made him into a virtual embodiment of Danish furniture functionalism. As head of furniture design at the Consumer Cooperative, Mogensen, a former pupil of Klint, tried to apply his teacher's theoretical precepts to the production of practical everyday furniture, probably the most important project in the Danish furniture trade in that generally very productive period. In the 1940s Mogensen developed several furniture series that were brought into Danish homes by way of the cooperative's channels of distribution. In 1940 he designed furniture for young people—back then a novelty—under the label "Hansen's Attic." He continued the series with "Peter's Room." It is one of his many accomplishments to have overcome ordinary folks' fondness for imitation mahogany by offering them attractive, blond beech furniture.

A connoisseur of modern art, Mogensen drew on popular originals for inspiration, for example, Windsor chairs and Shaker

1914 Born in Aalborg

1938 Studies furniture in Copenhagen under **Kaare Klint** after having completed apprenticeship as cabinetmaker

1942 Director for furniture design at the Consumer Cooperative/FDB (until 1950)

1945 Assistant to Kaare Klint, partnership with Hans J. Wegner

1958 Works for **Fredericia** and also for **Fritz Hansen**

1971 Furniture prize together with Andreas Graversen

1972 Honorary member of the Royal Society of Arts, London; died in Copenhagen

Easy Chair for Fredericia, 1964

Serving Trolley *5370* for Fredericia, 1963

furniture. At some point his sturdy furniture became fashionable in the open-minded middle-class circles that set the tone in home decor, and this was the cue for private manufacturers—among them **Fredericia**—to take an interest in the modernist's designs. After the war Mogensen worked as a consultant for the Institute of Building Research, where he collaborated with the architect Grethe Meyer on trendsetting modular furniture systems.

The wall unit *Boligens Byggeskabe,* a sizable built-in shelf system equally suitable for living room, dining room, and bedroom, became a best-seller. A close friendship linked Mogensen and **Hans J. Wegner,** and for a while the two were the stars at exhibitions of the Copenhagen cabinetmakers' guild. Mogensen, who would have loved to liberate humanity from big business, was ahead of his time and a pioneer in the fight against pollution. He used only materials that could be disposed of in an environmentally sound way. Wood posed no problems in this regard, because, according to Mogensen, "wood burns."

Products

1945 *Spindle-back Sofa* for Fritz Hansen

1952 Wall unit *Boligens Byggeska*be together with **Grethe Meyer** for Boligens

1958 *Spanish Chair* for Fredericia

1962 *Wing Chair*

1964 Easy chair for Fredericia

1965 Table *Shaker*

Bench *3171* for Fredericia, 1956

Per MOLLERUP

Graphic Designer / Denmark

Per Mollerup invades the parlors of his fellow Danes. He created the logo of Danish public television's first channel. A playful variation on the numeral "1," the logo remains on screen—sometimes as a positive image, sometimes as a negative—throughout the program. What the graphic artist Mollerup here did with a numeral he usually does with typefaces. Taking advantage of the complex nature of the characters, he plays off meaning, visual appearance, and phonetics. The same approach works for company logos, where he often condenses the content of the message in visual symbols. For example, turning the letter h in the trademark of furniture manufacturer **Schiang** into a chair triggers momentary confusion and establishes a memory link. In Scandinavia Mollerup, known for his play with language, is one of the leading visual communications specialists. One of his most extensive projects was the graphics "clearance work" at the Copenhagen airport, where Mollerup reduced the number of signs drastically, avoiding pictograms.

1942 Born in Valby Bakke

1986 ID Prize (a total of eight times)

1996 Bindesbøll Medal

Products

1986 Visual guidance systems for the Copenhagen airport

1992 Logo for Schiang (also for Danish Film Institute, Oslo airport, and others)

1994 Corporate identity for the first channel of Danish public television

Logo for Danish television, 1994

NILFISK

Manufacturer of Vacuum Cleaners

Nilfisk-Advance AS, Brøndby

1906 Founded as Fisker & Nielsen

1920 Listing on the stock exchange

1925 Exports amount to more than sixty percent of sales

1994 Takes over Advance Machine Company, one of the largest American cleaning machine manufacturers

Products

1910 First vacuum cleaner *C 1*

1922 First household vacuum cleaner

1960 Model *GM 80* (still on the market)

1998 Portable vacuum cleaner *Backuum* (ID Prize)

Jasper Morrison named it the "King of the Vacuum Cleaners" even though the 1960 model *GM 80*, a very robust and extremely durable appliance, is not a widely celebrated design classic. In its natural simplicity the design, though anonymous, reflects a piece of Danish design culture. It was neither the first nor the last design milestone to come from Nilfisk. An upscale brand, the company (which has also tried its hand at manufacturing motorcycles) has incorporated aesthetic quality and innovation into its program and works with experienced designers like **Jacob Jensen** as well as with younger ones that continue along the lines marked out by him. In fact, the current Nilfisk vacuum cleaners resemble Jensen's famous hi-fi equipment. With their sleek, smooth surfaces they do not look like traditional vacuum cleaners and, much like a black box, they give no visible indication of machine inside.

Vacuum cleaner *Backuum*

Vacuum cleaner *GM 410*

Page 280

Professional Vacuum Cleaner *GM 80*

NILFISK
GM 80
ORIGINAL
NILFISK

NOKIA

Manufacturer of Telecommunications Equipment / Finland

The silver-plated cellular phone *8810* is designed to look like "an elegant watch or an exclusive fountain pen," explains Frank Nuovo, Nokia's American designer-in-chief. The cell phone privilege may be a thing of the past, but not so the demand for status symbols. Telephone specialist Nokia (in 1997 sales of around twelve billion dollars, 36,000 employees, and subsidiaries in more than 100 countries) has become the most successful manufacturer of cellular phones worldwide and markets the new mass product, according to the group's chief executive, Jorma Ollila, as a "fashion accessory." In 1997 Nokia sold eleven million pieces and developed thirty-two new telephone models in a total of four design centers. That year sales in the cell phone business rose by almost one third. Now the phone company has sighted a new trend. Nokia's plan is to tailor its products' shape and color even more specifically to certain target groups and thus to provide a status symbol for the international business class by way of "design." "Designers recommended by Nokia" develop individual covers for the pocket telephones, in materials ranging from plastic to platinum. Political parties, businesses, football clubs, etc. can order such special designs directly.

Nokia Mobile Phones

1865 Started as a mill
1967 Paper and rubber factories merge into Oy Nokia
1979 Cellular phone division established
1988 First ISDN-network
1995 Divestiture of cable and television units
1996 Smart traffic products division established
1997 New headquarters in Espoo
1999 Design studies for multimedia cell phone

Products

1996 *Communicator 9000*
1997 Colored cell phone series 5510
1998 Cell phone series *6100;* silver-plated cell phone *8810* by Frank Nuovo

Communicator 9000

Page 283

Silver-plated cell phone *8810* by Frank Nuovo

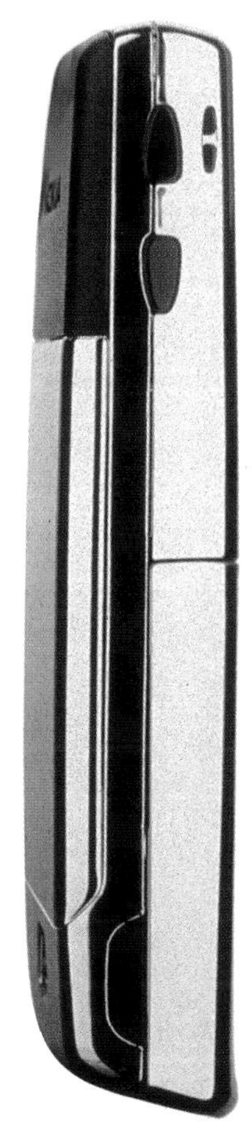

NORDISCHES DESIGN

1867 Excavations of Viking boats in Norway
1891 First open-air museum in Skansen near Stockholm
1892 Hotel Holmenkollen near Oslo
1894 **Akseli Gallen-Kallela** builds a studio in the Finnish wilderness
1897 Nordiska Museet (Nordic museum) opens in Stockholm
1900 National-romantic Finnish pavilion at the World's Fair in Paris
1901 **Carl** and **Karin Larsson** move to the country
1946 First Nordic Design Conference in Copenhagen
1951 Lunning Prize
1952 Nordic Council for the Cooperation of Scandinavian Parliaments
1953 Exhibition *Scandinavia at Table* in London (without Finland)
1954 Touring exhibition *Design in Scandinavia,* United States
1990 Exhibition *Nordform,* Malmö
1999 Shared embassy complex of the Scandinavian countries in Berlin

Plans for a postwar "Nordic Union" fell through because of the Cold War. However, designers succeeded where politicians had failed. When the Svenska Slöjdföreningen celebrated its 100th anniversary in 1945, everybody who was anybody in the Scandinavian art industry went to the banquet in Stockholm's Nordic Museum. The festivities were the prelude to several trans-Scandinavian conferences held regularly in the various capitals. The boom of Scandinavian design in the 1950s was the logical consequence of this development. To be sure, the export success had a share in bringing about this solidarity. As the critic Henrik Sten Møller commented, "Danish design became a marketing concept, often under the guise of 'Scandinavian.'"

The concept of an overarching, unified Nordic style appeared for the first time shortly before 1900. Political and economical radical changes back then went hand in hand with a reappraisal of each country's glorious past that led to a "Viking revival" in architecture, art, and the crafts. These movements had distinctly nationalist characteristics, especially in Norway and Finland, countries that had only just attained their independence or were about to. Therefore this style is also called **National Romanticism.**

Today the Scandinavian Design Council, a committee that awards prizes and organizes exhibitions, applies this term above all to the "Nordic heritage." In the 1950s the airline SAS found out how quickly this heritage changes when a company decision to

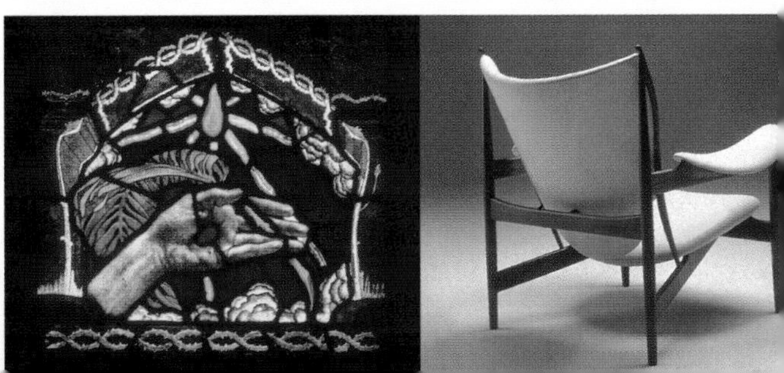

design the planes' interiors using "Nordic," i.e., national-romantic motifs, unleashed a storm of protest. Evidently the SAS management had not realized that the definition of "typical Scandinavian" had changed drastically. SAS responded promptly and subsequently left its interiors in the hands of designers such as **Sigurd Persson,** a card-carrying modernist.

A young generation of designers from Sweden has made the Nordic tradition as an "always valid vision" **(Claesson Koivisto Rune)** its cause in the 1990s. Simplicity is their byword; the new Nordic purism not only harks back to the golden era of the 1950s but even farther into the past for its legacy. The barrenness and rural poverty of the Scandinavian countries whose industrial development got underway only fairly recently, according to the hypothesis, still makes itself felt in contemporary styles. The role that preindustrial crafts played for a long time, and the great number of classic designs it produced, seems to support the argument. Inspiration from the outside, for example from the arts and crafts movement and the Bauhaus, gets short shrift in this analysis, and the same is true for luminaries like **Josef Frank, Timo Sarpaneva** and **Verner Panton,** who cannot be called minimalists by any stretch of the imagination.

"In Scandinavian Design rural culture and crafts of the nineteenth century have combined with industrial efficiency and a more or less socially oriented functionalism."

Ulf Hård af Segerstad

From left to right:

Glass window *Hand of Jesus* by Akseli Gallen-Kallela, 1897

Chief Chair by Finn Juhl, 1949

Jug *Stoneware lined with firebrick shards,* by Kyllikki Salmenhaara, 1960

Chair *Karm* and Table *Ängel* by Thomas Sandell for Källemo, 1995

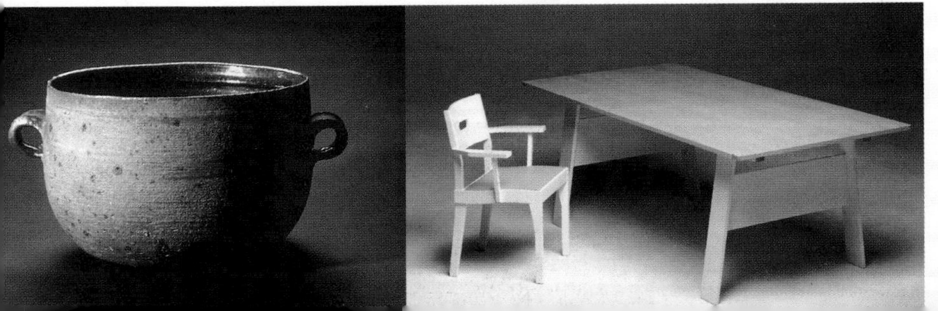

Antti NURMESNIEMI

Product Designer and Interior Decorator / Finland

1927 Born in Hämeenlinna
1951 Works in the architecture firm of Viljo Revell (until 1956)
1952 Hotel Palace
1954 Trip to Italy
1953 Marries **Vuokko Nurmesniemi**
1956 Design studio
1957 Exhibition at **Artek** together with Vuokko Nurmesniemi
1960 Finnish booth at the *Triennial,* Milan (also in 1964 together with V. Nurmesniemi), after that numerous exhibition concepts
1972 Professor for Design in Helsinki
1975 Studio house Nurmesniemi in Helsinki
1977 President of the Finnish Designer Association ORNAMO (until 1982)

Travelers to Finland will not be able to avoid his designs. Antti Nurmesniemi's works are part of Finland's landscape—he has designed the interiors of important buildings, *Finnjet* ferries, and Helsinki's urban railway. But his most recent project is the most striking: the high-voltage transmission towers (illustration page 38) he designed for IVO, Finland's largest electric utility company. His towers are huge pylons with no similarity at all to the conventional utility poles. The sheer attempt to consider aesthetics in designs for power distribution is an innovation. Nurmesniemi conceives of his monumental yet delicate structures as "architectural objects without enclosed space." Six of the towers were built on the coast near Turku as part of an art project, and one stands near Jyväskylä. There, in the middle of a beautiful lake area, is the starting point of a new transmission line. While power lines are usually considered a disfigurement of the landscape, Nurmesniemi's designer towers aim at reconciling technology and nature. The IVO management sees in Nurmesniemi's "landscape towers" opportunities for export.

Antti Nurmesniemi's first striking design was clearly on a much smaller scale. The inconspicuous coffee pots he displayed at **Artek** in 1957 nevertheless pointed "Finnish industrial design into a new direction," according to the consensus of the critics. And their trendsetting power was due precisely to their understatement. The monochrome enameled metal containers presented a tangible alternative to the traditional, big-bellied porcelain coffee pots.

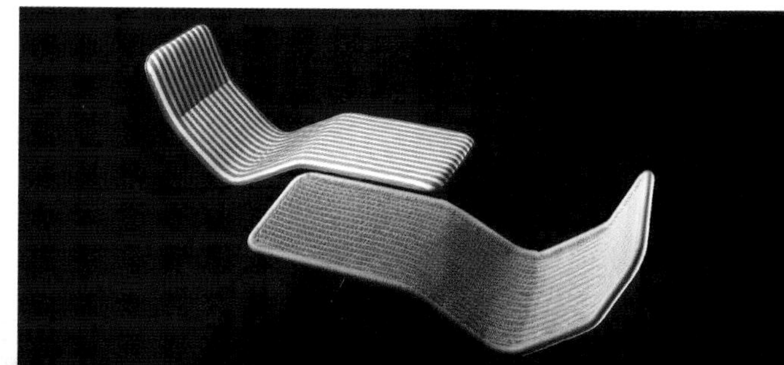

Deck chair *001,* 1967

Page 287

Telephone *Antti* for Fujitsu, 1984

Chair *Triennial 001* for Piiroinen, 1960

Walking stick, 1986

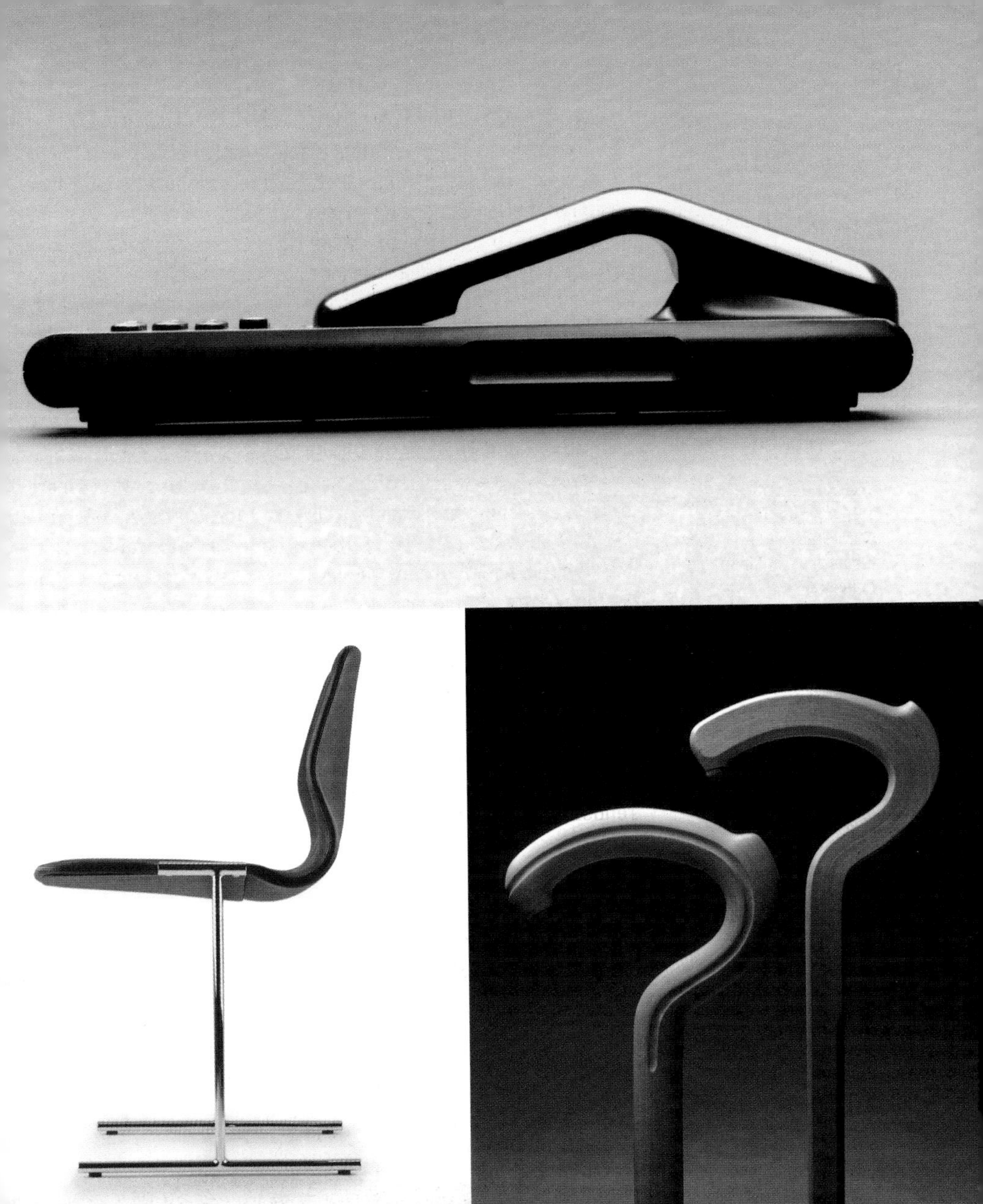

1979 On the board of the International Council of Societies of Industrial Design (President 1989–1992)

1985 Works for Cassina, Italy

1989 Guest House for Neste

1995 Retrospective, City Hall, Oslo

Products

1951 Stool *Horseshoe* for Palace Hotel

1957 Enameled coffeepots for Wärtsilä; plastic lamps for Artek

1960 *Triennial Chair* at **Piiroinen** (grand prize *Triennial,* 1964)

1964 Pots and pans for Högfors

1967 Deck chair *001* for **Vuokko**

Nurmesniemi's design sold well and soon became a cult object progressive architects decorated their homes with. In the early 1950s, after Nurmesniemi had worked in a cabinetmaker's shop and an airplane factory, he began his career in the architectural firm of Viljo Revell, an ardent champion of rationalist building principles. An important project was the Palace Hotel; Nurmesniemi designed the sauna and the stool Horseshoe (illustration page 2), a small seat in modern form but with a definitely Finnish accent.

In those hopeful postwar years, the twenty-five-year-old Nurmesniemi felt himself part of a generation that was going to build the new "international Finland." Even before he became a jet-setter in the 1960s and started representing his country in committees, symposia, and congresses all over the world as a kind of design ambassador, he had gained experience abroad, particularly on his trips to Italy and India. During the 1950s he and his wife, the textile designer **Vuokko Nurmesniemi,** participated together in numerous wallpaper competitions, and he later

Tables on casters, 1985

became a sought-after exhibition designer. After the Artek Exhibition, Antti Nurmesniemi began to develop his own design grammar, combining modernism with a rather subtle Nordic touch, a blend that is clearly visible in his furniture designs. The chair *Triennial* (reedition by **Piiroinen**) epitomizes the synthesis of two clearly distinguishable influences, the sculptural **organic design** (seat) and the constructive **functionalism** (legs). In this design Nurmesniemi exploits the structural potential of the two materials (leather and aluminum) to the full. A few years later, he introduced his deck chair *001,* a seemingly weightless, floating form in the striped "Vuokko-look." It is not without good reason that Nurmesniemi has been called the most "un-Finnish" among Finland's top product designers. For example, his super-flat push-button telephone of the 1980s is the epitome of pure "international style." But he also knows all about life at home in Finland—case in point: his birch walking stick with a rubber loop to hang it on a peg.

1968 Metro Helsinki (until 1977)
1978 Deck chair *002* and new deck chair *001*
1980 Easy chair *004* for Vuokko
1983 Wire furniture
1986 Walking stick
1987 Paper roll packaging for Enso
1991 Espresso machine *Tazza* for Paulig
1995 Transmission towers for IVO (ongoing project)

High-voltage transmission towers in Laukaa, 1990s

400 kV high-voltage transmission towers

Vuokko NURMESNIEMI

Textile and Fashion Designer / Finland

1930 Born in Helsinki as Vuokko Eskolin

1952 Ceramist at **Arabia**

1953 Artistic Director at Marimekko (until 1960); marries **Antti Nurmesniemi**

1956 Glass design for **Nuutajärvi**

1957 Exhibition at **Artek,** together with Antti Nurmesniemi (also in 1958, 1960, 1981); Grand Prize at the *Triennial,* Milan, for glass design

1964 Lunning Prize; starts her own textile and fashion house **Vuokko;** Finnish booth at the *Triennial,* Milan, together with Antti Nurmesniemi

1969 Finnish National Prize for Design

1994 Exhibition *Three Women: Three Lifeworks,* Ikaalinen

1997 Kaj Franck Prize and retrospective in the Design Forum, Helsinki

Products

1955 All-purpose dress / Fabric *Rimini*

1956 Striped shirt *Jokapoika* (every boy)

1957 Tent dress *Thread of Life* / Fabric *Kikeriki* all for **Marimekko**

Postwar Finland was "all black and dark brown," recalls Vuokko Nurmesniemi. Rich ladies had their dresses made by seamstresses; the rest sewed their own clothes, and that was not easy at all in those days. A huge number of pleats, vents, and hand-hemmed buttonholes were the rule then. In 1953 Nurmesniemi, a potter by training, joined **Marimekko,** a textile company specializing in cotton prints. The twenty-one-year-old became its first designer-in-chief and was responsible for the new, saucy style of Marimekko fashions and ultimately also for its international breakthrough.

Her first fabric, *Tibet,* had simple stripes, an unusual pattern in those days. Such large patterns, however, could not be printed with the existing machines. Together with the printers Nurmesniemi developed a method that became the foundation for almost all her subsequent designs. Nurmesniemi banished the gloomy dark-brown once and for all with her "antifashion" and developed an exciting, unpretentious, and universal clothing style. Her early designs from the 1950s still appear astonishingly modern. As a Finnish daily newspaper wrote in 1956, what Nurmesniemi was doing was "clothing as industrial art."

She was Finland's first fashion designer. Her fashion shows were happenings at which the beautiful, the clever, and the rich of Helsinki met. Nurmesniemi invented functionalist dresses she called "movable dresses." Because of their simple style and cut they were ideal for mass production. As a byproduct, Nurmesniemi also liberated women of traditional notions, demonstrating that a dress did not have to have a wasp-waist and that not only men could wear pants. The combination of large-scale patterns and strong colors gave her designs a bold, eye-catching effect. After the first fashion show in the United States, the *New York Herald Tribune* found that Vuokko Nurmesniemi was

"Finland's Matisse." In her daring creations she anticipated many a trend; most especially she was a pioneer of pop art. By the mid-1960s she had become one half of Finland's ideal designer couple through her marriage to **Antti Nurmesniemi** and had founded her own company, **Vuokko.** She continued to pursue her goal of thoroughly revamping feminine fashion, often resorting to means considered unfeminine. For example, she employed practical snap fasteners, zippers, and Velcro fasteners, which allowed unconventional solutions. But Vuokko Nurmesniemi also looked after men. In Finland her brand *Vuokko* became the unorthodox "architect's uniform"—menswear with a difference.

No other Finnish designs were as successful internationally as hers (illustration page 35), but Vuokko Nurmesniemi never followed the trend of the day. She sees herself as an artist who experiments with fabric and color and has never forgotten her most important principle: "A piece of clothing should be simple and functional, but never boring."

1967 Dress *Mini*

1975 Dress *Boticelli* / Fabric *Ministripes*

1983 Dress *Veistos* / Fabric *Solid*

1997 Dresses *Reliefi* and *Höyhen* all for Vuokko

Pages 292/293, from left to right:

Dress *Veistos,* 1986

Dress *Mini,* 1967

Dress *Horisontti,* 1997

From left to right:

Red dress, 1980s

Dress *Humaus,* 1968

Dress *Reliefi,* 1997

ORGANIC DESIGN

1936 Vase *Savoy* by **Alvar Aalto**

1939 Finnish pavilion at the World's Fair in New York by Alvar Aalto

1940 Exhibition *Organic Design,* MOMA, New York

1945 Teak easy chair by **Finn Juhl**

1946 Vase *Kantarelli* by **Tapio Wirkkala**

1952 Chair *Myren* by **Arne Jacobsen**

1956 *Ericofon* by **Ericsson**

1962 TWA terminal at the John F. Kennedy Airport, New York by Eero Saarinen

1967 Easy chair *Pastilli* by **Eero Aarnio;** *Panton Chair* by **Verner Panton**

1995 Exhibition *Mutant Materials* in the MOMA, New York

1996 Deck chair *Chip* by **Valvomo**

1997 Saltshaker *Toi* by Pekka Paikkari for **Arabia**

Eero Aarnio's seat *Pastilli* and **Verner Panton's** cantilever chair that bears his name—both designs of the 1960s in which plastic is rigidified into perfectly flowing and blending lines—are masterpieces of organic design, albeit late works of this style. In 1940 the Museum of Modern Art organized the exhibition *Organic Design in Home Furnishings.* Its most important exhibits, shell chairs made of three-dimensionally bent plywood (a new chair concept and a new technique, based on new glues), were an American-Scandinavian coproduction by Charles Eames and Eero Saarinen. The son of **Eliel Saarinen,** the Finnish director of the influential Cranbrook Academy, Eero Saarinen also cast his shells in concrete, for example, for the TWA terminal at the John F. Kennedy Airport in New York, the apotheosis of 1950s architecture.

The organic style was a blend of several different streams: the plant forms of art nouveau and the sweeping curves and lines of the coming space age entered into an aesthetic liaison with streamlining. At the 1939 World's Fair in New York the Scandinavians stole the show. One of the fair's highlights was **Alvar Aalto's** Finnish pavilion, a huge wave in wood. "Swedish Modern," the antigeometric style epitomized by **Josef Frank** (whose fabrics cater to the Swedish predilection for anything flowery), drew hardly any less attention. The exhibits that won the most applause in the 1954 touring exhibition *Design in Scandinavia* also had soft curves, for example, **Henning Koppel's**

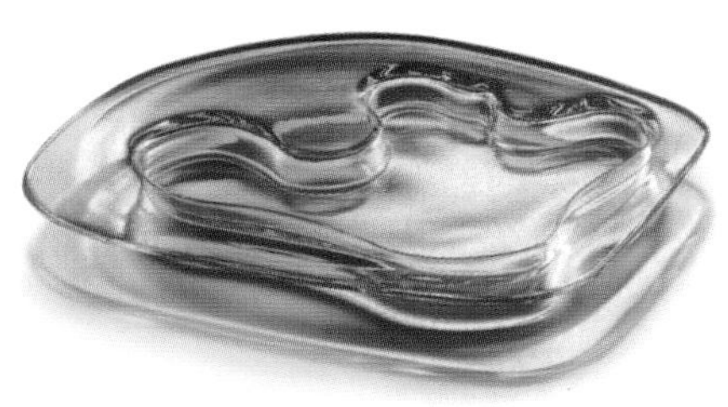

silver bowl or **Tapio Wirkkala's** plywood leaf. And when shortly thereafter furniture from Denmark became a big seller in the United States under the label "Danish Modern," **Finn Juhl's** curvy chair sculptures were among the most admired and best-selling pieces. Designers like Koppel and Juhl were connoisseurs of contemporary art and conceived of their designs as a direct response to it. Furniture became an aesthetic creation, design sculptures whose significance—and that of their creators—was redefined in artistic terms.

"Things should be humane," said **Kay Bojesen,** "warm and alive." In other words, they should be objects whose delicately rounded edges have the ambiance of an English garden and the same erotic tautness as Anita Ekberg's waist. The feminine "New Look" with which the new world of products cosseted consumers was also an organic design. One of the most successful products of that time, the Ericofon, aroused rather phallic associations, however. Organic design is making its comeback in the CAD-generated, biomorphous design of the 1990s, for example, in the countless cell phones of the Scandinavian telecommunications industry. To paraphrase Bojesen: "There should be life in things. Handling them should be enjoyable."

"Our chairs, tables, and cabinets will be sculptures in the interiors of the future."

Gerrit Rietveld

From left to right:

Bowl by Alvar Aalto, 1936

Deck chair *Pernilla* by Bruno Mathsson, 1944

Easy Chair *Cleopatra* by Ola Rune, 1994

Traffic light (prototype) by No Picnic, 1990s

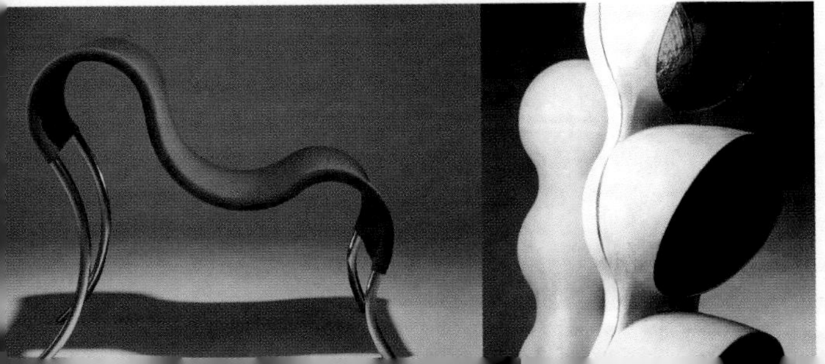

ORREFORS

Glass Manufacturer / Sweden

Orrefors-Kosta Boda AB

1726 Founded in Halleberg as ironworks

1898 Beginning of glass production

1916 New owner hires the artists **Simon Gate** and **Edward Hald** (1917)
1918 Acquisition of Sandvik glassworks

1925 Several prizes at the *Exposition des Arts Décoratifs et Industriels Modernes,* Paris

1927 Exhibition in New York

1928 **Vicke Lindstrand** hired

1936 Edward Hald develops *Slip-Graal-Glas*

1947 Henning Beyer new head of the company (in 1948 his son Johan Beyer); first designs by **Ingeborg Lundin** (until 1971)

1948 Sven Palmquist develops "Ravenna" technique

1990 Merger with **Kosta Boda**

1997 Taken over by **Royal Copenhagen**

Page 297

Vase *Appel*
by Ingeborg Lundin, 1957

Orrefors is Sweden's most famous design brand and almost as well known as **Volvo** or **Ikea**. Orrefors' story begins with an ordinary bottle factory. It was sold just prior to World War I, and this sale brought about extensive changes. The new owner had close contacts to the Swedish artisans' association, which worked on establishing an ongoing dialog between artists and industry. Soon after the change in ownership, the illustrator **Simon Gate** and the painter **Edward Hald** were hired. This was the first time they worked closely with glassblowers. In the 1920s glass from Orrefors became an export article, and had a leading position in Scandinavian aesthetics until after World War II. Orrefors began its ascent to aesthetic supremacy in 1925 when it caused a sensation at the Paris *Exposition des Arts Décoratifs* and won no less than six grand prizes as well as applause from both the jury and the public for its delicate engravings on crystal glass. The motifs were playful and figurative, balancing classicism, elements of modern art, and a tendency toward the exotic, especially in the preferred subject of nude engravings.

Edward Hald had studied architecture and painting in Dresden, Copenhagen, and Paris and was an established artist when he joined Orrefors (he directed its artistic affairs until his death in 1980), having already exhibited his work in Herwarth Walden's Berlin gallery Der Sturm (The Storm). For Orrefors he designed utilitarian articles, for example his early dinnerware set *Strawberry,* as well as decorative objects. His bowls, such as the 1928 *Girls Playing Ball,* fascinated with their shallow, modern silhouette and precisely detailed ornaments. They shared an almost poetic style for which an English critic coined the term "Swedish grace." Within only a few years the small glassworks in Småländ had established itself in the international market, thanks not only to its high-quality products but also to the clear-

sighted management, which established Orrefors' own glass school.

In the 1930s Edvin Öhrström and **Vicke Lindstrand** developed lavish techniques such as "Ariel." Orrefors had arrived as a world-class company and in Sweden was considered a national institution. Nothing expressed this more clearly than the huge glass globe Orrefors displayed at the 1930 *Stockholm Exhibition.* The globe is now in the National Museum. The company was then on the sunny side of life, and the golden 1950s seemed to confirm this with a spate of impressive designs, such as the 1957 vase Appel by **Ingeborg Lundin,** which caused a great sensation at the *Triennial,* where Orrefors' designs had often been awarded prizes. By then glasses were produced in many different techniques, and everything seemed possible. When the great brand (long since merged with **Kosta Boda**) was swallowed by the Danish concern **Royal Copenhagen** near the end of this glorious century, the shock was therefore all the greater—and

Products

- 1915 *Orrefors HW* by Heinrich Wollmann
- 1917 Vase *Graal* by **Knut Bergkvist**
- 1922 Paris cup by Simon Gate
- 1930 Vase *Cirkus* by Vicke Lindstrand
- 1953 Vases *Timglas* (hourglass) by Ingeborg Lundin
- 1954 Series *Fuga* by **Sigurd Persson**
- 1957 Glasses *Tulips* by Nils Landberg
- 1961 Bowl *Ravenna* by Sven Palmquist

the merger fell into the year of Orrefors' 100th anniversary to boot.

Crisis symptoms had of course appeared already long before that. The wild 1960s—**Gunnar Cyrén** invented the *Pop*-glass—were the watershed and led to a changing of the guard. The second generation of artists left the company, among them Ingeborg Lundin and the photographer and glass designer John Selbing. Orrefors has never been famous for experimental escapades. To this day Orrefors still reverberates with the old call for "beauty for all" (illustration page 4). Currently eight artists have a decisive influence on Orrefors' designs. Among them are the young Finnish designer Martti Rytkönen, who tells stories with her cartoon-like drawings on glass, and Lena Bergström, who creates "poetry in glass" and finds "beauty even in imperfections."

1985 Glass *Intermezzo* by Erika Lagerbielke

1992 Glass *Nobel* by **Gunnar Cyrén**

1997 Vases and bowls *Squeeze* by L. Bergström

1998 Art glass *Fabula* by Per B. Sundberg; vases and bowls *Esprit* by Jan Johansson

From left to right:

Bowl *Cirkus*
by Vicke Lindstrand, 1930

Pop-glass by Gunnar Cyrén, 1966

Bowl *Ravenna*
by Sven Palmquist, 1961

Plate *City Views* by Martti Rytkönen, 1998

PANIC DESIGN

Group for Furniture and Product Design / Denmark

1995 Launched in Copenhagen by the design students **Sebastian Holmbäck, Torben Quaade, Mathias Bengtsson, Frank Valentin Holgersen,** and **Rasmus Larsson**

Products

1996 Café table *Viskoser; Spiral Chair;* seats *Fragment;* chairs *Line I & II*

Torben Quaade produced a chair out of prepressed wood. Its structure resembles a snail shell and does not reveal the forces at work in it: four people were needed to hold the highly stressed wood slats. As Quaade himself admits, he "pushes cabinetmaking to the last extreme." Objects designed by the Panic group do not follow the iron rules of Danish **functionalism.** The newly graduated designers call their work "experimental furniture." **Mathias Bengtsson** assembles his bizarre club chairs from wire pieces he fits together without drawings but with much feeling. His one and only principle: always begin from the back. **Sebastian Holmbäck** produces thermoplastic café tables, taking advantage of the material's viscosity. The table base is extruded by hand while the plastic was heated, a process that requires great skill but also allows spontaneous, spur-of-the-moment design. The five extremist designers launched their attack on the design establishment in 1996, and if nothing else, it has been a wake-up call for Denmark's design industry.

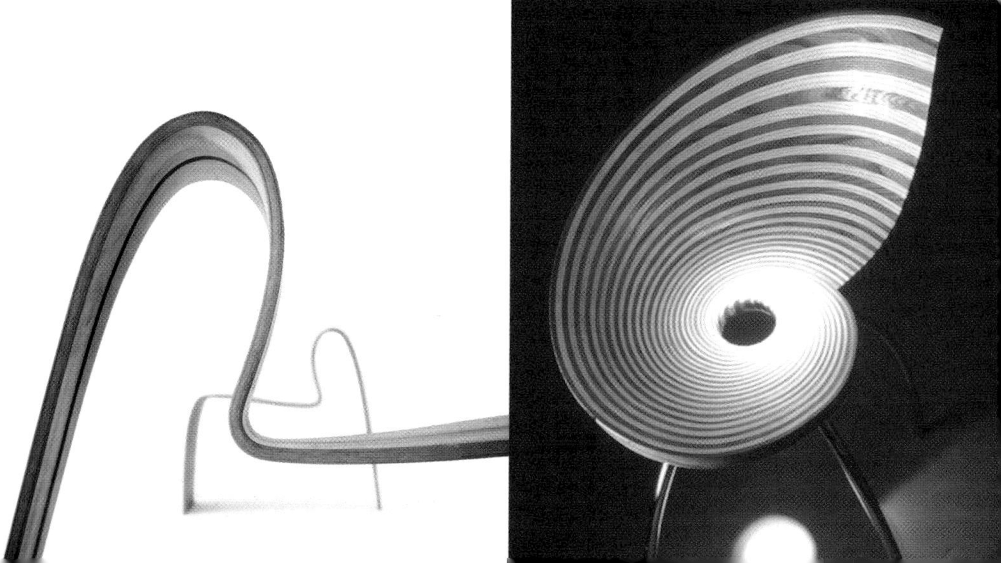

Bench *Resting Area* by Sebastian Holmbäck

Spiral Chair by Torben Quaade

Verner PANTON

Architect and Furniture Designer / Denmark

Reinforced concrete, glass walls, and an interior bathed in deep red. Red tablecloths, red lamps, red curtains, and waitresses outfitted in red. When the tourist café Komigen in the village of Langesø opened in 1958, the newspapers described it as "the most untraditional restaurant in Denmark." Its architect, Verner Panton, had designed a house so fantastic that guests came in droves to see it. In this design he had already anticipated several features for which he later became famous: a totally designed room, a production in color, and markedly original furniture designs, for example, the easy chair Cone that stands on its apex.

In the early 1950s Panton worked as an assistant for **Arne Jacobsen** and subsequently crisscrossed Europe several times in his VW van until he was offered the opportunity in Langesø. At a furniture exhibition later that year, the bearded, rebellious artist affixed his easy chair *Cone* upside down to the ceiling, and thus in no time at all acquired the reputation that has stayed with him to this day, that of being the most controversial designer in

1926 Born in Gamtofte

1950 Works for **Arne Jacobsen** (until 1953)

1953 First trip to Europe (second trip in 1957)

1955 Opens design studio

1958 Restaurant Komigen, Langesø; marketing company Plus-linje founded

1960 Restaurant Astoria, Trondheim; project *Plastic House*

1962 Moves to Basel

1968 *Visiona 0,* Cologne

Laminated chair for Thonet, 1966

Chair *Lupoflex*

1963 International Design Award, United States (also in 1968 and 1981)

1969 Interior of the editorial offices of Spiegel, Hamburg

1970 *Visiona II,* Cologne

1974 Editorial offices Gruner & Jahr, Hamburg; color system Mira-X

1984 Circus, Copenhagen

1992 IF Prize, Japan

1997 Book *Lidt om Farver (Comments on Color),* interior for Erco showroom, London

1998 Died in Basel; retrospective in the Traphold Museum, Kolding

Products

1955 *Bachelor chair* for **Fritz Hansen**

1957 *Cone* easy chair for Plus-linje

1959 Lamp *Topan*

1960 Lamp Moonboth for **Louis Poulsen**

1961 Carpet *Geometri* for Unica Vaev

Page 303

Panton Chair, 1967

Denmark. The 1950s were a period of visions, when the impossible seemed about to become reality. Panton designed inflatable furniture, a portable plastic house for everyone, and the house *Spheres,* a glass dome reminiscent of Buckminster-Fuller.

In 1960 he furnished the restaurant Astoria in Trondheim, creating a dramatic effect through various *Cone* club chairs, op-art patterns on carpets, walls, and curtains, and well-directed lighting. **Poul Henningsen** commended his young colleague expressly for both his "instinct for lighting" and, even more important, his "sense for darkness." For the doyen of light, Panton was above all a divinely gifted mood designer.

In the early 1960s Denmark became too crowded for Panton, and by way of Paris and Cannes, he finally arrived in Basel. There he managed to interest a number of illustrious companies in his idea of a totally designed, prefabricated house. However, the project turned out to be too ambitious and failed. But only a few years later, what had been considered outlandish only a short while ago before—for example, his excesses where color is concerned and his unrestrained desire to experiment—suddenly was in vogue. Panton now staged his designs regularly at the furniture fair in Cologne. At times this enfant terrible of design stuck crumpled up aluminum foil on the walls there; other times he put on a "pillow orgy."

Finally he was discovered by Bayer as the ideal protagonist to showcase their technologies. The chemical company from nearby Leverkusen wanted to show what could be done with plastic, plastic foam, and synthetic fibers. Under the programmatic title *Visiona,* Verner Panton then created a "total interior" (illustration page 32) in the hull of a Rhine steamer, the first one in 1968 and then another one two years later. Every room had its own color scheme and was filled with furniture, Dralon (polyacrylate fiber) rugs,

1963 *Cone* easy chair of wire for Plus-linje; radio-phonograph for Wega

1966 Laminated *S-Chair* for Thonet

1967 *Panton Chair* for Herman Miller

1968 Lamp *Flower Pot*

1969 Upholstered element *Living Tower* for Herman Miller

1970 Lamp *Panthella*

1973 Modular furniture *1-2-3*

1979 Upholstered furniture *Emmenthaler* for Cassina

1981 *Art Chair* (prototype)

1984 Lamps *New Wave* for **Holmegaard**

1994 Easy chair Z for Fritz Hansen; easy chair *Shogun* for **Erik Jørgensen**

1995 Chair *Pantoflex*

1998 Seat and table *Phantom* for Innovation

Page 305

Top left: Easy chair *Cone,* 1958

Top right: Room arrangement *Geometrie 1* for Plus-linje, 1961 (exhibition in Zurich)

Bottom left: Lamp *Panthella* for Louis Poulsen, 1970

Bottom right: Modular furniture *1-2-3,* 1973

pleasant fragrances, and—in keeping with the latest developments in psychedelics—with sound effects. The overall impression was overwhelming, but individual objects also drew attention, such as the lamp *Flower Pot*—two enameled hemispheres made up its shade, and it was available in many different colors.

The showstopper, however, was the chair *Panton,* the first plastic cantilever chair in one piece, one of the great successes of 1960s design—clearly not a phase lacking in innovations. Panton had been working on this chair for several years, and a few other designers back then had also been working on this technically and aesthetically ambitious concept. Panton was the first to realize it, thanks to his knuckle-down pragmatism, a trait he shared with his former boss **Arne Jacobsen,** all their other differences notwithstanding. Two years earlier he had introduced the *S-Chair,* a plywood design to which he later added twist with the series *Art Chair,* a design that anticipated the basic form of the *Panton Chair.* With these elegant plastic forms Panton achieved an astonishingly harmonious seating design.

But Panton went beyond that. The installation *Visiona 2* is considered the first synthetic interior landscape, a trendsetting, integrated furniture environment. Created one year after the moon landing, the design also involved "interplanetary" imagination. Spiegel and Gruner & Jahr, two renowned German publishing houses, had their offices decorated by Panton. After the 1970s brought utopias crashing down, Panton's work now seems to recover its earlier sensuous attraction. Shortly before his death the great experimenter furnished the Erco's London branch with gaudy plastic elements. As the Danish cultural magazine *Mobilia* commented, "Verner Panton wanted to reawaken all our senses, from the experience of claustrophobia all the way to erotic desire."

PELIKAN DESIGN

Studio for Furniture and Product Design / Denmark

1978 Founded in Copenhagen by **Niels Gammelgaard** and **Lars Mathiesen**

1980 ID Prize (also in 1991 and 1996)

1986 Liquidation of the company (reestablished in 1992)

1993 Danish Furniture Prize

1994 Design Studio Copenhagen founded, which develops products for **Ikea**

1996 Red Dot Award, Germany; Brunell Award, Great Britain

Pelikan is the exception—it is the only Danish furniture design studio with a permanent staff and it has deliberately dissociated itself from the perennial myth of Danish cabinetmaking. A plastic chair and an upholstered sofa are typical Pelikan products. The studio consists of the two architects **Niels Gammelgaard** and **Lars Mathiesen** and a handful of employees. For the pair Gammelgaard-Mathiesen, furniture is primarily an industrial product and in principle no different from a desk lamp or a refrigerator. It is probably in part due to this unsentimental attitude that these two untypical Danes have been working for **Ikea** for over twenty years now (since 1994 under the name Design Studio Copenhagen).

The products they have developed for the Swedish furniture discounter range from the very simple folding chair *Ted* (which is among Ikea's best-sellers, and that's saying something) to tables, mirrors, shelves, and coatracks to transparent plastic cases for records, diskettes, and CDs. In fact, plastic gets a lot of attention at Pelikan; the shell of the swivel chair *Nevil* is also made of plastic. That chair consists of only four components and was praised by Philippe Starck as "design with a future." As a supplier for the manufacturing industry, Pelikan also feels the

Children's bicycle and tricycle

Page 307

Chair *Napoleon* by Niels Gammelgaard

Chair *Nuovo* (No. 6212) by Niels Gammelgaard

Sofa system *Decision* for Fritz Hansen, 1986

Products

1977 Folding chair *Ted* for Ikea

1980 Children's tricycle *Tribike* for Rabo

1983 Chair *Café* for **Fritz Hansen**

1986 Easy chair *PK-7* for Cappellini

1987 Candlestick *Kräsen* for Ikea

1990 *Transitcarrier* for the Copenhagen airport (together with **Komplot** Design); upholstered furniture *Oasis* for **Erik Jørgensen**

1993 Partition *Wing* for Fritz Hansen

pressures of production schedules; the Pelikan design team has thus become used to managing several concurrent design projects with logistic mastery.

The products Pelikan has designed over the past two decades would fill a small department store. There are ashtrays, bicycle trailers, and hospital beds as well as children's bicycles, window blinds, and train seats. Still, the company has focused mainly on the design of chairs and tables. With very few exceptions, the upper crust of Denmark's furniture trade is represented on Pelikan's client list. Pelikan products are available at the posh upholsterer **Erik Jørgensen** (combination sofa *Oasis*), at **Bent Krogh** (stacking chairs *Opus* and *Nuovo*), at **Fredericia** (chair and sofa *Sofia*), and by **Fritz Hansen** (combination sofa *Decision, Café* chairs and tables.) The bulky executive chair Upsilon, designed for the Italian manufacturer Matteograssi, now sits in the foyer of Alfa Romeo, the car manufacturer. However, Pelikan's specialty is the workspace

Chair *Café* for
Fritz Hansen, 1983

rather than the entrance area. The desk system *Collage* Pelikan developed for a Norwegian manufacturer, can be arranged in a circle, a diamond, or an S-shape, offering more variability than organizers of symposia and conferences had dared to dream of.

But Pelikan has also created designs for privacy, for example, with a series of new room dividers. The partitions *Labyrinth* (for Fritz Hansen) are available in wood, linoleum, and fabric. The partition *Wing* comes on casters and has won several prizes. One of the lavish projects where Pelikan brought to bear its competence in all aspects of seating was the furnishing of the new Copenhagen city and suburban railway, for which Gammelgaard, Mathiesen, and their staff worked out an intelligent space concept. Its highlight is asymmetrical benches whose unusual arrangement increases the number of available seats and encourages passengers to move toward the windows. As a result the aisles are left free and there is noticeably less pushing and shoving.

1993 Folding chair *Sennik*

1994 Easy chair Upsilon for Matteograssi; chair Opus for Bent Krogh

1995 Interior of the Copenhagen city and suburban railway; easy chair *Sofia* for Fredericia

1996 Desk system *Collage* for Møremøbler (with Komplot Design); office furniture *IQ* for Duba

Partition Wing for Fritz Hansen, 1993

Transitcarrier for the Copenhagen airport, together with Komplot Design, 1990

Sigurd PERSSON

Product Designer and Jewelry Designer / Sweden

1914 Born in Helsingborg
1927 Craft apprenticeship with his father
1937 Studied in Munich and Stockholm
1942 Studio for industrial design
1954 Silver medal *Triennial,* Milan (also in 1957 and 1960)
1963 Consultant for the Ministry of Culture
1967 Training commission for artists and designers
1968 Works for **Kosta** (until 1982))

Products

1953 Flatware set *Servus* for Kooperativa Forbundet
1959 Dinnerware set for SAS
1979 Frying pans *Charlotte* for Ron-Produkter
1985 Brush and dustpan for Kronborsten

In the 1920s Persson learned his trade in his father's silversmith workshop, and the craftsman's son later became one of Sweden's best metal designers. His meticulous **functionalism,** which manifested itself, for example, in his flatware designs, had a pioneering impact, comparable to that of **Kay Bojesen's** work in Denmark. As freelance glass designer for **Kosta Boda,** Persson created simple glasses in bright primary colors. The interrelationship between the crafts and industry can be traced in no other person's career as clearly as in Persson's. Strongly influenced by modernity, he nevertheless insisted on concepts seemingly as old fashioned as "good taste" and "craftsmanship." His emphasis on the designer's social, indeed, moral responsibility made him one of the prominent representatives of **democratic design.** His 1977 series *Gunda* of stainless steel and cast iron saucepans were sold through the consumer cooperative after they had been tested and warmly recommended by the consumer protection agency.

Coffeepot and dinnerware set for SAS, 1959

PIIROINEN

Furniture Manufacturer / Finland

The catalog text is in Finnish, English, Swedish, German, French, and Russian. Piiroinen, located in Salo in southern Finland, invests heavily in export. The factory employs 130 people, but it achieved its 1997 sales figure of approximately $17 million not only through design. Piiroinen has three divisions: finishing of technical metal products (this is what the company, which celebrates its fiftieth anniversary in 1999, started out with), production of tubes for other furniture manufacturers, and production of its own collection. The latter is marketed under the brand name *Arena* and has a distinctive image. The product range includes a multitude of tubular steel tables and chairs, the latter with wooden (birch, birch veneer) or upholstered seats. These combinations of wood and metal are the products of in-house designers, particularly **Pasi Pänkäläinen.** Piiroinen has now expanded its severe product line and included **Antti Nurmesniemi's** classic furniture *Triennial* and **Sari Anttonen's** chair named *Kiss*—a chaste one, however, and thus no breach of what's proper at Piiroinen.

Arvo Piiroinen Oy, Salo

1949 Founded as manufacturer of metal parts in Salo

1978 Metal parts for furniture

1992 Furniture collection Arena

Products

1992 Chair Arena 011 by Pasi Pänkäläinen

1996 Chair *Triennial* by Antti Nurmesniemi (designed in 1960)

1997 Table and chair Arena *022/220* by P. Pänkäläinen

1998 Chair *Dome* by Asko Lax

Chair *Outdoor*

Chair *011 B* by Pasi Pänkäläinen

Ingegerd RÅMAN

Glass Designer / Sweden

1943 Born in Stockholm
1962 Studied in Stockholm (until 1968)
1965 Istituto Statale D'Arte Per La Ceramica, Faenza (until 1966)
1968 Works for glass manufacturer Johansfors (until 1972)
1972 Opened studio
1975 Exhibition in the Gelleri Petra, Stockholm
1981 Works for **Skruf** (until 1998)
1993 Prize for Outstanding Swedish Design (until 1997 seventeen times)
1993 Exhibition Svenskt Tenn (1994 **Artek,** Helsinki); glass for Sweden's foreign ministry
1995 Was made a Professor
1996 Exhibition in the Swedish Cultural Center, Paris
1998 Works for **Orrefors**

Page 313

Water carafe *Chambermaid*

She is considered one of the best in the field, yet outside of Sweden Ingegerd Råman is known only to insiders. One of her early works is a vase shaped like a test tube; a silver-plated brass insert turns it into a candlestick. As in this design, Råman knows how to transform objects through minor interventions. One of her design principles is that things must have several different uses, such as her series *Jar,* all-purpose cylinders for fruit or flower bouquets, and the carafes "with hats," whose lids also serves as drinking glasses. The pragmatist Råman designed them as water supply for the bedside table.

When she changed over from pottery to glass design at the end of the 1960s, there were about fifty independent glass manufacturers in Sweden. Today, only a handful of small glassworks remains. At the beginning of the 1980s when the industry was still in the midst of a structural crisis, former employees took over the glass factory **Skruf,** which had already been given up. The new owners asked Ingegerd Råman whether she wanted to be their in-house designer. Since then she has worked exclusively for Skruf. For her, the convincing proof of her success lies not so much in the awards heaped upon her in her native Sweden, but rather in the fact that her exhibition in Helsinki was unusually well attended. Nobody would have thought that a Swedish glass designer would be so honored by the glass nation of Finland.

Her workshop is located on the island Skansen, on the outskirts of Stockholm. In this suburban milieu Ingegerd Råman finds the perspective and inner distance she needs. She has been swimming against the tide for a long time. For example, in the 1980s, when large glass objects were in, she created small ones. This restraint did not fit into that era of grand gestures. Functionality was frowned upon—which is why there were no

Products

1983 Glass pitcher

1984 Glass series *Mezzo;* carafe and glass

1989 Vase *Samuraj*

1991 Glass service *Strof;* carafe and cocktail glasses *Fars glas*

1992 Service *Bellman*

1995 Glass service for Swedish Parliament

1996 Service for the restaurant of the Moderna Museet, Stockholm

1997 Brandy snifter; all for Skruf

designs of plain cocktail glasses back then. Råman remedied this lack with her series *Bellman.* According to Råman, "It is very easy to make grotesque things." What is spectacular about her work is precisely the absence of any spectacle and the nonchalance with which she unites form, function, proportion, and decoration into a perfect whole (illustration page 23). One must "listen to the material," as she says; similarly, she does not work with plastic, for "plastic is mute."

By varying her designs slightly again and again, she has created object families of vases, bottles, and carafes that each have their own pedigree, so to speak. As disarmingly simple as these objects seem, the surprise is often in the details. The glass ball that closes an oil flask, for example, is flattened in one place to prevent it from rolling off the table. Recently somebody was overheard to say, "I can't see the difference, but I know that there is a difference." And to the artist that is pretty much the highest assessment of her work that she has heard in a long time.

The raw material for her designs is clear glass. Råman also likes to use opaque glass, but at first was not satisfied with the results, which in turn are highly dependent on the technical skills of the people producing the glass. For example, at one point Skruf had only one master left who knew how to grind, and he was over seventy. Precisely because Råman's objects are so fundamentalist, she depends on perfect craftsmanship. Simple designs are particularly difficult because even the slightest imperfection mars the overall impression. When everything is just so, however, the clarity of the glass, enhanced by the unpretentious form, shows off the characteristics of the material, its lightness and fragility, to best advantage.

Page 315

Top: Brandy snifter

Bottom left: *Vase Grass*

Bottom right: Oil flask with top

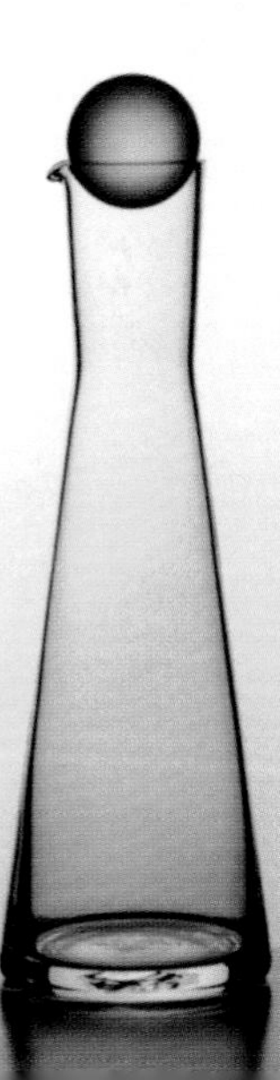

RÖRSTRAND

Porcelain Manufacturer / Sweden

Rörstrand's porcelain workshops are among the oldest in Europe. At Rörstrand production and fine art worked together as early as 1900 when the painter **Alf Wallander** contributed designs. However, it is only since the 1920s that artists like **Edward Hald** have been working for them on site. Among Rörstrand's best-known modern products are the dinnerware sets *East India* and Hertha Bengtson's *Blå Eld.*

A long phase of expansion peaked in the 1950s when 1,500 people were employed. When the company was taken over by a competitor in 1964, artists' freedom in designing was curtailed, and in the 1970s the design department was eliminated. Since then the company has started working with **Bertil Vallien,** indicating a new beginning. Currently the company—now integrated into **Hackman**—is under Finnish ownership. Among the staff designers are **Karin Bjørquist** and Pia Rönndahl. the current product line is called "Pro Arte," designs for which the prodigy **Pia Törnell** broke new ground in ceramics (illustration page 34).

1726 Founded in Stockholm (ceramics production since 1758)
1895 **Alf Wallander** artistic director (until 1910)
1917 **Edward Hald** hired
1939 Moved to Lidköping
1964 Bought up by Upsala Ekeby AB (in 1970 artists' positions cut)
1983 Taken over by Arabia
1988 Merged into Rörstrand-Gustavsberg
1994 Collection *Pro Arte*

Products
1900 Tea service by Alf Wallander
1931 *National service* by Louise Adelborg
1932 Dinnerware set *East India*
1951 Dinnerware set *Blå Eld,* both by H. Bengtson; dinnerware set *Mon Amie* by Marianne Westman
1980 Dinnerware set *Primeur* by Signe Persson-Melin
1994 Bowls *Sinus* by **Pia Törnell**

Bowls *New York* by Karin Bjørquist, 1986

ROYAL COPENHAGEN

Manufacturer of Porcelain and Housewares / Denmark

Founded in the mid-eighteenth century along the lines of a French model, the Kongelige Porcellains Fabrik (Royal Porcelain Factory) was closed again only a few years later and later rebuilt in a different location. Uncertain times for the manufacturer were followed by a golden age when the painter **Arnold Krog** overhauled the collection in the late nineteenth century. Krog's innovations, especially underglaze painting, and the introduction of new glass colors, such as light green and reddish brown, were applauded at international exhibitions.

On a trip to Paris Krog met the art dealer Siegfried Bing, a connoisseur and later a central figure of the Copenhagen circle of Japanists who made sure that the Royal Danish Porcelain also included designs inspired by the Far East. Under the leadership of Patrick Nordström, intensive studio experiments made the company a worldwide leader in stoneware, which was the basis for its great commercial success in the 1920s and 1930s. Among the most successful art potters were **Axel Salto,** Jais Nielsen,

1755 First Danish porcelain factory (closed in 1766)

1775 Refounding (in 1807 destroyed by English battleships)

1884 **Arnold Krog** artistic director (until 1916)

1911 Technical director Patrick Nordström establishes artistic studio

1923 Shared marketing with **Holmegaard** in export (taken over in 1975)

1933 **Axel Salto** hired

1957 Experiments with utility porcelain, for example, by **Grethe Meyer** and **Ole Kortzau**

1969 Takeover of jewelry manufacturer **A. Michelsen** (in 1986 also **Georg Jensen,** in 1987 **Bing & Grøndahl**)

1997 Merger with **Orrefors-Kosta Boda,** BodaNova, and Venini; renaming of the company as Royal Scandinavia

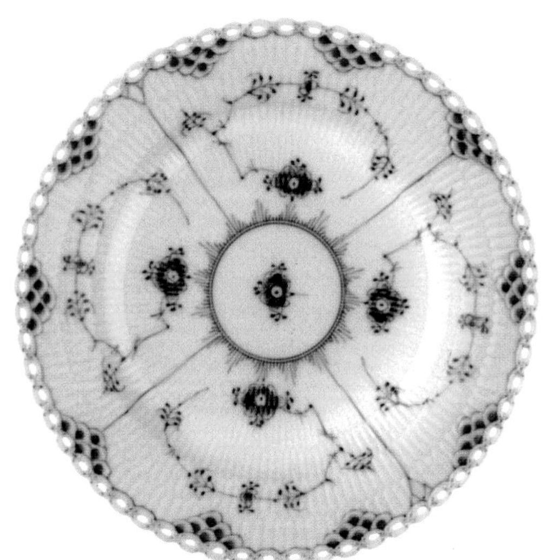

Plate *Musselmalet Full Lace,* Anonymous, 1775

Products

1775 Tableware *Musselmalet*

1802 Tableware *Flora Danica*

1887 Vase *Fishnet* by Arnold Krog

1911 Clay vase by P. Nordström

1927 Porcelain figurine *Island Girl* by Arno Malinowski

1957 Heat-resistant tableware set by **Magnus Stephensen**

1960 Service *Gemina* by Gertrud Vasegaard

1965 Dinnerware set *Blåkant* (Blue rim) by Grethe Meyer

1977 Service *Konkylle* by Arje Griegst

1993 Faience dinnerware set *Ursula* by **Ursula Munch-Petersen**

1997 Kitchen utensils *Ole* by **Ole Jensen**

Bowls *Complet* by Jörgen Möller

Page 319

Top left: Kitchen utensils *Ole* by Ole Jensen, 1997

Top right: Flatware *Vivianna* by Vivianna Torun Bülow-Hübe, 1997

Bottom left: Trivet by Grethe Meyer

Bottom right: *Blue Pitcher* by Ursula Munch-Petersen, 1993

and René Gauguin (the son of the famous painter). Their works drew great attention at the Paris Art Deco exhibition in 1925. After World War II domestic servants were a thing of the past, and the dinner service, until then so popular in Denmark, became obsolete and impractical. Dishes and bowls now had to be used for food preparation as well as serving. Royal Copenhagen's first attempt to meet this demand was the production in 1957 of heat-resistant bowls and plates designed by **Magnus Stephensen.** This series, which turned the whole Danish porcelain industry upside down, was followed later by a sturdy faience service that put an end to the predominance of conventional porcelain—a revolution accomplished by the company that had until then been the most conventional in its industry.

In the 1960s new designers appeared on the scene whose specialty was to apply modern design principles to the widely varied areas. **Grethe Meyer,** a practicing architect, brought these principles to Royal Copenhagen (by then the company had anglicized its name in line with its growing export sales). Meyer worked in glass and ceramics and ultimately was responsible for the series *Blue Rim.* At the same time, the company worked with other designers, for example, **Ole Kortzau.** Today Royal Copenhagen offers a very varied collection, a unique mixture of separate artistic pieces, services, and household accessories in contemporary design. In addition, the company also continues to manufacture its world-famous, popular figurines and reissues as

series from its historic production, such as the famous gala tableware set Musselmalet, which was at the beginning of it all.

After numerous takeovers, the traditional company has grown since the 1980s into a veritable art industry multinational (which renamed itself **Royal Scandinavia** and whose leading shareholder is the **Carlsberg** brewery). Meanwhile the Danish brands **Georg Jensen** and **Holmegaard,** Sweden's **Orrefors/Kosta Boda,** and Italy's Venini are members of the design family, a Nordic business association that can be compared only to the **Hackman** group. In Royal Scandinavia's marketing a kind of star system has established itself in which the artistic reputation of successful designers rubs off on the company. For a long time **Ursula Munch-Petersen** was one of its most successful designers; her tableware sets *Ole* and *Ursula* have been awarded several prizes. At the same time, the company continues to work with young innovators, among them the ceramist *Ole Jensen,* who combines functionality and biomorphous shapes in his designs.

Porcelain *Blåkant*
by Grethe Meyer, 1965

SAAB

Automobile Manufacturer / Sweden

The first mass-produced Saab in 1949, *Type 92,* was not quite 13 feet long, weighed 1,687 pounds, and had 20 horsepower. The model 9-5 is almost three feet longer, twice as heavy, and comes with ten times the horsepower. But even though the automobiles of yesterday and today are hardly comparable, the new model is still—in the words of the company in the Swedish Trollhättan—a "genuine Saab."

The idea and designs for the first Saab came from **Sixten Sason,** an artist, engineer, and visionary, who rigorously applied to his design the streamlining ideal of the 1930s. Even the underside of the vehicle was smooth, a novelty in the automobile history up to that point. Another attractive aerodynamic detail was the removable wings. The racy shape made the vehicle one of the most streamlined of its time. The Saab *92* had the profile of an airplane wing, a contour that remained Saab's standby until the discontinuation of the model *96* (illustration page 47) in the 1960s. This streamlined shape gave Saab cars a distinctive and

Saab Automobile AB

1937 Airplane manufacturer Svenska Aeroplan AB founded in Trollhättan

1945 Project "Small Car" with designer **Sixten Sason**

1949 Beginning of series production

1966 First car with four-stroke engine

1969 Merger with truck manufacturer Scania; **Björn Envall** designer-in-chief

1973 Side impact protection introduced (in 1978 also pollen filter)

Saab *92-001* by Sixten Sason, 1947

1985 Prototype *EV-1*

1987 Two million cars sold

1989 Model *9000* "the safest car" (again in 1992)

1989 Taken over by GM

1995 Norwegian Einaar Hareide is designer-in-chief

1997 Three million cars sold

Models

1947 Prototype

1949 *Sedan 92*

1955 *Sedan 93*

1956 Sports car *Sonnett 1*

1959 *Station wagon 95*

Page 323

Top: Saab *93,* 1956

Bottom: Saab *99,* 1968,

both by Sixten Sason

unmistakable look. From 1962 to 1967—the year of his death and the year his new design was introduced—the designer-in-chief, Sason, worked on the next generation of vehicles, model *99.* As a motor magazine at the time noted, the car had a "sporty note" and, the magazine added, many fans had probably "dreamed of a more daring profile." In fact, the overall look was rather restrained, but even this automobile had an original silhouette that, like its predecessor, was in use for about two decades. Typical features of the new car were trapezoidal lines running counter to each other and a stumpy tail end that flowed smoothly into the rear window. This was later transformed into a steep, square back. In 1979 Model *900,* a stretched-out version, was introduced and five years later Model *9000,* the first whose bodywork was not designed in-house. It had been ordered from Italy's Giorgietto Giugiaro, one of the most sought-after automobile designers. Giugiaro's Saab, part of a joint venture with Fiat, for the first time had a slight suggestion of a wedge shape. It was a massive sedan, the only import car in the United States classified as a "large car." Saab had progressed from a manufacturer of cars for everyone into a producer for a niche market, offering cars with above-average features for the upper class. Perhaps the relatively square design of model 9000 was too reminiscent of the vehicles of Saab's neighbor and competitor **Volvo.** In any case, preliminary studies for the next model were soon begun. Björn Envall, head of design and formerly Sason's assistant, had sketches and models made. The result was

Saab *92* by Sixten Sason (model), 1954

Dashboard of Saab 92

1960 Sedan *96*
1966 Sports car *Sonett II*
1968 Sedan *99*
1978 Sedan *900*
1985 Sedan *9000* by Ital-Design
1993 New sedan *900 S*
1994 Convertible *900*
1997 Sedan *9-5*
1998 Sedan *9-3*
1999 Station wagon *9-5*

a series of dream cars with as little chance commercially as the two prototypes (among others by Pininfarina). Model *900* was designed to preserve the characteristic features of its predecessor. The ambitious goal was "to continue Sason's lines into the next millennium." The shape of the car is crucial for Saab's brand identity, which the company interprets fairly conservatively.

Saab has long since placed high value on **ergonomics,** from the door handle to a selectively lit-up instrument panel, to vented seats, a functional concept promoted as typically "Scandinavian." The advertising for turn-of-the-century models *9-3* and *9-5* focuses on technology. Those who had to design bodywork in keeping with the company's identity once again did not have an easy job of it. The models, even more wedge-shaped and with the usual broad grin in the front, are a difficult compromise between global trends and Sason's legacy.

Saab *900 Cabrio,* 1987

Timo SALLI

Furniture and Product Designer / Finland

The box is made of steel and acrylics. At the touch of a remote control the lid opens, and a television set rolls out (and later disappears again the same way). By no means just a gag, *Jack in the Box* is Timo Salli's parody of the condition of our apartments that, according to the pensive designer, "are filled with things we no longer really see." In other words, the box for the (idiot) box is intended to make us think. What is important to Salli is above all the "design of our perception." The fondness of the former welder for mechanical details is also evident in his collapsible chair *Zik-Zak*. Like an Erector set toy, this "low-tech" piece of furniture shows its inner structure openly. Salli's easy chair *Tramp* also leaves nothing hidden. The removable net covering allows the construction to shine through and creates a shimmering moiré effect. Timo Salli, one of the designers in the circle around **Snowcrash,** considers his lightweight, portable easy chair part of the basic equipment for "urban nomads."

1963 Born in Helsinki

1981 Works as welder

1989 Studies furniture design in Lahti and Helsinki

1991 Works for **Stefan Lindfors**

1998 Presentation at the furniture fair in Milan with **Snowcrash**

Products

1996 Easy chair *Tramp* for Cappellini

1997 TV set *Jack in the Box;* chair *Zik-Zak*

1998 *Nomad House* with **Ilkka Suppanen**

Folding chair *Zik-Zak*

Easy chair *Tramp*

Thomas SANDELL

Architect and Furniture Designer / Sweden

1959 Born in Jakobstad, Finland; moved to Sweden in the same year

1981 Studied architecture in Stockholm

1985 Architectural firm

1989 Interior of the restaurants Rolf's Kök and Tratan together with **Jonas Bohlin**

1993 Design concept for SAS

1994 Works for **Artek**

1996 Works for B & B Italia

Products

1989 Cupboard *Panik*

1992 *Key cupboard* for Cappellini

1994 Glass for Pukeberg; bench *Air* and *Blue Cabinet* for **Asplund**

1995 Product series *PS* for **Ikea**

1996 Chair and table *Ängel* for **Källemo;** chair *Moderna M* for **Gärsnas**

Page 327

Chair *T.S.* for Asplund

Chair *Akvarium*

Armoire *PS* for Ikea

When construction of the Stockholm art museum Moderna Museet began, it almost went without saying that Thomas Sandell would provide the seating because Sandell, more than anyone else, embodies Sweden's new self-confidence in design. Already in 1996 on the "Top 40" list of the British magazine *I.D.,* Sandell has made it. Considered a particularly gifted interior designer, the architect and disciplined worker—who is married to a fashion designer—staked out his turf early on in the scramble for government contracts. The blond, almost stereotypical Swede achieved the greatest publicity with his restaurant interiors (for example, he designed the Shaker-inspired Rolf's Kök together with **Jonas Bohlin**) as well as with his simple furniture designs.

Sandell's name stands for luxurious simplicity. He plays with designs from Sweden's preindustrial past, and what he does with them is at times nostalgic but always bright and optimistic. Thomas Sandell, whose designs bear the names of Scandinavian upscale brands such as **Artek, Asplund, Gärsnäs**, or **Källemo,** was one of the initiators of the series *PS* (for **Ikea,** illustration page 39). It is no surprise that in the early 1990s he was also among Cappellini's illustrious designers (for example, with a steel key cupboard). It was thus all the more astonishing that David Eliot, the director of the Moderna Museet, publicly criticized Sandell's designs and showed him and his new chair the door.

That was the first time Sandell received negative headlines, but he had no time to worry about them, because he was currently busy working on a furniture series for the renowned Italian company, B & B. Sandell considers his reception south of the Alps "super-professional" and "unlike that among many Swedish manufacturers."

Timo SARPANEVA

Glass Designer / Finland

1926 Born in Helsinki

1948 Institute for Industrial Arts, Helsinki

1950 Design studio; works for **Iittala**

1954 Gold medal at *Triennial*, Milan (also in 1957)

1956 Lunning Prize

1963 International Design Award (won three times)

1976 Professor

1994 Retrospective in the Atheneum, Chicago

He is a living monument of Finnish glass design, a notorious eccentric and experimenter. His relationship to creativity is evident in the fact that he has dedicated his most recent glass series to the avant-gardist Marcel Duchamp. However, Timo Sarpaneva's successes are usually coupled not only with artistic inspiration but also with innovations in production engineering. A virtual Renaissance man, he made his mark in neighboring fields, such as sculpture, painting, and graphics, and knows how to handle different materials, such as porcelain, iron, and plastic.

But glass is Sarpaneva's true forte. In the early 1950s he created a series of art glass objects for **Iittala** by using the steam blow method, a method that had never before been used for art glass. One of his best known designs, a vase, the glassblowers called *Maailmankaunein* ("the most beautiful of the world," now called *Orkidea*). The U.S. magazine *House Beautiful* selected it as "the most beautiful object of the year" in 1954. In fact, in this design beauty had become an end in itself; it was all about pure form, a glass object as a showpiece whose use was unimportant. Sarpaneva had crossed the line separating design from art.

Just as innovative and yet diametrically opposed was Sarpaneva's commercially successful work, the *i-line* of the late 1950s. The artist himself counted the plates of this series among his best designs. They are watercolor paintings on glass whose colors run into each other as in a rainbow. The truly new aspect was the high aesthetic quality of these utilitarian glasses. The design star Sarpaneva, back then already part of the jet set, had been criticized severely in social-democratic Finland because of his elitist designs which only the high society could afford. With this new set of bottles, glasses, and plates, he had overcome the schism between luxurious art glass and cheap mass-produced glassware.

page 329

Glass series *i-Line* for Iittala, 1956

Cast iron Dutch oven, 1973

Vase *Orkidea* for Iittala, 1954

Products

1951 Art glass *Hiidenkirnu (Devil's Head)*

1952 Glass sculptures *Lansetti*

1954 Glass sculptures *Kajakki* and *Maailmankaunein*

1956 *I-line*

1963 Stackable bottle, all for Iittala; cast iron pot for Rosenlew (International Design Award)

1967 Fabric *Ambiente* for Tampella

1968 Cotton textiles *Bolero*

1974 Service *Suomi* for Rosenthal

1983 Glass sculptures *Claritas,* series *Hummingbird* for Iittala

1990 Vases *Marcel* for Iittala

1992 Silver service for Kultakeskus

In the early 1960s, Sarpaneva succeeded with a further stroke of genius when he discovered a completely new world of shapes in the wooden molds the glass blowers used to throw away after use. This scrap material inspired him to create one of his most fascinating series of objects that includes his 1964 glass sculpture *Liberation.* In his work Sarpaneva oscillates "between the realm of the objet trouvé and art work," commented the critic Ulf Hård af Segerstad in a review. For his collection *Finlandia,* famous for its smooth surface, reminiscent of ice, Sarpaneva used the new burnt wood technique. In the 1980s the series *Claritas* (illustration page 27) followed, combinations of black, clear, and opal glass, and then *Libertá,* stark glass sculptures (*Creatura* weighs about half a ton), in which the master hammered and chiseled away at the cold mass.

Glass sculpture *Claritas*

Page 331

Coffee and tea service for Finland's head of state, 1992

Plates of the *i-line* for Iittala, 1956

Glass sculpture *Kajakki* for Iittala

STELTON

Manufacturer of Housewares / Denmark

AS Stelton, Hellerup

1960 Founded by Peter Holmblad in Hellerup near Copenhagen

1963 Collaboration with **Arne Jacobsen**

1967 ID Prize (for *Cylinda* line, 1977 for thermos)

1971 After Jacobsen's death, collaboration with **Erik Magnussen,** who developed a series of stainless steel household utensils

Products

1967 *Cylinda* line by Arne Jacobsen

1977 Stainless steel thermos with automatic cap (later also in plastic)

1987 Plastic bowls

1998 Thermos *2000,* all by Erik Magnussen

Peter Holmblad *is* Stelton. In the early 1960s the design entrepreneur had an idea: he wanted to produce cylindrical stainless steel housewares. And he managed to interest the best possible designer in this project: **Arne Jacobsen.** Holmblad wanted to go against the grain of traditional Danish silverwork but, he recalls, "Arne had no idea about stainless steel." Jacobsen provided the basic ideas for the individual products, often sketching them hurriedly on napkins after dinner. One of the problems was the design of items such as cocktail shakers and martini mixers, which had to be included in the series, but Jacobsen was simply not interested.

It took three years from idea to first product. In 1967 the product line *Cylinda* was introduced with seventeen different products. Placed next to each other they formed a short skyline. After a certain warming-up period, the sales began to pick up. Thanks to *Cylinda,* Stelton expanded and sold its products abroad (currently the export rate is fifty percent). After Jacobsen's death, **Erik Magnussen** took over. His first design, a thermos (illustration page 13) made of stainless steel as a complement to the *Cylinda* line, exceeded all expectations. The thermos, now also available in plastic and in various colors, is still Stelton's unchallenged best-seller. Thanks to the successful team Holmblad-Magnussen, careful product development, and a long-term design policy, the medium-sized company has managed to establish itself as a high-class brand for bowls, pitchers, and pepper mills. Whether the new thermos, the model *2000,* will also turn out to be a long-running success nobody knows for sure, but one thing is certain for Holmblad: the thermos, like all other Stelton products, "will never be in the bargain bin."

Page 333

Flatware *541-543* by Erik Magnussen

Thermos model *2000* by Erik Magnussen, 1998

Pitchers and tray, *Cylinda* line by Arne Jacobsen

STOKKE

Furniture Manufacturer / Norway

Stokke Fabrikker AS

1932 Founded in Skodje

1986 Exclusively ergonomic furniture

Products

1972 Children's chair *Triptrapp*

1980 Chair *Variable Balans*

1983 Chair *Pendulum*

1984 Chair *Duo Balans,* all by **Peter Opsvik**

1987 Chair *Ekstrem* by Terje Ekstrøm and stool *Move* by Per Øie

1990 Chair *Flysit*

1993 Children's chair *Sitti,* both by Peter Opsvik; children's rocking chair *Hippo* by Wolfgang Rebentisch

Stokke is a showpiece company and by far the largest furniture manufacturer and exporter in Norway. This success has been possible because of a design-oriented, strictly ergonomic concept originally based on the studies of the **Balans**-Group. With its designer-in-chief **Peter Opsvik,** himself a former member of the group, Stokke has developed this concept further. Stokke's designs are based on the basic consideration that sitting is an activity: even when seated, people are constantly in motion. A chair should allow these movements without requiring any extra effort. In addition to *Ekstrem* (by Terje Ekstrøm), an easy chair for stretching out, and the abstract rocking horse *Hippo* (by Wolfgang Rebentisch) the anti-tension seats Stokke offers are mostly Opsvik's designs. True, sometimes it looks as though the users would have to be strapped into the chairs to escape the risk of falling out of them. Sitting on Stokke chairs must be learned just like riding a bicycle must be learned. At forty inches long and forty-nine inches high, *Duo* is the largest work chair in the

program and exemplifies how these "seating machines" are constructed. Because of its bent runners (a basic feature of almost all chairs in the series), the chair responds to even minute weight shifts. Thus everyone finds his or her right personal point of equilibrium, in leaning forward to work as well as in leaning back to relax. The space between back and headrest supports the natural curvature of the back, and the headrest is cell-phone compatible. Based on **Alvar Aalto's** teachings, the construction is made of glue-laminated wood and thus is sturdy without looking bulky. Parts that can wear out, such as the seat cushions, are replaceable.

Another easy chair design by Opsvik is *Flysit* whose legs rest on spirals, allowing the user to jump from one position to another. This elicits body language and loosens up any stiff meeting. For those who didn't know yet or have forgotten again: chairs are also a means of communication.

From left to right:

Chair *Ekstrem* by Terje Ekstrøm

Chair *Wing* by Peter Opsvik

Stool *Move* by Per Øie

Ilkka SUPPANEN

Furniture Manufacturer / Finland

1968 Born in Kotka

1989 Completed architecture and design studies in Helsinki

1990 Student at the Rietveld Academy, Amsterdam

1996 Lecturer at the Design Faculty in Helsinki

1998 Presentation at the furniture fair in Milan, with **Snowcrash**

Products

1994 *Nomad Chair*

1996 Office furniture *Miss Match*

1997 Easy chair *Airbag* for **Valvomo**

1996 Sofa *Flying Carpet* for Cappellini; folding bed; *Nomadhouse* with Timo Salli

The dream of the nuclear family, of the cozy home, and the lifelong job still seems to be alive and well, especially in Scandinavian Design. But Ilkka Suppanen questions all these certainties. He designs his furniture for the nomads of tomorrow—"nomadic objects" for nervous, rootless urbanites. His shelves play a double role as wall news-sheets, a folding bed mutates into a sofa, and an easy chair is so lightweight that it can be worn strapped around the hips. Suppanen makes sure that furniture is not too heavy, otherwise its mobility suffers. He experiments with porous and versatile materials, such as synthetic fibers or copper cloth. Suppanen, who studied at the famous Rietveld Academy and is widely considered an oddball, sees anthropological dimensions in his design for nomads, because ultimately his designs are all about the relationship "between the transitory and the timeless." Every object is only the "crystallization of perception," says Suppanen, "just like a poem." One result of such practical poetry is, for example, his "laminated feather glass."

Sofa *Flying Carpet* for Cappellini

Cabinet *AV Rack*

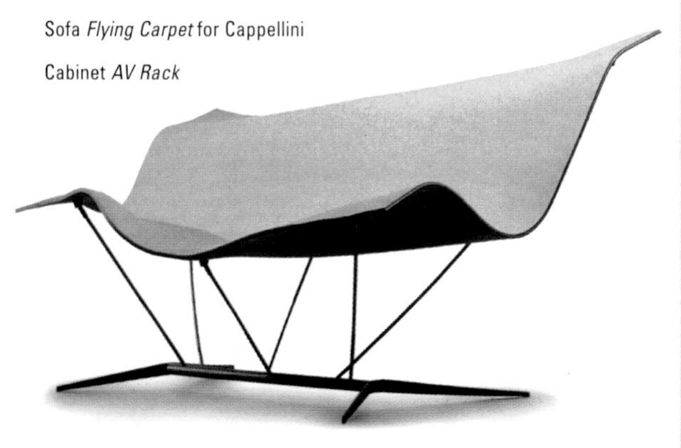

Mats THESELIUS

Artist, Furniture Designer, and Interior Designer / Sweden

"Swap your life" was the title of his official contribution to 1998, the year in which Stockholm was Europe's cultural capital. Mats Theselius opened a travel agency of a different kind for the occasion, one that offered expeditions into other people's everyday life or their jobs or their shoes, a kind of brokerage of experience. Theselius is a bohemian by profession and is a V.I.P. in Sweden. The son of an artist and a sought-after interior designer and passionate collector of everyday design, he does not like to be pinned down; is very fond of Russian consumer goods; and in general likes to provoke irritation (for example, with an exhibition on Sweden's dreary satellite towns).

While others keep an eye on international trends or concentrate on what is authentically Swedish, concept designer Theselius playfully mixes the global with the homemade. This is exemplified in his famous cabinets custom-made to serve as storage for issues of *National Geographic*—extremely functional pieces of furniture (in the same yellow as the magazine cover).

1956 Born in Stockholm

1979 Studied interior design in Stockholm (until 1984)

1992 Participated in the World's Fair in Seville

1993 Book, *Miljon Programmet (Housing Program for One Million)*

1994 Book, *Kamrad Mats (Comrade Mats)* for exhibition in Moscow

1995 Professor for Industrial Design in Gothenburg; participated in exhibition Good Design, Athenaeum, Chicago

1997 Exhibition Röhsska-Museum, Göteborg; Bruno Mathsson Prize

1998 Project *Swap Your Life* for Cultural Capital Stockholm

Easy Chair *Ritz* for Källemo, 1993

Products

1986 Easy chair *Fåtölj* for **Källemo;** lamp *Moulin Rouge*

1987 Cabinet *National Geographic* for 25, 50, 70 and 100 years, for Källemo (1991)

1988 *Chair* for Källemo, couch (painted wood)

1991 Couch in steel and leather for Källemo; *Eremitens Koja (Hermit's Hut)*

1993 Easy chair *Ritz* for Källemo

1994 Shelf *Art Against Aids* for Källemo

1995 Easy chair *Rex* for Källemo; umbrella stand *Excalibur*

His design of a comfortable easy chair with elk fur has almost achieved the status of a classic. Theselius frequently uses traditional material in new and irritating combinations. In 1991 he surprised the visitors at the Stockholm furniture fair with his *Erimitens Koja (Hermit's Hut),* a simple house made of polystyrene and a metaphor for loneliness. He continuously walks the fine line between design and art (illustration page 42) and therefore can claim two superlatives for himself: the perfect eclectic is not only one of the most noted but also one of the most controversial furniture designers in Sweden. Thus it is no surprise that **Källemo** was the first to take on his designs.

The objects by Mats Theselius, such as the *Aluminum Easy Chair* and the couches, do not hide their construction. The designer left connections and functional elements exposed not so much to express his ultimate "honesty" but more to foreground the synthetic-smooth surfaces of the alienated, mass-produced items that surround us. Theselius's furniture is avant-garde because it is anachronistic. His objects do not remain neutral; they have something individual, a narrative dimension (and in that they are reminiscent of Josef Frank's work). The spindle-back chairs for which Theselius has taken his cue from the Småländ peasants (who in earlier times produced them in cottage industry) are something for enthusiasts of design quotations. These are the chairs, painted green, red, or yellow, Astrid Lindgren's *Children of Bullerbü* would have loved to climb on.

Page 339

Iron plate easy chair *200* for Källemo, 1994

From left to right:

Easy chair *Rex* for Källemo, 1994

Chaise lounge, 1991

Umbrella stand *Excalibur,* 1994

Helene TIEDEMANN

Furniture and Product Designer / Sweden

1960 Born in Malmö

1983 Lived in London (until 1997)

1985 Central St. Martins School of Art & Design, London (until 1988)

1992 Works for Habitat and Liberty's

Products

1993 *Cat Bed; Skyscraper for Goldfish*

1994 Lamp *Taiwan*

1996 Lamps *Lowlight* and *Highlight;* shelves *Front-de-bœuf;* mirror *Mirror, Mirror*

She has designed a *Skyscraper for Fish* and hates furniture that "makes you feel sorry for it." Helene Tiedemann introduces the necessary decadence into the new Swedish design to keep it from being overwhelmed and drowned out by its own beauty. She has seen a lot of the world and has worked in London for Habitat and Liberty's. Along the way she has now and again missed the "respect for design" but has also learned to complete tasks efficiently. Behind every one of her objects there is a surprising idea, sometimes an exalted but always a useful one, as for example in the shelves *Front-de-bœuf,* a storage system that snaps together in the shape of an oversized puzzle. The floor lamps *Highlight* and *Lowlight* look like stylized dogs. Their four legs make them look like animals but also provide great stability. One of her most captivating objects consists of only three parts that are snapped together to form an elegant cylindrical lamp: a support, a fixture, and a plastic sheet as shade. Tiedemann christened the minimal object *Taiwan,* because it can be copied so effortlessly.

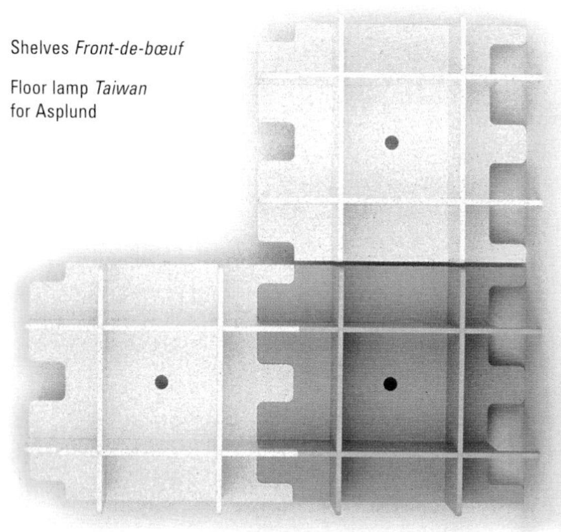

Shelves *Front-de-bœuf*

Floor lamp *Taiwan* for Asplund

Pia TÖRNELL

Ceramic and Glass Designer / Sweden

She belongs to the new generation of designers that, like movie stars, is exalted. With her studies barely completed, Pia Törnell was already under contract with Sweden's largest porcelain manufacturer. Since then she has far exceeded everyone's hopes. Since Törnell has begun working for **Rörstrand's** collection "Pro Arte" (illustration page 34), she has received the award for Outstanding Swedish Design three times in a row, a completely new phenomenon in the history of this prize. She herself characterizes her work as the continuous search for something she can hardly even envision herself at the beginning, before that clarifying "moment of silence." The results of her quest are original, simple, and harmonious objects, such as the prizewinning series *Sinus,* a set of serving bowls in pastel colors. The flowing lines are typical of her designs. Törnell would not be Törnell if she had not already gained international attention. In Paris she was awarded the *Prix de la Décoration* for the Vase *Cirrus,* a fan-like ceramic sculpture that looks as though it could be folded up.

1963 Born in Stockholm
1994 Completed design studies in Stockholm
1997 *Prix de la Décoration,* Paris

Products
1994 Serving bowls *Sinus*
1996 Vase *Cirrus*
1997 Vase *Mantello,* all for Rörstrand

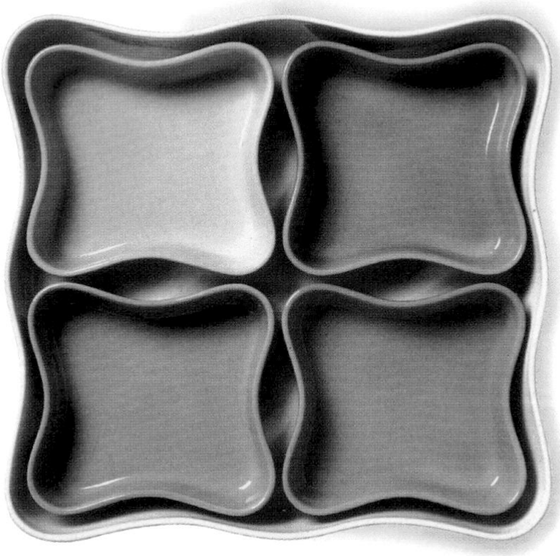

Vase *Cirrus*

Ceramic bowls *Sinus,* both for Rörstrand

Bertil VALLIEN

Glass Designer / Sweden

1938 Born in Stockholm

1961 Trip to the United States (until 1963)

1967 Teaches glass design at the Art Academy in Stockholm

1979 Shows ceramic boats in the Galerie Konsthantverkarna, Stockholm

1981 The magazine *Japan Interior Design* chooses him as the most influential representative of his field

1988 One-man show in the Rosenfield Gallery in Chicago (also in 1994)

Products

1986 Glass boat *Voyage of Dreams*

1988 Sculpture *Madre;* sculpture *Blue Venus*

1989 Sculptures *Pendulums*

1992 Champagne glasses for **Kosta Boda**

A summer job led him to glass as design material, and since then Bertil Vallien's work has broken new ground for Swedish glass design. The son of a painter and minister, Vallien trained as decorator in a Stockholm department store before he studied ceramics at the Art Academy. On trips through the United States and Mexico in the early 1960s, he came to know the creative freedom of American artists and studied the culture of Native Americans. Upon his return to Sweden he was recruited by the legendary glass manager Erik Rosén, and he moved into the Småländ glass district together with his wife, Ulrica Hydman-Vallien.

In the foreground of his work are free-form objects; even his designs for mass production are often the result of experiments with form. Vallien has become famous as a master of sandblasting, especially because of his long glass cuts, sometimes measuring several feet (illustration page 14). This form, fraught with symbolic meaning, which he has been developing since the late 1980s, has been included in the collections of renowned museums all over the world. Later there followed *Viewpoints,* massive, archetypal glass blocks, in which Vallien once again featured, what he calls, his medium's "marriage of heat and cold."

Glass bottles, collection Kosta Boda, 1980

Page 343

Top left: Vase with Figure, 1970s

Top right: Plate *Crossboat,* 1984

Bottom: Glass object *Crossboat,* 1985

VALVOMO

Studio for Interior Design, Furniture Design, and Product Design / Finland

1993 Founded in Helsinki by **Teppo Asikainen, Vesa Hinkola, Timo Mänttäri, Markus Nevalainen, Kari Sivonen, Ilkka Terho, Jan Tromp, Rane Vaskivouri,** and **Timo Vierros** as studio for interior decorating and furniture and product design.

1996 Interior of the nightclub DJ, booth and film studios in Helsinki

1997 Presentation at the furniture fairs in Milan and Cologne

1998 Project **Snowcrash**

The word "crisis" was still on everyone's lips in Finland, when a group of unknown designers, founders of the young studio Valvomo, dared to open their own booth at the furniture fair in Milan in 1997. For their unexpected expedition to the South they adopted the name **Snowcrash** and even hauled several other designer colleagues into their boat for reinforcement. Even more surprising than their daring were the subsequent reactions. Design magazines applauded them in unison, and even the *New York Times* weighed in on the subject of new Finnish Design. The principles of the impatient Aalto heirs were "no bent plywood," but instead "visionary things for the network age."

There is, for example, the lamp *Glowblow* that inflates when it is switched on and deflates when switched off. The lamp is based on one of those astonishingly simple concepts that simply work. Its worldwide success is no accident but is based on experience (though founded in 1993, Valvomo's design history dates back into the 1980s) and, moreover, proves that success

Easy chair *Airbag* by Ilkka Suppanen for Valvomo

Page 345

Light *Glowblow* by Vesa Hinkola, Markus Nevalainen, and Rane Vaskivuori

Products

1995 Computer workstation *Netsurfer* by T. Asikainen and I. Terho

1996 Library table *UFO* by T. Asikainen and T. Vierros; lounge *Chip* by T. Asikainen and I. Terho

1997 Lamps *Glowblow* by V. Hinkola, M. Nevalainen and R. Vaskivuori

1998 Chair *Droppe* by I. Terho for **Artek**

can be planned. The designers had spent years putting together international networks that included artists, artisans, business people, and filmmakers. Now they work with such renowned companies as **Artek** and at the same time have expanded the Snowcrash project to a company for experimental design that will offer opportunities to Finland's future creative talents.

One of the most applauded exhibits at the 1997 show was the computer workstation *Max,* an aerodynamic lounge for workers in the digital world. "I want to apply the vision of the network age to living design," commented **Ilkka Terho** about this design; he and **Teppo Asikainen** had created this horizontal browser's station together. And there *was* plywood after all: Terho and cohorts took their cue from the snowboard and expanded it to *Chip,* a legless lounge chair. Compared to **Alvar Aalto's** chair designs, *Chip* represents as much a higher stage of evolution as the swatch car does in relation to the good old Citroen *2 CV.* It's been prophesied that this new generation of furniture will be classic Nordic design.

Lounge *Chip* by Teppo Asikainen and Ilkka Terho, 1996

VOLVO

Automobile Manufacturer / Sweden

When Volvo introduced the new models of the 1990s, many believed that designer-in-chief Peter Horbury and his crew had gotten off the right track. The Göteborg carmaker had until then staunchly held fast to the box shape of its cars but was now abandoning it for a curvier design. In the flagship *S 80* those who looked for it could even detect an **Aalto** wave. It is a long time since Sweden's oldest automobile manufacturer has gone in for curvy lines.

Founded in the 1920s, Volvo concentrated at first exclusively on the production of trucks. When the experimental car *Venus Bilo* came out in 1933, it had an extremely streamlined body with a tail, and even the sedan *Carioca* derived from it had American styling. In fact, designers from the United States were flown in to help design the car. Subsequent models were limousine-size until the *PV 444*—the "hunchback Volvo" of the postwar era and the first Volvo to achieve considerable export sales in Europe and the United States.

The rough Swedish climate, impassable terrain, and long distances called for the development of automobile models that would stand up to these conditions. That is one of the reasons why Volvo pursued functional concepts emphasizing passenger

Volvo Personvagnar AB

1926 Founded in Göteborg

1934 Experimental car *Venus Bilo*

1935 Admission to official listing on stock exchange

1941 Airplane manufacturer Svenska Flygmotor taken over

1959 Three-point safety belt

1967 Jet plane *Viggen*

1972 DAF taken over

1974 Group production

1979 Participated in Arianespace

1994 New management after failed merger with Renault; company reduced to core business, that is "transport-related products"

Volvo *Station wagon 960*

VOLVO
OA 49664

Products

1927 Small car *Jakob*

1935 Sedan *Carioca*

1947 Sedan *PV 444*

1953 Station wagon *Duet*

1956 Sedan *121 Amazon*

1962 Station wagon *P 22*

1968 Sedan *144*

1971 Station wagon coupe *P 1800 ES* ("Snow White's Coffin")

1974 Sedan *244*

1982 Sedan *760*

1985 Station wagon *760*

1990 Sedan *940*

1995 Sedan *S 40*

1997 Coupe *C 70* by Peter Horbury, José Diaz de la Vega, and Anders Gunnarson (Prize for Outstanding Swedish Design)

1998 Sedan *S 80*

safety. Usefulness was also the basic idea behind the station wagon *445*, a new type of car that entered Swedish car folklore under the name *Duet*. In the 1950s Volvo hired its first designer, Jan Wilsgaard. More than for other car manufacturers, the image of the car as reliable transportation was to determine the Volvo brand for years to come. The most beautiful but also short-lived design of this species was the low-slung station wagon coupe *1800 ES*, whose large rear window was very striking ("Snow White's coffin"). The station wagon version of the series *240/260* became the ideal family vehicle. Its massive front part was designed along the lines of the safety car *VESC*, an epitome of angularity that was long to remain typical of Volvo. At the end of the 1970s Volvo won a design competition at the Museum of Modern Art in New York by submitting the best design for a new New York City taxi. However, much to the regret of everyone involved, it was never built. In 1985, under the direction of designer-in-chief Wilsgaard, the *700* Series was introduced, the first luxury station wagon. Volvo now stood for highest comfort and safety. The new round, sporty design will achieve cult status as soon as James Bond switches back to Volvo, his car of choice in the 1960s.

Page 348/349

Volvo *1800 ES*

Volvo *P 130*

Volvo *S 80*

Jakob WAGNER

Product Designer / Denmark

Design, especially in Denmark, is "static," according to Jakob Wagner. He calls his own work "action design," by contrast. His specialties are diving and fire fighting: extreme situations that have a number of things in common besides the short supply of breathable air. Meeting technical requirements, such as the legibility of instrument panels, can be of life-saving importance in both cases. For example, Wagner has designed a transmitter that can receive signals under water and help divers find their boat without having to stick their head above water. All technical refinement notwithstanding, the actionist admits that as a hobby diver he simply likes beautiful equipment, something he shares with firefighters who are proud of their profession and therefore appreciate the design of their equipment. A designer who names his studio **Q-Lab** (after the crazy scientist in the *007* movies) works of course with the latest 3-D software. Nevertheless the workbench in the adjoining room is not just a prop. There he still fashions clay models by hand.

1963 Born in Copenhagen

1988 Design studies in Copenhagen (until 1990)

1992 Founds studio *Q-Lab*

1995 Erik Herlows Prize

1996 Participated in exhibition *Tool Toys,* Denmark and Japan

Products

1995 Play equipment *Fly me;* inflatable surf T-shirt

1997 Outdoor thermometer (in C-Shape) for Vilbor

1998 *PSS 500* breathing apparatus for firefighters, for Draeger; *Neverlost* position finder for divers, for Uwatec

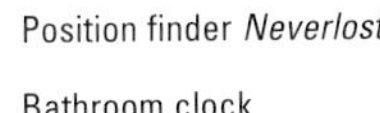

Position finder *Neverlost*

Bathroom clock

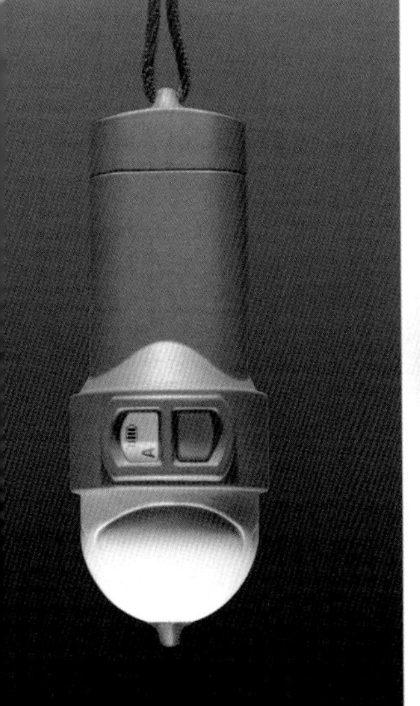

Hans J. WEGNER

Furniture Designer / Denmark

1914 Born in Tondern
1927 Apprenticeship as cabinetmaker
1936 Commercial arts school, Copenhagen (until 1938)
1938 Participation in exhibition of the cabinetmaker's guild, Copenhagen(by 19 68, he had won 27 prizes)
1940 Works for **Arne Jacobsen** and Erik Møller; interior of Århus city hall
1943 Studio in Gentofte
1946 Teaches at the Commercial Arts School, Copenhagen; works with **Børge Mogensen** for the exhibition of cabinetmakers
1951 Lunning Prize
1953 Trip to America
1959 Named *Honorary Royal Designer for Industry* by the Royal Society of Arts, London
1994 Retrospective of the Danish Design Center
1997 International Design Award, Japan

Page 353

Top: D*e runde stol,* 1949

Bottom left: Office chair *502,* 1955

Bottom right: Easy chair *Cirkel,* 1986

all for PP Møbler

The son of a Danish-German family, Wegner grew up in a small town in Jutland after World War I. His father, a shoemaker, "used his tools without looking at them," recalls Wegner. In the late 1920s he began an apprenticeship as cabinetmaker, and in 1936, at the age of twenty-two, he went to Copenhagen to study at the Industrial Arts School. During the war he worked for **Arne Jacobsen**, on the city hall in Århus, among other projects. There he set up shop on his own because under the German occupation travel to Copenhagen was not permitted. However, in 1946 he caught up on that and in the same year introduced, together with **Børge Mogensen,** with whom he maintained a close friendship, the furnishings for a three-bedroom postwar apartment: handmade and trendsetting simple furniture of solid wood.

Hans J. Wegner's career is closely tied to the annual exhibitions of the cabinetmakers guild, which he hardly ever left without an award (two dozen prizes by 1968). The pair Mogensen-Wegner represented a new type of furniture maker; formerly most furniture designers were architects and worked on furniture as a sideline. The two novices were of the first generation that was called in Danish *formgiver* (form giver) and would today be called designers. For the realization of their ideas they needed master cabinetmakers.

Wegner's approach consisted in "stripping the old chairs of their outer style." He reduced them to the "pure construction" he could then experiment with. At the annual exhibition in 1947 he introduced an unusual interpretation of the English Windsor chair. The chair, known under the model name *Pheasant* (Wegner never named his works), was his first big success. But Wegner's *Round Chair* was to be the one to cause a big stir. Based on Chinese models, this design stood out because of its extremely elegant lines, for example, the lines of armrest and back that

Products

1944 Rocking chair for Tarm; *China Chair* for **Fritz Hansen**

1947 Chair *Påfugle (Peacock)*

1949 *De runde stol (The Round Stool);* folding easy chair for hanging up; all for **PP Møbler;** shell easy chair for Johannes Hansen

1950 Easy chair *Flagline* for Getama; for Getama; Y-chair for Carl Hansen

1952 Chair *Cow Horn* for PP Møbler

1953 Chair *Jakkens Hvile (Valet)* for PP Møbler

1955 Office swivel chair for PP Møbler

blend gracefully into each other. Notwithstanding the design's originality, the chair was suitable for series production. Because of its balance between formal discipline and a clever play with lines, this chair appeared luxurious and Spartan at the same time. Was it not therefore "the chair," the quintessence of Scandinavian design as such? This view of Wegner's design soon was widespread, due largely to the U.S. magazine *Interior,* which featured the master chair on its title page in 1950. As a result a restaurant in Chicago ordered 400 chairs, an inconceivable amount by Danish standards.

By the mid-1950s Wegner's furniture designs were being produced by **Fritz Hansen** and no less than five other companies. The manufacturers formed a joint distribution company to deal with the rapidly growing demand in the export market. Now many Wegner models are marketed by **PP Møbler.** Whether Wegner is indeed the "most gifted cabinetmaker of the world," as the critic Henrik Sten Møller once called him, is hard to say, but that he is undoubtedly among the most copied. His work encompasses about 500 chair designs, some of which he took up repeatedly and varied slightly. A number of innovations go back to Wegner, such as the jacket chair *Valet* (with a back rest in the shape of a

coat hanger, illustration page 36), the shell chair (with handles), the easy chair *Cirkel* (which has casters on the back legs and whose front legs can be lifted like wheelbarrow handles), and the folding chair *PP 512* (which can be hung on the wall). From the beginning Wegner also tackled modern materials. His tubular steel and plywood furniture, however, has gained far less attention.

Ultimately, what made him famous was his absolute demand for perfection, from the concept down to the last detail. The value of his work lies to no small extent in its durability even with only a minimum amount of care. By now there is a booming market for secondhand Wegner chairs in Denmark. Hans J. Wegner is known for his precise, full-size design sketches, and he is considered one of the few who can fit a chair in only one drawing. "A piece of furniture must never have a back side," so one of his mottoes, because "one experiences it from every side and it must be able to live up to that." In line with this he offered the following practical tip: "In buying furniture," advises Wegner, "one should hold the pieces upside down, for if the underside is okay then the rest is probably okay also."

1960 Easy chair *Pølle (Ox)* for Erik Jørgensen

1961 Chair *Tyre (Bull)* for PP Møbler

1963 Three-legged shell chair for Johannes Hansen

1965 Armchair for PP Møbler

1976 *Wegner Lamp* for Louis Poulsen

1986 Easy chair *Cirkel* for PP Møbler

1988 Rocking chair for PP Møbler

From left to right:

Easy chair *Polle* (Ox) for Erik Jorgensen, 1960

Lounge chair *512* for PP Møbler, 1949

Easy chair *460* for Getama

Yrjö WIHERHEIMO

Architect and Furniture Designer / Finland

1941 Born in Helsinki
1969 Freelance designer
1980 Designer-in-chief at **Vivero** Oy
1997 Professor UIAH, Helsinki

Products
1984 Chair *Pinna,* together with Rudi Merz
1987 Chair *Tina*
1991 Chair *Flok* together with Simo Heikkilä
1993 Collection Birds for Vivero
1994 Table system Ilo

Chair *Visio-100,* 1980

Armchair *Verde-600N,* 1980

both for Vivero

Yrjö Wiherheimo is among the most influential designers in the country, both through his own studio and through his teaching at Helsinki's Design Academy where he has been preparing new generations of designers for two decades. His furniture is called *Skin and Bones, Ilo (Fun)* or *Hei (Hello).* The contrast between funny name and kosher form is typical of this practicing design professor. Yrjö Wiherheimo, at once eclectic and functionalist, plays with meanings, styles, and materials. For example, his *Ilo* designs are oval office tables with fifties appeal whose legs can be attached at different points depending on space and computer constellation. The decision for wood, metal, or plastic is not based on a doctrine but depends on the task at hand. That Wiherheimo uses a lot of bent birch in his furniture (most of it for **Vivero**)—for example, in the best-selling chair *Tina* of 1987—goes without saying for this Finnish designer. After all, the insight that design "is crucial for national identity" is part of what he teaches.

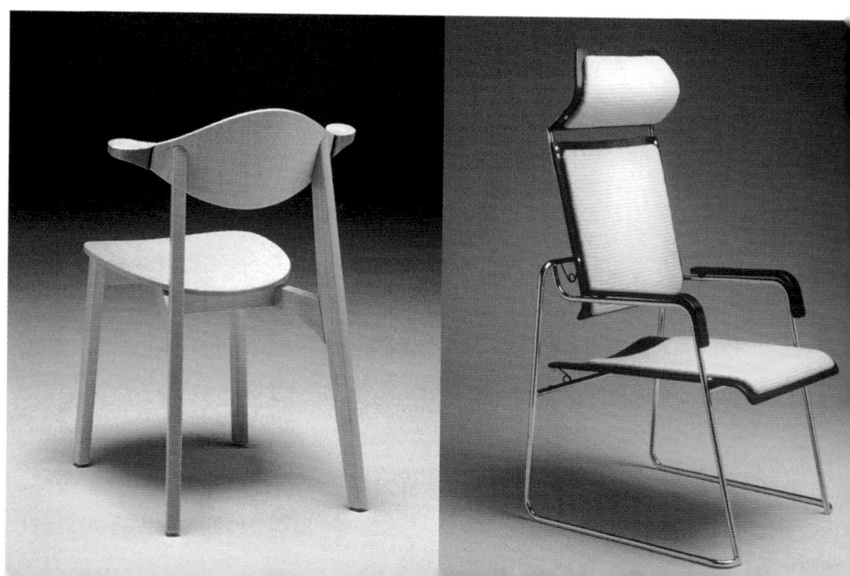

Tapio WIRKKALA

Glass Designer and Product Designer / Finland

The Italian designer Gio Ponti called his friend a "child of nature," a man who came from the forest country but grew up in Helsinki and was bursting with creativity. Among many other things, Tapio Wirkkala, indisputably Finland's most productive designer after World War II, was also a highly gifted photographer and documented his work in artistic photos. Moreover, he was a national symbol because he employed the materials, methods, and designs of traditional Finnish crafts and because he epitomized Finland's recovery after the terrible war years.

Tapio Wirkkala studied at the Central School for Applied Arts in Helsinki, whose director he later became. He turned to glass design after he won the first prize at a competition sponsored by the **Iittala** Works in 1947 (jointly with **Kaj Franck**). Wirkkala gained international renown in the late 1940s, especially with the mushroom-shaped vases *Kantarelli,* in whose paper thin glass he etched decorative lines of varying depths. Their organic form, an

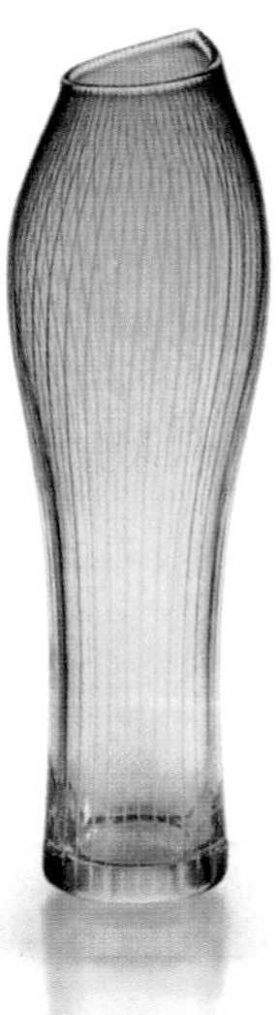

1915 Born in Hango

1936 Institute of Industrial Arts, Helsinki

1946 Works for **Iittala**

1951 Grand prize at the *Triennial,* Milan (also in 1954, 1960, and 1963); Lunning Prize; "Most Beautiful Object of the Year" (U.S. magazine *House Beautiful*); friendship with Gio Ponti

1955 Starts own studio

1963 Gold medal at Faenza International Design Competition (also in 1966, 1967, and 1973)

1967 Plywood sculpture *Ultima Thule* for the World's Fair in Montreal

1968 Heads state commission for "Industrial Arts"

1980 Prince Eugen Medal, Sweden

1985 Died in Helsinki

Left: Vase *Kantarelli,* 1946

Right: Vase *Varsanjalka,* 1946,

both for Iittala

expression of the neo-romantic trend of that time, gave them the appearance of erotic objects. Typical of Wirkkala's aesthetic approach is the use of natural materials, which he managed to force into new shapes. For example, he created sculptures out of plywood in such a way that the critic Edgar Kaufmann opined, "He practically composes his own wood." The finely veined, leaf-shaped plywood bowl that became the logo of the 1954 exhibition *Design in Scandinavia* (illustration page 8)—thus serving a kind of coat of arms for the triumph of Scandinavian design—was one of Wirkkala's most famous pieces. In 1951 the American magazine *House Beautiful* had declared it the "most beautiful object of the year," and in that year alone Wirkkala won three grand prizes at the Milan *Triennial* (and also designed the Finnish pavilion).

Tapia Wirkkala also designed a series of knives, specifically the Finnish "puukko"—a knife that is best worn at the belt and that Wirkkala himself knew how to use masterfully—which has always been a national symbol of freedom.

Products

1946 Vases *Kantarelli*

1949 Beer bottle for Lahden

1951 Plywood bowl; glass sculptures *Campanile* and *Reindeer;* vase *Tuonen Virka* for Iittala

1952 Glasses *Tapio* for Iittala; Finnish paper money

1956 Coffee cups *Finlandia*

1960 Glass sculpture *Paaderin Jaa* for Iittala

1961 Knife *Puukko*

1963 Flatware *Composition* for Rosenthal

1966 Vodka bottle *Finlandia*

1968 Black teapot; *Camping Ax*

1970 Vase *Bolla* for Venini

1972 Glasses *Gaissa* for Iittala

1975 Bird figurines in wood

1978 Drinking glass *Primavera* for Iittala

1980 Pitchers *Viva* for Iittala; coffee service *Century*

1984 Pitchers *Kelo* for Iittala

Glass pitcher and glasses *Ultima Thule* for Iittala, 1968

WOODNOTES

Textile Manufacturer / Finland

Spinning paper cord is an old technique. Textile designer **Ritva Puotila** rediscovered this material, which was used in hard times when textiles were rare, and which was therefore considered an inferior substitute. Puotila rehabilitated paper cord in her art objects and in 1987 also in a rug collection to which she later added window blinds, bags, and upholstery fabric. For four years Woodnotes operated in the red. Now the family business is a perfect example of how a market niche can be conquered through technological innovation coupled with design. Woodnotes exports ninety percent of its products and serves its design-oriented customers through specialty shops in more than thirty countries. The material, produced from wood, is a purely natural product. It is densely woven and therefore particularly sturdy and impermeable. Retro patterns with a "Scandinavian" look turn the paper textiles into a lifestyle product that harmonizes perfectly with the evergreen trend toward the "simple life."

Woodnotes Oy

1987 Founded by Mikko Puotila; exhibition at **Artek**

1992 Commercial breakthrough at the furniture fair, Cologne

1996 Woodnotes chairs at the fair in Cologne

Products

1987 Paper cord rugs

1993 Bags and textiles

1998 Upholstery fabrics all by **Ritva Puotila**

Easy chair and small chair by Ulla Koskinen

Rug *New York* made of paper cord by Ritva Puotila

ZERO

Lighting and Furniture Manufacturer / Sweden

Zero AS, Pukeberg

1978 Zero founded

1988 Furniture manufacturer Lustrum founded

1989 Glass factory Pukeberg taken over

1997 Interior of the city library of Malmö

Products

1989 Spotlight *Trix*

1992 Hanging pendant *PS,* both by Per Sundstedt

1993 Wall light *Keps* by Börge Lindau

1995 Pendant light *Peanut* by Thomas Sandell

Zero is the mother of three offspring, namely, a furniture manufacturer, a glass factory, and a company specializing in lighting systems for public spaces, offices, and stores. For example, with its varied product line of shelf lighting, the company ensures that library users can always find the right book (and it can supply the shelves too). This is not to say, however, that Zero's lamps cannot also be used for lighting up the home.

After all, with **Börge Lindau** and **Thomas Sandell** two luminaries of the new Swedish design are represented in the product line, names that define historical phases of design. Lindau, the rebel of the 1970s and 1980s, has contributed a series of white wall lights made of hole-punched steel. The pendant lights by Sandell, a figurehead of Swedish neo-purism, are usually made of opaque opal glass and have simple, sometimes curvy silhouettes as, for example, the model *Peanut.*

Left: Pendant light *Peanut* by Thomas Sandell

Right: Wall lamp *Arcad* by Per Sundstedt

Page 361

Glasses for the Kiasma Museum, Helsinki, by Sari Anttonen

Guide

Scandinavia Design Addresses

Danish Design Addresses

Copenhagen

DANSK DESIGN CENTER
H.C. Andersen Boulevard; Spearhead of Danish Design: the PR department of the Danish Design Council organizes exhibitions, publishes the magazine *Design DK,* and also serves as an information clearinghouse (www.ddc.dk).

DANSK MØBELKUNST
Bredgade 32; the place that proves again that what is good remains good: Modern Danish furniture is again trendy and therefore not cheap.

DET DANSKE KUNSTINDUSTRIMUSEUM
Bredgade 68; Denmark's glorious design history as permanent exhibit: in addition to a new exhibit of twentieth-century objects also includes crafts from Denmark, Europe, and Asia. Knud Holscher revamped the corporate identity of the museum (www.mus-kim.dk).

GEORG JENSEN
Amagertorv 4; the best address for silverware, which is also sold at Danborg Antikviteter (Holbergsgade 17) and at Peter Krog (Bredgade 4).

HOLMEGAARD
Østergade 1; "Danish Modern" in glass.

ILLUMS BOLIGHUS
Amagertorv 10; this design department store is a Copenhagen institution and a pleasure zone for aesthetes. Solid design from cake forks to duvet covers.

KLASSIK
Christian IXs gade 5; the right place if you are looking for Jacobsen, Juhl, Wegner, etc.; "classic" here means "Danish Modern."

LE KLINT
St. Kirke Straede 1; Kaare Klint's lighting designs: folded lamps of coated paper in many variations.

LOUIS POULSEN
Nyhavn 11; legendary address with showrooms: the historical headquarters of the upscale lighting factory is located on the waterfront.

MOESGAARD ANTIKVITETER
Bredgade 24; great selection for all lovers of Danish furniture.

ROYAL COPENHAGEN
Amagertorv 6; the definitive shopping paradise for porcelain. The manufacturing facility is also open for tours (Smallegade 47).

ROYAL COPENHAGEN ANTIQUES
Bredgade 11; a great selection of exclusive furniture.

SAS ROYAL HOTEL
Hammerichsgade 1; Arne Jacobsen's total art work opened in 1961: unfortunately the twenty-two-story hotel building has suffered renovations.

TRE FALKE MÖBLER
Falconer Allé; furniture store with Danish furniture from various periods.

ZIRKUS BYGNINGEN
Jernbanegade 8; color philosopher Verner Panton turned this circus into a pop-palace with loud yellow pillows and a purple dome.

Danish Hinterland

HOLMEGÅRD
Fensmark near Naestved; the glassworks is open also on holidays (11 A.M. to 3 P.M.)

ART MUSEUM TRAPHOLT
Æblehaven 23, Kolding (Jutland); one of the largest Danish museums with an extensive collection of craft and design objects; Danish furniture is presented in a separate wing.

LEGOLAND
Billund (Jutland); children love this leisure park just as much as the colorful Lego bricks.

LOUISIANA
Gammel Strandvej 13, Humlebaek (19 miles north of Copenhagen); Denmark's most important museum of modern art, on the outskirts of Copenhagen, offers special exhibits on design themes.

Finnish Design Addresses

Helsinki

DESIGN FORUM FINLAND
Fabianinkatu 10; the communications center for Finland's design ambitions, publishes the magazine *Form Function Finland* and has ongoing exhibits on display, up to thirty in the course of one year (info@designforum.fi).

ALEKSANTERINKATU
This large shopping street is dominated by the Stockman department store (No. 52); this Harrod's of Helsinki is Scandinavia's largest department store and also offers design classics. Only a few houses down the street the Skanno furniture store (No. 40) and furniture manufacturer Vivero (No. 52) outdo each other in modern decor.

ARABIA MUSEUM
Hämeentie 135; the company museum shows the product history of the famous brand. Factory tours by appointment. The Arabia store also offers inexpensive factory seconds.

ATENEUM
Kaivokatu 2; this museum of Finnish art across the street from the central station was Finland's first museum and had an allied school for applied art, which was the cradle of Finnish design. The works of the legendary Akseli Gallen-Kallela are also displayed here.

AVARTE
Kalevankatu 16; Finnish functionalism from the furniture manufacturer Kukkapuro.

CAFÉS
Hot coffee is almost as important to Finns as the sauna. Recommended addresses: the Art-Deco Café Fazer (Kluuvikatu 3), the Aalto (Academic Bookstore), the National-Romantic Socis (Kaivokatu 12, Hotel Seurahuone), and the totally cozy Café Engel (Aleksanterinkatu 26), which also offers free light therapy for darkness-induced depressions.

DESIGN MUSEUM/TAIDETEOLLISUUSMUSEO
Korkeavuorenkatu 23; this house dating from the late nineteenth century, completely renovated in 1998, presents Finland's design trophies. Only a minute's walk down the street, the Museum of Architecture (Kasarmikatu 24) offers displays on some of the same heroes of modern design

ESPLANADI
On Helsinki's shopping mile between Market and Swedish Theater, the cult addresses vie for space. For Aalto fans, Artek (No. 25) offers his classic furniture collection; the Academic Bookstore across the street (No. 3) is a late work of the master (1996); particularly noteworthy are the prisms in the ceiling and the Jacobsen chairs in the Aalto Café. The chain of Marimekko stores (Nos. 2, 14, and 31) was furnished by different designers for different groups of customers. In addition: ceramics at Arabia (No. 25), furniture at Piiroinen (No. 21), and fashion at Vuokko (No. 27). In the house on the corner of Fabianinkatu are the showrooms of the very active Design Forum Finland.

FISKARS
Mannerheimintie 14; beautiful scissors for every occasion.

GALLERI INTO
Boulevardi 22b; display windows for the designs of tomorrow; here Helsinki's design students show their work.

CENTRAL STATION
Kaivokatu/Mikonkatu; Eliel Saarinen's art-nouveau train station built in 1914: the low building with tower is considered one of the most beautiful train stations of the twentieth century. The restaurant has also been preserved in the authentic style.

KIASMA
Mannerheiminaukio 2; the art museum opened in 1998; it has spectacular glass-concrete architecture (by Steven Holl) and several fine design details, such as Sari Anttonen's drinking glasses and children's chairs by Stefan Lindfors.

NATIONAL MUSEUM
Mannerheimintie 34; a granite bear guards the entrance; this picturesque cross between a castle and a church, an early work of the trio Eliel Saarinen, Herman Gesellius, and Armas Lindgren (inaugurated in 1916), takes national-romanticism to the limit.

RESTAURANTS
The Kappelli (Esplanadi 1) is a light-filled pavilion of glass and iron dating from the turn of the century; the slightly chipped art-nouveau restaurant Kosmos (Keskuskatu 4) still serves as a meeting place for artists; the exotic interior of

the Pigéon (Eerikinkatu/Yrjönkatu) had its origin in Stefan Lindfors's imagination; in Alvar Aalto's Savoy (Esplanadi 14) on the top floor of the hotel of the same name, ice cream in the shape of the master's most famous vase is served as dessert.

SEURAARI OPEN-AIR MUSEUM
Island Seuraari; the oldest (1909) of approximately 250 (!) open-air museums in Finland provides in 100 historical buildings a comprehensive overview of the country's rural culture and architecture, which has had such a determinative influence on modern design. In addition to craft courses, there are classical concerts and a nudist beach right next door. Also offers tours in German and English.

HOTEL TORNI
Yrjönkatu 26; art-deco hotel with a grand past; Josephine Baker slept here, as did the head of the Soviet controlled commission. The bar on the 14th floor offers the best view of the city.

Finnish Hinterland

ALVAR AALTO MUSEUM
Jyväskyla, Alvar Aalon katu 7; in the birthplace of the great architect the lifework of Alvar Aalto and his wife Aino is on view.

FISKARS / HISTORICAL IRONWORKS
Fiskars; the wheels are still turning but where workers once slogged away numerous artists and designers now have their open studios: the factory situated in an idyllic spot in the forest has become a tour destination for craft fans. Exhibitions take place frequently, and a store has local wares for sale. A museum documents the history of Fiskars.

HVITTRÄSK
Luoma; villa on the lake; the studio of the architects Gesellius, Lindgren, and Saarinen is filled with the romantic spirit of the turn of the century. The furniture also was designed by the trio, even the children's furniture. The restaurant is often booked for office parties and celebrations.

IITTALA GLASS MUSEUM
Kalvola/Iittala; the Valhalla of Finnish glass art; additional glass museums are close by, such as Nuutajärvi and Riihimäki, and are also worth exploring.

Norwegian Design Addresses

Oslo

NORSK FORM
Uranienborgveien 2; this center for design, architecture, and environmental design—like its Scandinavian sister organizations—organizes exhibitions and conferences, issues publications, and handles publicity work (E-mail: norform@telepost.no).

APROPOS ARCITECT
Riddervoldsgate; furniture more or less Nordic.

ARISTA
Karl Johansgate in the Paleet department store; design objects of all kinds.

BYGDE ALLEE
Here furniture store follows upon furniture store, from Berg Studio, Studio Sit-in, and Vidivici (furniture) to Expo Nova (furniture and lights) and Interlight (lamps).

DAVID-ANDERSEN
Karl Johansgate/Akersgaten; best address for Norwegian jewelry.

HOLMENKOLLEN PARK HOTEL
Kongev 26; typical romantic wood architecture from the turn of the century in Viking-revival style.

KUNSTINDUSTRIMUSEET OSLO
St. Olvasgate; the museum, founded in 1876, would be the oldest design museum of the world if one would include crafts under the heading design; in addition to historical and modern applied art from Norway, the royal wardrobe is also on exhibit here. The museum provides a guided tour through the branches and epochs of the modern era, including crafts, early Norwegian functionalism, furniture of the golden postwar years, and Stokke's feel-good chairs, the most recent, most radical, and also most successful Scandinavian furniture concept. Another Norwegian icon: the flexible Luxo-lamp designed by Jacob Jacobsen in 1937 represents a highlight of design history.

NORWAY DESIGNS
Stortingsgt. 28; art glass, housewares, silver jewelry, and rugs in the vicinity of the national theater.

Norwegian Hinterland

BERGEN DESIGN CENTER
Bergen, Cultural Center; a forum for architecture, landscape, and design that also organizes exhibitions.

DUSAVIK-OILBASE
Stavanger, Harbor; industrial design in the raw. Norway's largest open oilbase is also the basis of the country's prosperity. On the huge pontoon tied fastened to the dock the ships are loaded that supply the oil platforms in the North Sea. Admission free.

HADELAND GLASSMUSEUM
Jevnaker; the oldest and most important Norwegian glassworks displays utility and art objects dating from 1750 to the present, including an exhibit on the history of drinking glasses.

HENIE-ONSTAD KUNSTSENTER
Høvikodden; in addition to a collection of modern and contemporary art, a permanent exhibition featuring industrial design is on display in one wing of the museum.

NORDENFJELDSKE KUNSTINDUSTRIMUSEUM
Trondheim, Munkegaten 5; highlights of the collection are art nouveau and Japanese art as well as contemporary design and crafts, including a rug collection by Hannah Ryggen and a room with furniture by the Danish designer Finn Juhl.

PORSGRUND BYMUSEUM
Porsgrund, Storgarten 59; this municipal museum features an exhibition of traditional and contemporary art as well as displays on the product history of the well-known ceramics factory Porsgrund from 1887 to the present.

VESTLANDSKE KUNSTINDUSTRIMUSEUM
Bergen, Nordahl BrunsgaTe 9; the permanent exhibition comprises a broad range of Norwegian crafts. Early works of pioneers, such as the silversmith Jacob Prytz, are presented, some in the "Viking style." Famous manufacturers of the art industry, such as Hadeland and Porsgrund, are represented as are small, independent workshops and studios. In flatware designs, as in those by Anne Korsmo, the soft, organic shapes of the coming epoch were already anticipated in the 1940s. Moreover, the museum offers a glimpse into the development of Norwegian furniture and textile design.

Swedish Design Addresses

Stockholm

SVENSK FORM
Norrlandsgatan 18; this association with a rich tradition publishes the magazine Form (www.svensk-form.se).

ASPLUND
Sibyllegatan 31; neo-Nordic furniture store with its own furniture collection by leading young designers.

BARS
Among the long-running successes are the good old Café Opera (Kungsträdgården) and Jonas Bohlin's Sturehof (Stureplan 2).

BIONDI
Odengatan 43; a personally chosen selection of contemporary design objects.

BLÅS & KNÅDA
Hornsgatan 26; glass and ceramics for the modern home of the coming century; the store is run by potters and studio glass artists.

DUX
Strandvägen 7 c; Mathsson and mattresses.

EKERÖ MÖBLER
Malmvik, Ekerö; new Swedish furniture in a modern building situated in the midst of a park.

HOTEL ESPLANADE
Strandvagen 7a; this pretty but unpretentious art-nouveau hotel is located between Dux and Svenskt Tenn in a courtyard screened off from the street noise.

GALLERI STOLEN
Birger Jarlsgatan 57; chair variations à la Åke Axelsson.

GÖSTA WESTERBERG
Fleminggatan 13; Aalto, furniture, and Marimekko.

IKEA
Skärholmen (free bus from Regeringsgatan 13); the first and by far the largest among the blue-yellow furniture stores is Kungens Kurva dating from 1965, a round building inspired by the Guggenheim Museum.

KALIKÁ
Österlånggatan 18; fabric toys directly from the manufacturer plus toys from the good old days.

KLARA
Nytorgsgatan 26; the vital nucleus of the most recent Swedish design wave.

KULTURHUSET
Sergels Torg 3; changing exhibitions on art, photography, and design. The bookstore in the cellar was designed by Mats Theselius.

LILJEVALCHS KONSTHALL
Djurgårdsvägen 60; this museum with a rich tradition shows crafts as well as art. In 1917 the home show that jumpstarted modern Swedish design was held here.

MODERNA MUSEET
Skeppsholmen; this home for Swedish and international twentieth-century art opened in 1998. Notable for its restrained architecture (by Rafael Moneo) and neo-Swedish seating.

NATIONAL MUSEUM
Södra Blasieholmshannen; the national art collections are the focus of this museum. But there are also frequent exhibitions featuring the work of particular designers or important design themes.

NORDISKA MUSEET
Djurgårdsvägen 6-16; far from any Nordic mysticism, here the myths of Swedish everyday culture are presented and reappraised, from Abba to Ikea, from Pippi Longstocking to Ingemar Stenmark. And somehow design is always involved.

ORDNING & REDA
NK Hamngatan/Sturegallerian 47/Drottninggatan 82; a selection of beautiful Swedish paper products for everyday writing.

RESTAURANTS
Stockholm is proud of its trendy restaurants. Only two of them can be mentioned here: the highly praised Japanese restaurant One Happy Cloud (Karlavägen 15) designed by the minimalist trio Claesson Koivisto Rune and the Akvarium designed by Thomas Sandell (Hamngatan/ Kungsträdgården).

R.O.O.M.
Alströmergatan 20; new furniture in an old factory building.

SKANSEN
Djurgården; the oldest open-air museum of the world and with 150 historic buildings also one of the largest. It features folk culture from all regions of Sweden.

CITY LIBRARY
Odengatan/Sveavägen; Gunnar Asplund's all-around successful 1920s masterpiece.

SVENSK MÖBELCENTER
Storängsvägen 10; twenty-three firms display furniture and home decor.

SVENSKT TENN
Strandvägen 5; the legend lives; exclusive furniture store filled with the spirit of Josef Frank and "Swedish Modern."

TIO-GRUPPEN
Götgatan 25; ten designers, many beautiful fabrics.

Swedish Hinterland

FORM / DESIGNCENTER
Lilla Torg, Malmö; permanent exhibition of Swedish design objects and changing exhibits.

LILLA HYTTNÄS
Sundborn; Carl and Karin Larsson's nest has long since become a place of pilgrimage.

RÖHSSKA KONSTSLÖJDMUSEET
Vasagatan 37-39, Göteborg; Sweden's only design museum that also has the largest collection.

BRUNO MATHSSON-CENTER
Värnamo; the former home of the most famous Swedish designer now houses the headquarters of the Bruno Mathsson Foundation and Museum.

Page 367

Plastic radio by Sigvard Bernadotte for Brdr. Andersson, 1955

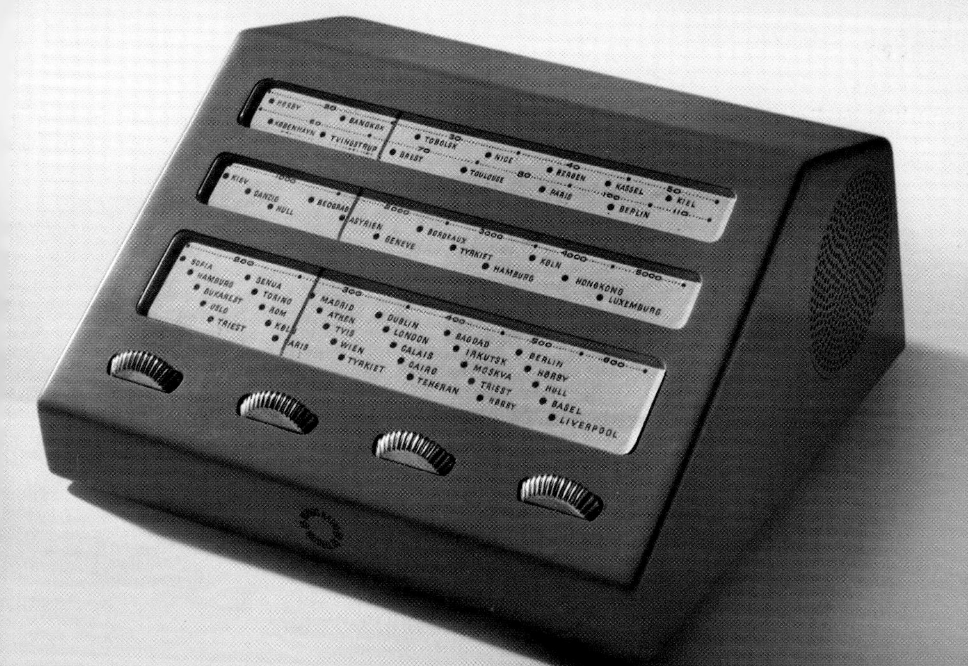

20
BANGKOK
KØBENHAVN
60
TVINGSTRUP
30
TOBOLSK
70
BREST
NICE
TOULOUSE
40
BERGEN
80
PARIS
KASSEL
100
BERLIN
50
KIEL
110
KIEV
GANZIG
HULL
BEOGRAD
2000
ASYRIEN
GENEVE
BORDEAUX
3000
TYRKIET
HAMBURG
KØLN
4000
HONGKONG
5000
LUXEMBURG
SOFIA
200
HAMBURG
GENUA
BUKAREST
TORINO
OSLO
ROM
TRIEST
PARIS
300
MADRID
ATHEN
DUBLIN
TYIS
LONDON
WIEN
CALAIS
TYRKIET
CAIRO
TEHERAN
400
BAGDAD
IRKUTSK
MOSKVA
TRIEST
HØRBY
500
BERLIN
HØRBY
HULL
BASEL
LIVERPOOL
600

AALTO, Aino;1894–1949, née Marsio; Finnish architect, interior designer, and glass designer (1932 glass series *Bölgeblick,* for Iittala). Married Alvar Aalto in 1924 and was his congenial partner; headed Artek. 1936 gold medal at the *Triennial.* 60, 98, 213

AALTO, Alvar; 9, 60, **98,** 120, 121, 192, 213, 228, 260, 273, 294, 335, 344, 346, 347

AARNIO, Eero; 72, 75, **105,** 158, 294, 304

A & E DESIGN; **110**

ABLOY; Finnish manufacturer of padlocks in Joensuu. Designer: Creadesign. 148, 192

ABSOLUT; **112,** 139, 174

AHLSTRÖM, Tom; 1943; Swedish industrial designer; studied at the Konstfackskolan in Stockholm, Department Metal; Partner in A & E. 110

ALLARD, Gunilla, 1957; Swedish set designer and furniture designer; works for Lammhults (1991 sofa *Cirkus*). 1996 Georg Jensen Prize for her "minimalist, elegant forms." 250

ANDERSEN, G. Aagaard; 1919–1982; avant-garde Danish painter and designer; worked with Fernand Léger. Experiments in graphics, textiles, light, and color. Belonged to the circle around the magazine *Mobilia.* (1963 plastic foam easy chair; 1980 *Milking Stool*). 72, 160.

ANIMAL DESIGN, Antti Eklund's design studio. 162

ANTTONEN, Sari; **114,** 254, 311

ARABIA; 10, 60, 76, **115,** 180, 197

ARBÈN, Love; 1952; Swedish interior decorator and furniture designer; representative of the new Swedish purism; works for Lammhults. Teaches at the Konstfackskolan in Stockholm. 250

ARCH DESIGN; **119**

ARTEK; 60, 76, **120,** 178, 286, 312, 326

ASIKAINEN, Teppo; 1968; Finnish furniture and product designer (1996 lounge chair *Chip;* 1997 computer workstation *Netsurfer*). Partner in Valvomo. 346

ASKO; Finnish furniture manufacturer and chain of stores. Designers: Ilmari Taapiovaara, Eero Aarnio (1963 plastic seat *Ball*). 105

ASPLUND, Gunnar; 57, 58, **121,** 192

ASPLUND; **122,** 145, 174, 326, 340

ATLAS COPCO; Swedish machine manufacturer (1997 low vibration pneumatic drill *Cobra* by Björn Dahlström). 150

ATLET; Swedish manufacturer of ergonomic, accident preventing forklifts (1997 model *Tergo*).

AVARTE; Finnish furniture manufacturer with own production; founded in 1980 in Helsinki. Ergonomics and ecology (1997 wooden coatrack by Petri Vainio). Designer-in-chief: Yrjö Kukkapuro. 248

AXELSSON, Åke; **124,** 194

BAHCO (Sandvik Bahco AB); Swedish manufacturer of tools and machines (1983 tools *Ergo* by Ergonomi). 169, 170

BALANS; **126** 170, 334

BANG & OLUFSEN; 10, 75, **129,** 134, 193, 231, 256

BATES; Danish manufacturer of paper bags (1997 combination system for household garbage with Christian Bjørn, awarded European Design Prize for this). 138

BENGTSSON, Mathias; 1971; Danish artist and furniture designer (1996 wire seat *Fragment*). Partner in Panic. 300

BENKTZON, Maria; 1946; Swedish product designer; developed ergonomic methodology (1987 crutches for arthritics for RFSU Rehab); pioneer of design for the disabled; extensive teaching activity; partner in Ergonomi. 168

BENT KROGH; **133** 308

BERNADOTTE, Sigvard; 70, 129, **134,** 232

BINDESBØLL, Thorvald; 1846–1908; Danish architect, graphic artist, ceramist, furniture designer, and bookbinder. One of the great precursors of Danish Design. In the 1890s developed his own graphics style in his pottery, a style he then also used in his textiles. His silverware shows oriental influences. 56, 121

BING & GRØNDAHL; Danish manufacturer of ceramics, founded in 1853; at first figurines based on Bertel Thorvaldsen; 1885 Pietro Krohn hired as artistic director; one of two important Danish porcelain companies. Renowned designers, among others Axel Salto, Kay Bojesen, Gertrud Vaasegaard and Pietro Krohn (1888 dinnerware set *Hejrestellet*/Heron). Erik Magnussen reformed tableware

1971 dinnerware set *Hank*). 1987, after takeover through Royal Copenhagen, production discontinued. 66, 76, 264, 318

BJERG, Thea; **136**

BJØRN, Acton; 1919-1992; Danish architect, urban planner, and product designer; as partner of S. Bernadotte in the vanguard of Scandinavian industrial design (1966 portable radio *Beolit 500;* won ID Prize for that). 129, 135

BJØRN, Christian; 138

PIA BJØRNSTAD; 1948; Norwegian textile designer; studied in Great Britain; works for Gudbrandsdalens Uldvarefabrik as designer and in management. Norwegian Design Prize in 1991 and 1996.

BJØRQUIST, Karin; 1927; Swedish ceramist at Gustavsberg (1959 stoneware *Ball*). 1954 gold medal at the *Triennial,* 1963 Lunning Prize. 316

BLÅ STATION; **139**

BOHLIN, Jonas; 75, 122, **140**, 234, 250, 326

BOJESEN, Kay; 58, 60, **143**, 295, 310

BONGARD, Hermann; 1921; Norwegian graphic artist and product designer (1956 plywood salad servers). Representative of "Beautiful Form;" worked for Hadeland (1951 carafe, gold medal at the 1954 *Triennial* for that). 1957 Lunning Prize, 1982 Jacob Prize.

BOTIUM; Danish furniture manufacturer, Copenhagen. Designer: Rud Thygesen (1983 *Royal Furniture)*.

BOX DESIGN; **144**, 145

BRINDFORS, Hans; Swedish graphic artist; successful advertising agency; worked for Absolut, SAS, and Ikea. 112, 218

BRUMMER, Arttu; 1891–1951; Finnish interior decorator and glass designer; worked for Riihimäki and for the Italian magazine *Domus;* was president of Ornamo. Prize at the 1937 World's Fair in Paris. As professor in Helsinki during the 1940s mentor of modern Finnish design. 268

BRYK, Rut; 1916; Finnish graphic artist and ceramist; worked for Arabia; tile reliefs (1978 wall relief *City on Water* for the Volvo headquarters); married Tapio Wirkkala.

BÜLOW-HÜBE, Torun Vivianna; 1927; Swedish jewelry designer; lived in Germany, France, and Indonesia; works for Georg Jensen (1969 wristwatch). 1960 gold medal at the *Triennial* and Lunning Prize.

CARLSBERG; **Danish Brewery** (Tuborg also belongs to the concern); founded in 1874 by J. C. Jacobsen, a patron of the arts; parent company of Royal Scandinavia. The *Carlsberg Foundation* is the most important private Danish cultural institution for the support of the arts and sciences. 320

CBI; **145**, 174

CLAESSON KOIVISTO RUNE; 81, **146**, 152, 280, 283

CLAESSON, Mårten; 1970; Swedish furniture designer, interior decorator, and author; studied in New York and Stockholm; assistant to Love Arbèn; partner in Claesson Koivisto Rune (1995 chair *Maxply,* won first prize in the *Försnäs Design Competition* for that; 1997 *Telephone table*); writes for trade journals and daily newspapers. 81, **146**

CREADESIGN; **148**, 192

CYRÉN, Gunnar; 1931; Swedish glass designer and silversmith; worked for Orrefors but broke with the purist style of the house (1966 *Pop glasses,* 1971 plastic bowls and pitchers *Medley,* 1990 vase *Fyra Björnar*). 1966 Lunning Prize. 296, 299

DAHLSTRÖM, Björn; 145, **150**, 197

DAVID DESIGN; 145, **152**, 340

DEMOCRATIC DESIGN; 64, **154**, 169, 220, 310

DESIGN DK; Magazine of the Dansk Design Council in Copenhagen (six issues per year and special issues, in Danish and English).

DESIGN MUSEUMS; see Guide

DESIGN PRIZES; The Lunning Prize (1951–1970) was the first pan-Scandinavian prize and much like a *Nordic Compasso d'oro;* Frederik Lunning founded the New York branch of Georg Jensen. Since 1992 the Scandinavian Design Prize has been awarded (by the Scandinavian Design Council). The most famous prize and also the one with the most money is the Danish Georg Jensen Prize. Among the many national awards, the following are the most important: In Denmark the ID Prize for product design and the Furniture Prize of the Danish furniture industry; in Finland the Kaj Franck Prize and Industrial Designer of the Year; in Norway the Jacob Prize and Classic Prize; in Sweden the Bruno Mathsson Prize and

Utmärkt Svensk Form (outstanding Swedish design) for product design..

DESIGN ASSOCIATIONS; the national associations for crafts and applied arts were founded in the 19th and early 20th centuries, for example, Svenska Slöjdföreningen (Swedish Work Association), Suomen Taideteollisuusyhdistys (Finnish Commercial Arts Association), Landsforeningen Dansk Brugskunst (National Association for Danish Utilitarian Art), Foreningen Brukskunst (Association for Utilitarian Art). After restructuring, especially in the 1970s, there are now the following trade associations: in Denmark the Danish Design Council, in Finland the Design Forum Finland and Ornamo, in Norway Norsk Form and Norsk Designråd, in Sweden Föreningen Svensk Form and the SID (Association of Swedish Industrial Designers). See also under Industrial Design and Crafts.

DESSAU, Ingrid; 1923; Swedish textile designer; worked for Kinnarand. 1955 Lunning Prize.

DISSING & WEITLING; **156**

DITZEL, Nanna; 64, **158,** 187, 196

DUX; Swedish manufacturer of furniture and mattresses; founded in Stockholm around 1900; worked with designers early on. Markets the furniture by Bruno Mathsson (1973 bed *Ulla*). Other designers: Gunnar Asplund, Carl Axel Acking, Carl Malmsten, and Alf Svensson. 217, 273

E & D; one of the largest Finnish studios for industrial and product design in Turku; high-tech, wood processing; household appliances (1992 electronic tickets for Buscom). 148

ECKHOFF, Tias; **161**

EHRICH, Hans; 1942; Product designer; in the 1960s worked in Italy; is considered the gray eminence of Swedish product design; partner in A & E. 110

EKHOLM, Kurt; 1907–1975; Finnish ceramics designer; functionalist; 1932–48 artistic director at Arabia; set up studios; established the company museum; later worked for Rörstrand and taught in Göteborg. 60, 116

EKLUND, Antti; **162,** 270

ELECTROLUX; 70, 77, **164,** 200

ERGONOMI; 11, 79, **168,** 171

ERGONOMIE; 170, 175, 256, 274, 324

ERICSSON; 77, 134, **172,** 280

ERIK JØRGENSEN; leading Danish manufacturer of upholstered furniture in Svendborg (1961 easy chair *Corona* by Poul Volther). Designers: Johannes Foersom, Jørgen Gammelgaard, Verner Panton, Peter Hiort-Lorenzen, Hans J. Wegner. 308

ERIKSSON, Thomas 174; 220

EXEL; Finnish manufacturer of ski poles in Mäntyharju; developed innovative plastic poles for the 1976 Winter Olympics. 148

FINCH, Alfred W.; 1854–1930; Belgian painter; active in the arts and crafts movement; contacts to Henry van der Velde and Akseli Gallen-Kallela; since 1897 in Finland; director of the ceramics department of the Iris Factory. 54

FISKARS; 79, 170, **175**

FLANDER, Brita; 178, 270

FLOR, Ellinor; 1946; Norwegian fashion designer. Knit fabrics; modern interpretation of traditional styles (1990 suit *Telemark*); initiated wool revival, among other things through her 1991 book *Rosa Heimafrå,* in which she reports on her experience with the Norwegian style of knitting. 1992 Jacob Prize.

FOERSOM, Johannes; 1947; Danish furniture designer; works for Erik Jørgensen and Lammhults. Partner of Peter Hiort-Lorenzen. In 1992 awarded the prize for High Design Quality by the Design Center NRW; 1998 Bruno Mathsson Prize. 250

FORM; Magazine of Svensk Form in Stockholm; appears since 1905 (six issues per year, Swedish with English summaries; special issues).

FORM FUNKTION FINLAND; Magazine of the Design Forum Finland in Helsinki and of the Finnish Society for Crafts and Design (four issues per year in English).

FORMBOLAGET ID; Swedish studio for industrial and product design; founded in 1989 in Stockholm (1997 bulldozer *Maro* for Svedala Compaction).

FRANCK, Kaj; 66, 116, 148, 154, **180,** 193, 216, 264, 283, 359

FRANK, Josef; 60, **183,** 283, 294, 338

FREDERICIA; 76, 160, **186,** 278, 308

FREDERIKSEN, Louise C.; 1966; Danish product and jewelry esigner; biomorphous forms (1998 flatware for children and randy snifter for Glaskoch); partner in Selle 16.

RIIS & MOLTKE; Danish studio for furniture and product esign; founded in Brabrand in 1957. Danish minimalism. utdoor lights for Lampas. 1972 Danish Furniture Prize, 1989, 994 ID Prize. 133

RISELL, Astrid; 1966; Norwegian product designer (1994 rotective clothing for firefighters, for Lillehammer rodukter and carrier strap for infants). Trained in marine echnology.

RITZ HANSEN; 70, 76, 78, **188**, 192, 236, 266, 308, 356

UNCTIONALISM; 121, 140, 154, 161, 170, 183, **192**, 226, 233, 51, 262, 277, 289, 300

ALLEN-KALLELA, Akseli; 1865–1931; Painter, furniture, and extile designer; symbolist; close contact to contemporary vant-garde in Scandinavia (August Strindberg, Jean Sibelius) nd Europe (member of the artist group *Die Brücke*). Inspired y the Finnish epic *Kalevala (Frescoes);* like Eliel Saarinen built studio in the wilderness. Although ardent champion of verything primevally Finnish, he was also an internationalist friendship with Gustav Mahler and Maxim Gorki); traveled widely, expedition to Kenya. Influenced design by founding the ris Factory and participating in the 1900 World's Fair in Paris 1899 wooden cabinet *Tree of Knowledge*). 1996 retrospective n the Ateneum Museum in Helsinki. 54

AMMELGAARD, Niels; 1938; Danish furniture designer. In 969 founded Box 25 together with four architects, 1978 ounds *Pelikan* together with Lars Matthiesen; considers imself an industrial designer (1986 chair *PK/7* of metal and ubber for Cappellini; 1996 partition *Wing* for Fritz Hansen, won Roter Punkt (Red Dot) for that); works since 1975 for kea, most recently under the name Design Studio Copenhagen (1995 director's chair *Tias*). 218, 306

ARDBERG, Bertel; 1916; goldsmith and product designer. Master of the metal trade; produced works for Georg Jensen, Lafayette, Fiskars, and Hackman (1963 flatware *Carelia*); 1954 and 1957 gold medal at the *Triennial* 1961 Lunning Prize. 1995 Exhibition *Classic Makers* in Helsinki. 175

GÄRSNÄS; 124, **194**, 326

GATE, Simon; 1883–1945; Swedish artist; 1916 together with E. Hald at Orrefors; together with glassblower Knut Bergqvist developed the Graal technique. His work launched the worldwide success of Swedish glass art ("Swedish grace"). 54, 57, 296

GEORG JENSEN; 10, 69, 78, 143, 158, 161, **195**, 243, 320

GOOF; Danish manufacturer of dental products; 1988 European Design Prize

GULBRANDSEN, Nora; 1894–1978; Norwegian glass designer. Modernized Norwegian utilitarian ceramics (1927 porcelain pot *Tureen*), 1928–45 artistic director at Porsgrund. 58, 60, 161

GUSRUD, Svein; 1944; Norwegian furniture designer and artist; worked in the Balans Group (1982 ergonomic seating for buses and trains); 1992 first prize in the chair competition for the Norwegian pavilion at the World's Fair in Seville; professor for furniture design in Oslo.

GUSTAVSBERG; Swedish manufacturer of ceramics, founded in 1640. Around 1900 successful through working with the artist Gunnar Wennerberg. Since then the flagship of the Swedish art industry. From 1917–49 Wilhelm Kåge artistic director (1945 dinnerware set with gray lines), later Stig Lindberg (1955 pan and plates *Terma*) and Karin Bjørquist (1978 tableware *BV*). Belonged since 1937 to the Consumer Cooperative *Kooperativa Förbundet* (KF), since 1987 to Arabia (merged with Rörstrand). 65, 192

HACKMAN; 76, 118, **197**, 216, 316, 320

HADELAND; 198

HAGERUP, Leif; 1962; Danish product and furniture designer; worked for Knud Holscher; bicycles and seating furniture (1994 spiral chair *Eddy*); partner in Linde, Hagerup, Petersen. 255

HAKATIE, Annaleena; 1965; Finnish glass designer, works for Iittala (1965 tealights *Ballo*). 216

HALD, Edward; 1883–1980; Swedish artist and glass designer; worked for Orrefors (1921 plates *Broken Bridge*), 1933–44 director at Orrefors. Responsible for the style of "Swedish Grace" and its worldwide success; worked also for Rörstrand and Lidköping. 54, 57, 296, 316

HANSEN, Fritz; See FRITZ HANSEN

HANSÉN, Kristofer; 199

HASSELBLAD; 200

HAUGESEN, Niels Jergen; 133, **202**, 230

HEIBERG, Jean; 1884–1976; Norwegian artist; studied in Munich and Paris under Henri Matisse, among others. One of the pioneers of Scandinavian industrial design (1931 Bakelite telephone for Ericsson). 172

HEIN, Piet; 1905; Danish mathematician, inventor, and poet (successful poetry under the pseudonym "Kumbel"). Together with Bruno Mathsson transposed his *Superellipsis* (form between oval and rectangle) onto porcelain, glass, textiles, and furniture (1964 table *Superellipsis* for Fritz Hansen). 190, 274

HENNINGSEN, Poul; 58, 129, 143, 192, **203**, 208, 260, 266, 302

HINKOLA, Vesa; 1970; Finnish interior decorator and product designer; co-creator of a current best-seller (1996 lamp *Glowblow*). Partner in Valvomo. 344

HIORT-LORENZEN, Peter; 1943; Danish shipbuilder and furniture designer. Partner of Johannes Foersom. 250

HØLASS, Kjellaug; 1906–1990; Norwegian textile designer and silversmith; numerous rugs; influential as teacher of a whole generation. 1964 Jacob Prize.

HOLMBÄCK, Sebastian; 1971; Danish furniture and product designer (1997 bench *Rest for Two*); partner in Panic. 300

HOLMEGAARD; **207**, 320

HOLSCHER, Knud; 78, 171, 193, **208**, 228, 255

HÖRNELL; Swedish manufacturer of welding helmets and breathing apparatus; founded in 1983; 1997 European Design Prize.

HOUGHTON, John R.; 1944; British product designer; lives in Norway; founded Ango-Nordic Design in 1980. Numerous prizes; among others award for best innovation in 1992 from the Design Center Nordrhein-Westfalen for his pan *Wing* (for Hackman).

HULDT, Johan; **210**

HVASS, Niels; **211**

HYDMAN-VALLIEN, Ulrica; 1938; Swedish glass designer; since 1972 at Kosta Boda. Successful glass-staining. Taught from 1981–88 at the Pilchuck Glass Center, Washington State. Married to Bertil Vallien. 246, 342.

IFORM; Swedish furniture manufacturer; founded in Malmö in 1975. Designers: Ruud Ekstrand, Peter Karpf.

IITALA; 180, 197, **213**, 328, 359

IKEA; 11, 52, 77, 93, 145, 154, 174, 210, **217**, 233, 250, 283, 29 306, 326

INDUSTRIAL DESIGN; in this book industrial design is define as design for processing industries, that is, design products and of the means of production. It developed as profession in Scandinavia only in the 1970s (as did also th trade associations). Industrial design in the narrower sens that is, the design of the means of production, such a machines and transport vehicles, is beyond the scope of th lexicon. The term industrial design is often use interchangeably with product design; in fact, produc designers usually belong to the trade association of industri designers. For information on individual designers and desig studios see: for Denmark (Christian Bjørn, Dissing & Weitlin Friis & Moltke, Knud Holscher, Jacob Jensen, Stev McGugan, Q-Lab), Finland (Creadesign, E&D, Muodos), an Sweden (A&E, Formbolaget; Monitor, Nya Perspektiv, N Picnic). See also Crafts, Art Industry, and Product Design.

INNO; 221

INNOVATOR; Swedish furniture manufacturer; founded i 1968 by J. Huldt; broke with traditional furniture industry an established a new high-tech style, which was later ofte copied and was particularly successful in export. 76, 210.

IRIS; Finnish manufacturer of ceramics, furniture, an textiles (1897-1902), followed the example of Liberty's worked with Louis Sparre (furniture) and Alfred Finc (ceramics); Finland's success at the 1900 World's Fair i Paris was based on their products. 54

ISHIMOTO, Fujiwo; 118, **222**, 270

ISOLA, Maija; 1927; Finnish painter and textile designer; i 1949 started working for Marimekko and Printex; famous fo large-scale patterns that anticipated pop aesthetics; late also folklore and in the late 1960s political motifs. 222, 268

JACOBSEN, Arne; 10, 60, 64, 156, 188, 192, 202, 208, **224**, 236 262, 264, 301, 304, 382, 352

JALK, Grete; 1920; Danish furniture designer. Experiment with laminated wood (1963 laminated chair for Jeppensen worked for Fritz Hansen (1964 tubular steel easy chair). 194 first prize of the Copenhagen cabinetmakers' guild; 198

book *Dansk Møbelkunst* (Danish furniture art). 1990 retrospective in the USA. 64

JÄRVINEN, Pasi; 1951; Finnish product designer; worked for Creadesign since 1983. Sport and leisure equipment, for example, ergonomic ski poles (1992 model *Avanti* for Exel); together with top skier Kari Ristanen developed new skis (1997 Cubix-Skis for Karhu). 1995 *Industrial Designer of the Year.* 148

JENSEN, Georg; see GEORG JENSEN

JENSEN, Jacob; 129, 135, 193, **231**, 284

JENSEN, Ole; 1958; Danish ceramics designer. 320

JOHANSSON, Willy; 1921-1993; Norwegian glass designer; son of a glassblower; was artistic director at Hadeland in the golden era of Scandinavian design (1952 wineglasses *Medoc*). 1957 *Jacob-Prize.*

JØRGENSEN, Erik; see ERIK JØRGENSEN.

JUGEND (Youth); Scandinavian term for Jugendstil (Art Nouveau) after the eponymous Munich magazine, which was widely circulated among artists (e.g., Carl Larsson and Eliel Saarinen) and also influenced design (1900 tea and coffee service with dragonfly by Alf Wallander for Rörstrand); counterconcept to classicism. This style, which gained ground in Scandinavia around 1900, above all in Helsinki (at that time undergoing a period of growth) and much less so in Denmark, blended with national-romanticism (1907 chair with dragon motif by Gerhard Munthe for the Fairy Tale Room of the Holmenkollen Hotel near Oslo); in architecture it led to the adoption of the concept of the total art work (1914 central train station in Helsinki by Eliel Saarinen). 244, 295

JUHL, Finn; 1912-1989; Danish architect and furniture designer. Broke away from strict functionalism, drew on British sculpture (e.g., Barbara Hepworth) and gave furniture a flowing, sculptural form (together with the cabinetmaker Niels Vodder); industrial use of teak (1953 easy chair *Model 133* for France). After 1945 he was one of the most famous representatives of "Danish Modern"; worked for Georg Jensen, IBM, General Electric, and Big & Grøndahl. 1957 gold medal at the *Triennial,* 1964 AID-Prize, Chicago. 63, 295

JUHLIN, Sven-Eric; 1940; Swedish ceramist and product designer; worked as design engineer at Electrolux, 1967-76 as designer at Gustavsberg (1970 shopping basket); since 1972 projects with Maria Benktzon. Design for the disabled, ergonomic method. Partner in Ergonomi (1988 coffee and tea pot for SAS). 168

JUTREM, Arne Jon; 1929; Norwegian artist, graphic artist, textile designer, and silversmith; since 1950 worked for Hadeland, most recently as artistic director. Internationally known for art glass (1990 *Objects in Blue*). Also furniture, fabrics, rugs, ceramics, jewelry, and graphic art. 1963 cofounder of the Association Norske Brukskunst. 1954 gold medal Triennial; 1967 Norwegian pavilion at the World's Fair in Montreal; 1959 Lunning-Prize, 1992 Jacob-Prize. 198

KÅGE, Wilhelm; 1889-1960; Swedish graphic artist, textile designer, and ceramics designer; worked from 1917 to 1960 for Gustavsberg, until 1949 artistic director; championed modern design and designed simple, stackable, and heat-resistant dinnerware. His dinnerware set *Liljeblå* (blue lily) of 1917 was an early attempt to elevate everyday items to a higher standard; later functionalist designs (1933 dinnerware set *Praktika*) as well as Mexican and Japanese motifs. 1925 grand prize of the *Exposition Internationale des Arts Décoratifs,* Paris. 57, 60, 154

KÄHÖNEN, Hannu; 1943; Finnish production designer; functionalist school; wide range of activity from transportation vehicles (1998 streetcar for Helsinki) to high tech (1996 cell phone *Alfa 900* for Benefon). Partner in Creadesign. 148

KÄLLEMO; 75, 140, **233**, 250, 326, 338

KANDELL, John; 1925-1991; Swedish architect and furniture designer; 1948-69 in the studio of Sven Ivar Lind. Reedition at Källemo (1985 chair and table *Solitaire*). Wall system made of driftwood. 1993 exhibition *Mathsson Chambert Kandell Bohlin* in the National Museum, Stockholm. 234

KARELIANISMUS; Movement in Finnish art, literature, music, and design in the late 19th century; variation on national romanticism. Elias Lönnrot collected folk poetry and published it in 1835 under the title *Kalevala.* After that great interest especially on the part of poets, artists, and folklorists, among others Jean Sibelius and Akseli Gallen-Kallela (*Kalevala*-frescoes). Karelian ornaments were also used in architecture and textile design. 54

KARULA; Finnish glass manufacturer; founded in 1899; merged in 1917 with Iittala. Design competitions 1932 (second prize for Aino Aalto's *Bölgeblick*) and 1936 (first prize for Alvar Aalto's vase *Savoy*).

KARPE, Peter; 1940; Danish furniture designer. 1957-61 cabinetmaker at Fritz Hansen; worked for Grete Jalk and Arne Jacobsen; since the 1960s works on an unusual series of plywood chairs. (1995 chair collection *Voxia* at I-Form).

KASTHALL; Swedish textile manufacturer in Kinna; rugs of classical and contemporary modern design. Designers: Gunilla Allard, Jonas Bohlin, Gunilla L. Ullberg.

KEY, Ellen; 1849-1926; Swedish author and social reformer; socialist, pacifist, and feminist (believed in the "all-motherliness" of women); worked in education for the industrial proletariat and fought for affordable popular design, for example, in her 1899 book *Skönhet för alla* (Beauty for all); beauty through honesty and simplicity; organized home decor exhibition (1917 *Hemutställningen* together with Svenska Slöjdföreningen). Wrote in 1900 her best known book, *The Century of the Child.* 56. 79, 154

KINNASAND; Swedish textile manufacturer in Stockholm, belongs to Proventus Design.

KITTELSEN, Grete Prytz; 1917; grande dame of Norwegian jewelry and ceramic design (1958 vase in silver and enamel). Developed efficient production methods for jewelry (around 1955 ring *Domino*) and studied enamel techniques. Worked for Paolo Venini. 1952 *Lunning-Prize,* grand prize *Triennial* 1954 (gold medal 1957, 1961), 1972 *Jacob-Prize.*

KJAER, Anja; 1956; Danish glass designer; 1983 workshop together with Darylle Hinz in Copenhagen; works since 1989 for Holmegaard. 1992 exhibition *10 Danish Women in Crafts,* USA. 207

KJAERHOLM, Poul; 64, 190, 230, **236**, 248, 274

KJELDBERG, Friedl; Austrian ceramist; née Holzer; worked from 1924-71 for Arabia (around 1940 *Mocha Cup* made of rice porcelain).

KLARA; Swedish furniture store; founded in 1991 in Stockholm; one of the top design stores of the new style, whose concept was largely developed by Christian Springfeldt; it's the display case of the new purism; belongs to CBI. 145

KLÄSSBOLS; **240**

CLASSICISM; strong movement in European and Scandinavian architecture and design that goes back to Friedrich Schinkel's romantic classicism (which corresponds to the imperial style of Karl Ludwig Engel in the center of Helsinki, around 1819) and showed up at the beginning of the 20th century in Denmark (Carl Petersen) and Sweden (Gunnar Asplund); ideal of "archetypal-Doric simplicity." Mixed with regional influences such as the Swedish Gustavian style (Swedish pavilion at the 1900 World's Fair in Paris by Ferdinand Boberg) and the Danish "Skønvirke." Until the Second World War dominant in many fields, for example, in silver and glass ("Swedish Grace") design, in textiles and furniture (1915 chair in walnut and wicker by Carl Malmsten). 57, 121

KLINT, Kaare; 56, 58, 63, 124, 143, 158, 170, 186, **241**, 274, 277

KLINT, Vibeke; 1927; Danish textile designer; established a simple repertoire of forms and colors in the 1950s. 1960 *Lunning-Prize.* 1998 one-man show in the Art Industry Museum, Copenhagen.

KOIVISTO, Eero; 1958; Swedish furniture designer and interior decorator; studied in Stockholm and New York (1995 bench *Kwai* for Nola, 1998 rug Golden Section for Asplund). Partner in Claesson Koivisto Rune. 81, 146

KOMPAN; 79, 170, **242**

KOMPLOT; Danish studio for furniture and product design; founded by Boris Berlin and Poul Christiansen, 1986-91 also Lars Mathiesen; designs for Klaessons, Tendo, and Bent Krogh (1989 table system *Lobster*); 1991 *Scandinavian Furniture Prize.* 133

KOOPERATIVA FÖRBUNDET (KF); Swedish consumer cooperative; design-focused since the 1920s. Production of furniture and housewares. 1927 opened Hyresgästernas Möbelaffär, a store offering affordable and practical furniture (1951 children's furniture by Erik and Tore Ahlsén); 1937 taken over by Gustavsberg (1955 dinnerware set Spisa by Stig Lindberg).

KOPPEL, Henning; 67, 196, **243**, 262, 295

KORTZAU, Ole; 1939; Danish architect and product designer; worked for Royal Copenhagen, Georg Jensen, and Holmegaard. 318

KOSTA BODA; **244**, 296, 299, 310, 320

KREBS, Nathalie; 1895-1978; Danish ceramist; worked for

en years for Bing & Grøndahl; together with Gunnar Nylund ounded in 1929 the influential studio Saxbo; specialized in glazes; later worked with Eva Staer-Nielsen. 1957 gold medal at *Triennial*. 161

KRITISK REVY; Danish cultural magazine, 1925-28; an nitiative of progressive architects; criticism of classicism and crafts as anachronisms. Focus on social, not aesthetic ideas. Editor-in-chief Poul Henningsen reproached the furniture and porcelain industries for their lack of interest in good, affordable everyday articles. 58

KROG, Arnold; 1856-1931; Danish ceramist; 1885-1916 artistic director at Royal Copenhagen; launched the success of the 1920s and 1930s with his innovative glazes. 317

KROGH, Bent; see BENT KROGH

KUKKAPURO, Yrjö; 248

KULIK, Barbro; 1942; Finnish furniture and product designer (1993 CD-rack *Hook* for Onoma); since 1980 editor-in-chief of *Form Function Finland* (until 1994); partner in Arch Design. 119

CRAFTS; originally rural and craft production of everyday items; revival in the 19th century through the English Arts and Crafts movement, which became very influential in Scandinavia, especially through the magazine *The Studio*. Since the late 19th century a strong tendency toward documentation and revival of old craft techniques, e.g., in Finnish Karelianism and the Swedish handwork and back-to-the-land movement. Crafts were the backbone of the classical Scandinavian design of the 1940s and 1950s; therefore emphasis on simple shapes and natural materials, such as glass, wood, textiles, clay. Transition to art industry (exemplary Scandinavian system of studios in factories) and to art all the way to the production of individual, purpose-free objects, at first by Timo Sarpaneva; most recently, for example, new impulses through the American studio glass movement.

ART INDUSTRY; term for producers of everyday articles, particularly housewares, of high aesthetic quality; including artists or architects in the production, around 1900 in Denmark (Royal Copenhagen), but also in Sweden (Orrefors) and Finland (Iris); later very influential in regard to industry-appropriate design through the German crafts association and the Bauhaus. Glass and porcelain manufacture considered core areas, but also furniture manufacture as well as textile-, leather-, and metal-processing factories (e.g., Hackman and Norsk Stålpress). Unlike in crafts, in art industry industrial techniques are used and large numbers of units are produced; this is what made sizable export, for example, in the furniture industry, possible. Traditional companies of Scandinavian art industry are Arabia, Royal Copenhagen, and Orrefors, for example. The art industry is rooted in crafts and at the same time, it itself the root of product design.

KVADRAT; Danish textile manufacturer in Ebeltoft. Designers: Nina Ferlov, Sharon Fisher, Anne Birgitte Hansen, Nanna Ditzel, Hanne Vedel.

LAMMHULTS; 250

LAMPAS; Danish lamp manufacturer in Ringe. Designers among others: Friis & Moltke.

LANDE, Catherina; 1963; Norwegian product designer (1998 flatware *San*); worked in Milan and Great Britain, among others with David Mellor; concepts for exhibitions (1997 *Waves: Furniture Design Beyond 2000* for Norsk Form).

LARSSON, Carl; 1853-1919; Swedish illustrator and painter; after a stay in Paris became an outdoor painter along the lines of the school of Barbizon; critic of modernism. Swedish patriot; awarded numerous public contracts. In 1901 moved to the country (house Lilla Hyttnäs in Sundborn, Dalarna); there painted watercolors that depict family life (delicate lines, clear structures, subtle colors, cheerful moods) and publication of which made him popular (books 1899 Ett Hem, 1902 Larssons, 1906 Spardarfvet, 1910 Åt Solfidan, 1913 Andras Barr; a German edition of Ett Hem / The House in the Sun reached sales of more than 200,000 copies); championed an avant-garde, eclectic furniture style based on tradition and crafts, in sharp contrast to the bourgeois-historic salon style; influenced by Arts and Crafts movement, Jugendstil (art nouveau) as well as magazines such as Deutsche Kunst und Dekoration (German art and decoration) and The Studio. 51, 52, 70, 124, 283

LARSSON, Karin; 1859-1928; Swedish artisan and designer, née Bergöö; married Carl Larsson in 1883. Designed rugs, wallpaper, children's fashions, and furniture (1906 rocking chair, painted red) for Lilla Hyttnäs and was largely responsible for the furnishing style now famous as "Swedish style." Sundborn, the village in which the Larssons lived, is now a national symbol and a tourist attraction. One of their stylistic devices that was much copied later on was painting furniture, particularly chairs, in bright colors. Avant-garde approaches also in textile design, for example, through loosely falling, simple, and practical clothes. 51, 124

LE KLINT; Danish lighting manufacturer; produces exclusively Kaare Klint's paper lamps.

LEGO; 10, 79, 171, **251**

LEINO, Jouni; **254**

LEWIS, David; 1939; British product designer. Since 1965 at Bang & Olufsen (hi-fi system *Beolab 5000)*; developed "slide-rule" control; since 1968 mainly in the TV sector together with Henning Moldenhawer; 1991 design director; since 1979 five *ID-Prizes* (1994 for *Beosound Century*); 1988 *European Design Prize,* 1995 named *Royal Designer for Industry* in Great Britain. 132, 256

LINDAU, Börge; 1932; Swedish furniture designer; partner with Bo Lindekrantz; innovator of Swedish furniture design (1968 stool *S 70*); 1969 *Lunning-Prize,* 1984 founded furniture company Blå Station; worked for Lammhults and Zero. 139, 250, 362.

LINDBERG, Stig; 1916-1982; Swedish artist, ceramist, and textile designer; since 1937 worked for Gustavsberg. Original motifs and bright colors (1949 plate *Laundry on the Line*). Creator of numerous ceramics designs (1956 heat-resistant dinnerware *Spisa*); developed also one of the most successful plastic services (1968 for Gustavsberg); taught since 1957 at the Art Academy (Konstfack), Stockholm. 65

LINDE, Morten; 1965; product designer; worked for Bang & Olufsen. Watches (1996 wristwatches for Mondaine) and telecommunications equipment (1997 cordless telephone *Detc-Z* for Kirk); partner in Linde, Hagerup & Petersen. 255

LINDE, HAGERUP & PETERSEN; 255

LINDEKRANTZ, Bo; 1932; Swedish interior decorator and furniture designer; partner of Börge Lindau. 139, 250

LINDFORS, Stefan; 80, 118, 197, **257,** 270

LINDSTRAND, Vicke; 1904-1983; Swedish artist and glass designer; worked from 1928 to 1940 for Orrefors (1935 vase *Pearl Diver*). 1943 artistic director at Upsala Ekby, 1950-53 at Kosta Boda. 1937 designed 23-foot-high window for the Swedish pavilion at the World's Fair, Paris; 1939 glass fountain for World's Fair, New York. 58, 244, 296, 298

LINDVALL, Jonas; 1963; Swedish furniture designer i Malmö, Studio Vertigo; champion of the new Swedis purism, which he considers to be an internation phenomenon. Designs for David Design (chair *Sputn* coatrack *Quasimodo*). 152

LINGE, Jan Herman; 1922; Norwegian boat designe internationally among the leading experts in his field (19 sailboat *Soling*). Among other things, developed speed extremely maneuverable torpedo boats for the Norwegia navy. 1988 *Jacob-Prize.*

LOUIS POULSEN; 204, **260**

LUNDIN, Ingeborg; 1921; Swedish glass designer; 1947-72 Orrefors; art as well as utility glass; worked with ornamen and pure forms, that greatly underscore the clarity of th crystal glass. (1957 vase *Apple*). 1954 *Lunning-Prize.* 296, 2

LUSTRUM; Swedish furniture manufacturer, founded in 19 in Pukeberg; belongs to Zero. 362

LÜTKEN, Per; 1916-1998; Danish glass designer, since 19 artistic director at Holmegaard. 207

MAGNUSSEN, Erik; 66, 78, 193, **264,** 332

MALMSTEN, Carl; 1888-1972; Swedish furniture and texti designer; traditional-functional, craftsman-like style opposition to the machine culture; drew on models from th Gustavian court. In 1916 won the competition for furnishir the Stockholm city hall; worked with non-European woo but also with pine and birch (1940 spindle-back chair in oile birch). Reformer and educator who trained generations Swedish furniture designers in his workshops. 57

MARIMEKKO; 10, 73, 163, 178, 222, **268,** 290

MATERIA; Swedish furniture manufacturer; founded in 19 in Stockholm.

MATHIESEN, Lars; 1950; Danish architect, furniture design and product designer; in 1978 founded Pelikan together wi Niels Gammelgaard. 306

MATHSSON, Bruno; 60, 65, 124, 170, 190, **272**

MATTSSON, Chiqui; Swedish textile designer ar consultant.

MCGUGAN, Steve; 1960; Canadian industrial designe worked for Bang & Olufsen (headphones *Form 2*); medic products (1990 injections for Novo Nordisk, won *ID-Prize* f these). 132

MENGSHOEL, Hans Christian; 1946; Norwegian furniture designer; Balans-Group. 126

MEYER, Grethe; 64, **276**, 278, 318

MEYER, Terje; 1942; Norwegian industrial designer; had key role in the development of Norwegian product design; about 100 designs in production; track vehicles (1991 Intercity train for Norwegian National Railroad; 1994 subway of Oslo Sporveier). 1981-85 on the board of the International Council of Societies of Industrial Design (ICSID); 1995 *Jacob-Prize.*

MOBILIA; Danish magazine for design, crafts, and art (edited by Gunnar Bartvold, later Per Mollerup; eight issues per year in Danish and English); in the 1960s forum for critics such as Poul Henningsen and Sven Erik Møller; discontinued around 1985. 72

MOGENSEN, Børge; 63, 186, 193, 276, **277**, 352

MØLLER, Jørgen; 1948; Danish furniture and product designer; minimalist of the old school; worked for Arne Jacobsen (around 1980 wristwatches for Georg Jensen; floor lamp *Flamingo* for Royal Copenhagen). 196

MØLLER-JENSEN, Jens; 1938; Danish architect and product designer; worked for Novo Nordisk, the Danish National Railroad, and Louis Poulsen (1973 lamp *Albertslund*). 262

MOLLERUP, Per; 279

MONITOR; studio for product and industrial design in Stockholm; partner Kristofer Hansén. 199

MORSING, Ann; 1956; interior decorator and furniture designer; studied in Stockholm and San Francisco. Partner in Box Design. 144

MOTZFELDT, Benny; 1909-1995; Norwegian glass designer; 1955-67 artistic director at Hadeland; shaped Norwegian art glass design with her large number of original works that inspired freelance glass blowers; in the 1960s her designs took on expressive shapes (around 1970 vase *Torso*); 26 one-man shows, among others in the Victoria & Albert Museum, London. 1969 *Jacob-Prize.* 198

MUNCH-PETERSEN, Ursula; 1937; Danish glass and ceramics designer. Utilitarian designs for Royal Copenhagen. 20

MUNTHE, Gerhard; 1849-1929; Norwegian painter and textile designer; studied in Düsseldorf and Munich; before 1900 developed a graphical, colorful style with Nordic motifs based on legends. 1900 gold medal World's Fair, Paris. 54

MUODOS; Finnish studio for industrial design in Helsinki (breathing masks *M 95* for Kemira). 148

MUONA, Toini; 1904-1987; Finnish ceramist; worked for Arabia since 1931; several stays in European countries and USA. New primitivism (1940 slim porcelain vases with copper glaze).

NATIONAL ROMANTICISM; style and way of thinking in architecture and design since about 1890. At first in Finland, where a group of artists around Akseli Gallen-Kallela and Eliel Saarinen, inspired by the folk epic *Kalevala* (Karelianism), developed a national lexicon of designs (1902 Villa Hvitträsk by Eliel Saarinen, Herman Gesellius, and Armas Lindgren); countermovement to classicism, which was felt to be imperialist; expression of national independence and therefore also strong in Norway. Drew on various sources, such as art nouveau, Scottish granite construction technique, wood construction techniques, and Nordic legends; therefore also known as "Dragon or Viking-Style" (1897 wall hanging *The Five Suitors* by Gerhard Munthe). 53, 282

NEVALAINEN, Markus; 1970; Finnish furniture designer and interior decorator (1997 fair booth for Marimekko); partner in Valvomo. 344

NILFISK; 78, 232, **284**

NO PICNIC; Swedish design studio; founded in 1993 in Stockholm; one of the most successful companies of the late 1990s (1995, 1996, and 1997 prizes for *Outstanding Swedish Design*); among the clients are Scania and Ericsson (1995 helmet-shaped simulation display *Avionics HMD* for Ericsson, 1997 air-brush large printer for Big Image). 28

NOKIA 149, **281**

NOLA; Swedish furniture manufacturer; founded in 1965 in Stockholm; benches for indoors and outdoors. Designers: Mats Aldén (1997 chair *Saga*), Ola Rune (1995 bench *Minimal*), Gertrud Olsson (1995 partition *Piano,* each awarded prize for *Outstanding Swedish Design*).

NORD, Beban; 1956; Swedish furniture designer, interior decorator, and art historian; worked in the cabinetmaking workshop of the royal palace. Partner in Box Design. 144

NORDIC DESIGN; **282**

NORDISKA KOMPANIET; Stockholm's largest department store began textile production in the 1930s; 1937-72 Astrid Sampe was artistic director and had enormous influence on Swedish textile design (1952 printed fabric *Pythagoras* by Sven Markelius); in addition also furniture manufacturing (1955 chair *Tokyo* by Car-Axel Acking). 65

NORSK DESIGNRÅD; Norwegian institution for consulting and information, in particular for Norwegian industry; publishes books and awards prizes (*Classic Prize* and *God Design / Good Design*).

NORSK FORM; the Norwegian "Center for Design, Architecture, and Constructed Environments" in Oslo aims to raise awareness for aesthetic values in society (e.g., through exhibitions, symposia, etc.).

NORSK STÅLPRESS; Norwegian manufacturer of flatware; founded in 1947 in Bergen; timeless functionality is the goal (1959 flatware set *Maya* by Tias Eckhoff). 161

NOVO NORDISK; Danish pharmaceutical manufacturer in Frederiksberg, whose in-house architect was Arne Jacobsen (1952 chair *Myren* for the company cafeteria); still focuses on design to this day. Designers: Steve McGugan, Jens Møller-Jensen. 188

NURMESNIEMI, Antti; 66, 193, 248, 258, **286**, 291, 311

NURMESNIEMI, Vuokko; 268, 288, **290**

NURMINEN, Kerttu; 1943; Finnish glass designer; worked for Nuutajärvi, now at Iittala; broad range of art and utility glass, commercially successful (1988 glass series *Mondo*). 1996 *Kaj-Franck-Prize.* 182, 216

NUUTAJÄRVI; oldest Finnish glass manufacturer; founded in 1793; from 1946-48 Gunnel Nyman artistic director, 1950-76 Kaj Franck and Saara Hopea formed a congenial team that gained international recognition with its captivating simple lines (1952 stackable drinking classes by S. Hopea). The elite of Finnish glass design worked for N., such as Kerttu Nurminen, Heikki Orvola, Oiva Toikka, Markku Salo. After complicated mergers and takeovers since 1987 part of Iittala, which in turn belongs to the Hackman concern (now also a glass museum). 66, 178, 182

NYA PERSPEKTIV; studio for product design in Stockholm.

NYMAN, Gunnel; 1909-1948; Finnish glass and product designer; worked for all important Finnish glass manufacturers; 1951 gold medal at the *Triennial.*

OCTO; Danish design group; founded in 1989; with Niels Hvass. 80, 211

OPSVIK, Peter; 1939; Norwegian graphic artist, furniture designer, and artist; worked in the 1960s for the radio manufacturer Tandberg; 1968 room installation *Furniture for Mix and Match.* Ergonomic seating furniture (1972 *Tripp-Trapp* for Stokke, the most copied children's chair). Co-founder of the Balans-Group (1979 *Balans Variable* for Stokke); developed the idea of variable seating and "social furniture"; furniture sculptures for the Art Industry Museum in Oslo (1986 chair *Embrace: The Chair to Whom You Matter,* 1996 wooden pyramids).11, 126, 171, 334.

ORGANIC DESIGN; 161, 272, 289, **294**

ORREFORS; 54, 57, 58, 76, 244, **296**, 320

ORVOLA, Heikki; 1943; Finnish designer of glass, ceramics, and textiles. Began working for Nuutajärvi in 1968; has the double talent — fairly common in Finland — for pure, practical designs (1996 vase *Carambola* for Iittala) and for artistic glass sculpture; fifteen years of government support allowed him the freedom to work artistically; designs for Arabia (1997 service *24h*) and in 1985-95 for Marimekko as well as on a freelance basis for Alessi (since 1994). 1998 *Kaj-Franck-Prize.* 118, 182

OTICON; Danish manufacturer of hearing aids in Hellerup; founded in 1904; *1997 European Design Prize* with Christian Bjørn. 138, 171

PANIC DESIGN; 81, **300**

PÄNKÄLÄINEN, Pasi; 1964; Finnish furniture designer; worked for Piiroinen (series Arena). 1994 SI Association Prize. 311

PANTON, Verner; 72, 107, 160, 262, 283, 294, 301

PAULSSON, Gregor; Swedish art historian, design functionary and critic; lived 1912 in Berlin and came into contact with the German Craft Association; compiled its credo in the 1919 publication Vackrare vardagsvara (*More Beautiful Everyday Things*). Became director of Svenska Slöjdföreningen. Believed that good design could improve people's lives. In 1930 organized Stockholm exhibition together with the architect Gunnar Asplund. 56

PAUSTIAN; Danish furniture manufacturer; founded in 1937 in Copenhagen. Designers: Arne Jacobsen, Ole Jensen, Poul Kjaerholm, Erik Magnussen (1992 tubular steel chair *Park*), Børge Mogensen, Hans J. Wegner. 266

PELIKAN DESIGN; 133, **306**

PENTAGON; studio for product design in Helsinki; among the most successful young Finnish companies (1197 plastic envelope *Bytepak* for computer diskettes, won Design Prize of the Industry Form, Hanover, for this).

PERSSON, Sigurd; 65, 282, 298, **310**

PETERSEN, Søren U; 1961; cabinetmaker, furniture designer, and product designer (1998 saltshaker for Royal Copenhagen); partner in Linde, Hagerup & Petersen. 255

PETTERSEN, Jon Å.; 1948; Norwegian textile and fashion designer (1998 fabric for the royal palace in Oslo); specialist for upholstery fabric.

PIIROINEN; 289, **311**

PORSGRUND; biggest Norwegian porcelain manufacturer, founded in 1886; around 1900 patterns in the Nordic and Symbolist style (1900 dinnerware set with blue Nordic motifs by Henrik Bull). Theodor Kittelsen artistic director from 1927–45, then Nora Gulbrandsen, since 1949 Tias Eckhoff (later in management); won acceptance for a progressive, sober line (1929 service with green stripes by Nora Gulbrandsen). Designers: Leif Helge Enger, Poul Jensen, Eystein Sandnes, Grete Rønning, 60, 161, 198

POULSEN, Louis; see LOUIS POULSEN

PP MØBLER; Danish furniture manufacturer in Allerød. Designer: Hans J. Wegner. 356

PROCOPÉ, Ulla; 1921–1968; Finnish ceramics designer; worked for Arabia under Kaj Franck; stackable and heat-resistant dinnerware sets (1957 Liekki, 1960 Ruska). 1957 honorary diploma of the Triennial. 116

PROVENTUS DESIGN; Swedish design company in Växjö, to which Artek, Kinnasand and Snowcrash belong.

PRODUCT DESIGN; a branch of industrial design (often used synonymously); design of industrially produced goods for daily use, going beyond the scope of traditional art industry; for example, concerns also technical equipment (Bank & Olufsen, Electrolux), toys, fashion, etc. The best known Scandinavian product designs prior to the Second World War were Poul Henningsen's *PH Lamps;* among the pioneers in the postwar years are Sigvard Bernadotte and Sixten Sason. In the 1950s additional consumer goods were included, such as electrical household appliances and mass-produced cars. Through opening of markets, especially the expansion of the EU, as well as through accelerated technological developments, in particular digitalization, new fields of activity arise; for example, medical products (among others by Christian Bjørn, Kristofer Hansén). In the Scandinavian countries promoting product design is considered a task of public and economic policy, in particular in Denmark and Finland. This includes, in addition to consulting (by the respective Design Councils) and frequent exhibitions, also design training, which is considered exemplary in Scandinavia. In the 1990s telecommunications boomed, an industry where Scandinavian manufacturers are leading (for example, Ericsson, Nokia). Successful Scandinavian specialties are design for the disabled and design of public spaces (for example, in Norway the design of gas stations was a widely discussed topic in the 1990s).

PUOTILA, Ritva; 1935; Finnish textile and glass designer; 1959 studio in Helsinki; worked for Tampella, Dansk International Designs, and Hadeland. 1987 family business Woodnotes was founded. Products and objects made of paper cord. In addition to rugs, mats, and upholstery fabric, also artistic objects. 1988 design consultant for the UN International Trade Center. 1995 participated in exhibition *Classic Makers* in Helsinki. 361

Q-LAB; studio for product design by Jakob Wagner. 351

QUAADE, Torben; 1968; Danish furniture designer (1996 *Spiral Chair*); partner in Panic. 300

RAKET; studio for interior decorating, lamp and furniture design; founded in Helsinki in 1997 by Vesa Damski (1998 chair *ADC* made of ash and steel), Ilkka Koskela (1998 lounge chair *Nasta Revolving* made of rubber and fiberglass), and Harri Koskinen (1998 *Fatty Containers* made of birch); designs for Artek. 81

RÅMAN, Ingegerd; 312

REFLEX; Sari Anttonen's design studio. 114.

RELLING, Ingmar; 1920; Norwegian interior decorator and furniture designer. Functional and popular furniture, especially easy chairs (1966 easy chair *Siesta* for Vestlandske Møbelfabrikk) with at times innovative technical solutions (around 1965 folding chair *Scandic* made of laminated beech, 1987 adjustable lounge chair *Optima* made of steel and leather). 1978 Jacob Prize.

RIIHIMÄKI; Finnish glass manufacturer; founded in 1910 as factory for window glass; since 1928 competitions, among the participants were Aino and Alvar Aalto, Arttu Brummer, and Gunnel Nyman; after 1945 innovative design and international reputation through designers such as Nanny Still (1961 candlestick *Ambra*) and Helena Tynell. 1976 fully automated (since then no more handblown glass).

RIMALA, Annika; 1936; Finnish textile designer; 1961 first collection for Marimekko with Oiva Toikka; her pop patterns and striped tricot shaped the style of the company (1966 fabric *Oasis*). In 1967 chosen by the Swedish press as one of the ten best fashion designers of the world. Founded around 1980 together with Teemu Lipasti the company Santtu; fabrics and ready-to-wear clothing with simple, timeless patterns; worked in the 1990s again for Marimekko (1996 fabric *Tarinat*), 1996 Retrospective *Design Forum Finland* in Helsinki. 268, 270.

ROHDE, Johan; 1856–1935; Danish doctor, artist, and silversmith, and furniture designer. Classicist; turned to clear forms in the 1920s (1925 silver pitcher for Georg Jensen); increasingly Scandinavian historical elements in the 1930s. Founded in 1882 Kunstnernes Studieskole (art school). Mentor and partner at Georg Jensen, where he had his own designs produced and among whose most famous designers he was (1935 flatware *Acorn*); 1918 store design for Georg Jensen in Copenhagen, 58, 196

RÖRSTRAND; 54, 115, **316**, 341

ROYAL COPENHAGEN; 55, 66, 244, 276, 296, 299, **317**

ROYAL SCANDINAVIA; since 1998 name of the company Royal Copenhagen. 76, 196, 244, 320

RUNE, Ola; 1963; Swedish furniture designer and interior decorator; studied in Stockholm, Copenhagen, and London (1996 shoehorn *James* made of birch). Partner in Claesson Koivisto Rune, 81, **146**

SAAB; 171, 200, 236, **321**

SAARINEN, Eliel; 1873-1950; Finnish architect and designer, third father figure of the Finnish modern style in addition to Akseli Gallen-Kallela and Alvar Aalto; grew up in eastern Finland; frequent visits to St. Petersburg. Protagonist of the national romanticism movement (1916 National Museum together with Herman Gesellius and Armas Lindgren, 1914 central train station, both in Helsinki); his studio was famous for furniture and housewares in a rustic, folklorist style; strongly influenced by art nouveau, especially by the Viennese Secession. Emigrated to the United States in 1923; there from 1932 to 1946 director of the Cranbrook Academy, which became one of the most influential art and design schools of the country under his leadership (organic design). Among his students were Charles Eames, Harry Bertoia, and Florence Knoll, and also many Scandinavians such as Maija Grotell and Marianne Strengell. In addition to his teaching E. Saarinen headed an architect and design studio, which his son Eero joined in 1936. Eero was also a successful architect and designer (1957 plastic shell chair for Knoll). 55, 60, 162, 294

SALLI, Timo; 325

SALMENHAARA, Kylikki; 1915–1981; Finnish ceramist; glaze experiments and new primitivism; worked since 1947 for Arabia (1957 coffee cup *SS*); influenced by English and Native American ceramics after trips to the United States; 1951 silver medal at *Triennial*. 1986 Retrospective in the Taideteollisuusmuseo Helsinki.

SALTO, Axel; 1889–1961; Danish ceramic designer; co-editor of magazine *Klingen;* worked for Bing & Grøndahl, Saxbo, and Royal Copenhagen. Experimented with unusual glazes and organic shapes (1943 stoneware vase for Royal Copenhagen). 1951 grand prize *Triennial.* 318

SAMPE, Astrid; 1909; Swedish textile designer. Studied in Stockholm and London; worked 1937–71 for department store Nordiska Kompaniet in its "Textile Chamber," which had a lasting influence on Swedish textile design (1939 textiles for the Swedish pavilion at the World's Fair in New York). Very active abroad: 1956 exhibition *Modern Swedish Home* in London; 1948 exhibition *Textil Bilderbok* at Knoll in New York; 1949 member of the Royal Society of Arts in London. In 1957 textiles for the Swedish building at the *Interbau* in Berlin. In 1963 member of the American Institute of Interior Designers. 1970 first *Data Designs* in collaboration with IBM. 1984 Retrospective in the National Museum in Stockholm.

SANDELL, Thomas; 220, **326**, 362

SARPANEVA, Timo; 67, 193, 213, 283, **328**

SAS; Pan-Scandinavian Airline; always used top designers for its Nordic image, such as Sigurd Persson, Hans Brindfors, Sven-Eric Juhlin, and Thomas Eriksson. 174

SASON, Sixten; 1912–1969; Swedish engineer and product designer. Since the 1940s pioneer of Scandinavian product design. Streamlining according to American example; created numerous classics (1948 *Hasselblad 1600 F*); worked for Electrolux (refrigerators and vacuum cleaners) and Saab, where he was designer-in-chief until his death. 70, 164, 200, 321

SAXBO; Danish ceramics manufacturer (1930–68); most important independent pottery in Denmark, influenced generations of ceramists; managed by Nathalie Krebs (responsible for glazes) together with Eva Staehr-Nielsen (responsible for forms); developed Saxbo style with its simple shapes and orientalist decoration; production of large numbers at moderate prices. 161

SCANVIEW; Danish manufacturer of color scanners; founded 1990. 78

SCHARFF, Allan; 1945; Danish jewelry and glass designer; works since 1987 for Royal Copenhagen (1996 silver objects *Snapshot of a Danish Bay*) and since 1991 for Holmegaard. 1980 one-man-show in Det Danske Kunstindustrimuseum, Copenhagen; 1995 *Bayrischer Staatspreis* (Bavarian State Prize). 196

SCHIANG; Danish furniture manufacturer in Copenhagen (1992 chair *Concept No. 18* by Jørgen Gammelgaard). 279

SELLE 16; Danish design group with Louise C. Frederiksen. 81

SETH-ANDERSSON, Carina; 1965; Swedish glass designer (1998 glass *For All Beverages*). 145, 197

SILTAVUORI, Antti; 1943; Swedish furniture and industrial designer (1998 pilot filter for Outokumpu Mintec); partner in Arch Design. 119

SIVONEN, Kari; 1969; Finnish furniture and product designer; partner in Valvomo. 344

SKANNO; Finnish furniture store and manufacturer; founded in 1956 in Helsinki. Furniture and lighting design. Designers: Brita Flander, Pentti Hakala, Simo Heikkilä, Stefan Lindfors, Merita Soini, Petri Vainio. 178

SKRUF; Swedish glass manufacturer; founded 1997; specializes in restaurant glasses. After liquidation reopened by glassblowers who had been employed there. Designer: Ingegerd Råman. 312

SNOWCRASH; Finnish design firm; founded in 1998 in Helsinki; experimental design; subsidiary of Proventus. Originated in 1997 as distribution company for young designers around Valvomo, who presented their work at the Milan furniture fair. 81, 193, 325, 344

SPARRE, Louis; 1866–1964; Swedish furniture designer; 1891–1911 in Finland; 1897 co-founder of Iris factory. 54

STELTON, 11, 78, 193, 230, 264, **332**

STENROS, Pirkko; Finnish interior decorator and furniture designer; 1993 Kaj Franck Prize for her unpretentious, timeless designs, most of which are based on modular concepts.

STEPHENSEN, Magnus; 1903–1992; Danish architect; worked for Kay Bojeson and Royal Copenhagen. 66

STILL, Nanny; 1926; Finnish glass and product designer; worked for Riihimäki (1960 vase *Ambra*) and Rosenthal.

STOKKE; 76, 79, 128, 171, **334**

SUPPANEN, Ilkka; 336

SVENSKT TENN; legendary Swedish furniture store of style-forming impact. Founded in 1924 by Estrid Ericson in Stockholm; early on exported designs to the United States. Since 1933 Josef Frank artistic director (1934 sofa *Liljevalchs*); had great success at the World's Fair in 1937 and in 1939 with "Swedish Modern." 60, 184

SWECODE; Swedish distribution organization; founded in 1994 by CBI; participating: Asplund, Box Møbler, and David Design. 81, 145, 174, 344

SYVÄLUOMA, Sari; 1966; Finnish textile designer, lives in Norway; knitwear. 1993 participation in the *Viking* exhibition in Helsinki, 1996 one-man-show, Norsk Form, Oslo.

TAAPIOVAARA, Ilmari; 1914; Finnish furniture designer and interior decorator; functionalist school; worked in 1937 with Le Corbusier. In the 1930s responsible for furniture collection of Asko; worked on mass production and export; started the Domus Academy in 1946; furniture went into production (stackable chair *Domus*). Numerous designs during the building boom of the 1950s (1955 *Fanett* for Asko). 1952 lecturer at the Institute of Technology, Chicago. Projects in Paraguay,

Yugoslavia, and Hong Kong. Co-editor of the magazine *Muoto.*

TANDBERG, Roy H.; Norwegian product designer; consumer electronics and communications systems. Won Prize for Good Norwegian Design nine times.

TERHO, Ilkka; 1968; Finnish interior decorator and furniture designer (1997 computer workstation *Netsurfer*); partner and spokesman at Valvomo. 344

THESELIUS, Mats; 80, 234, **337**

TIEDEMANN, Helene; **340**

TIOGRUPPEN (Group of Ten); Swedish textile manufacturer; founded in 1970 in Stockholm by Gunila Axén, Britt-Marie Christoffersson, Carl-Johan de Geer, Inez Svensson, and others.

TOIKKA, Oiva; 1931; Finnish set designer, designer of glass, ceramics, and textiles; worked from 1956-60 for Arabia, later for Marimekko and Rörstrand. 1963 art director at Nuutajärvi. Famous for extremely original, playful style (glass birds for Iittala). 1970 Lunning Prize. 182

TÖRNELL, Pia; 316, **341**

TORSTEINSEN, Frederick and **Solveig**; 1964 and 1966; furniture and exhibition designers (lightweight, stackable chair *b-dimension* for Fora Form won the Good Norwegian Design prize in 1997); 1998 awarded Furniture of the Year.

TROMP, Jan; 1969; Finnish furniture designer (1996 sofa *Plusminus*); partner in Valvomo, 344

VALLIEN, Bertil; 246, 316, **342**

VALVOMO; 81, 120, **344**

VASKIVUORI, Rane; Finnish furniture and product designer and interior decorator (1996 design of the exhibition *Japan Today*) in Helsinki; partner in Valvomo.

VEDEL, Kristian; 1923; Danish furniture designer. Developed modular systems (1956 children's chair made of plywood) and multifunctional objects, some of them made of plastic. In the 1960s director of the IDD (Association of Industrial Designers in Denmark). Taught around 1970 in Nairobi, Kenya; first chair of product design in Africa. 1962 Lunning Prize. Worked in the 1970s on the uses of wool. 64

VERDE, Johan; 1964; Norwegian product designer; worked for lamp manufacturers Luxo and Stokke. 1996 Norwegian Design Prize for cafeteria dinnerware set.

VIERROS, Timo; 1967; product and furniture designer (199 library counter for comic-library in Stockholm); partner i Valvomo. 344

VIKØREN, Dave; Norwegian furniture designer (collectior Jazz for Fora Form); Norwegian exhibition design fo furniture fair in Cologne.

VIVERO; Finnish furniture manufacturer; founded in 1980 ir Helsinki. Designer-in-chief: Yrjö Wiherheimo 358

VOLVO; 77, 134, 171, 296, 322, **347**

WAGNER, Jakob; **351**

WALLANDER, Alf; 1862–1914; Swedish artist, ceramist, furniture and textile designer. Art nouveau. 1879–85 one of the first artists in the industry to work at Rörstrand (around 1900 vase with pansies); since 1900 artistic director. 244, 316

WANSCHER, Ole; 1903–1985; Danish architect, furniture designer, and author; since 1931 exhibitor at the cabinet-makers' guild in Copenhagen (1942 Windsor chair for Fritz Hansen). 1956 book *History of Furniture Design.* 1960 gold medal *Triennial.*

WÄRFF, Göran; 1933; Swedish glass designer; worked since 1964 for Kosta Boda (1986 pressed glass series *Limelight*). 1974–78 in Australia; taught 1982–85 in Sunderland, Great Britain. 1968 Lunning Prize. 244

WEGNER, Hans J.; 64, 274, 278, **352**

WENNERBERG, Gunnar; 1863–1914; Swedish painter, cartoonist, ceramics and glass designer; 1895–1908 artistic director at Gustavsberg; simple forms and naturalistic motifs (1899 pitcher *Lindlof* with flowers); worked for Kosta and Orrefors. 52, 244

WIHERHEIMO, Yrjö; **358**

WIRKKALA, Tapio;9, 67, 216, 295, **359**

YTTERBORN, Stefan; 1963; Swedish design visionary. Consultant to many Scandinavian companies. 1991 founded Klara, CBI, later Swecode. Since 1996 consultant company Ytterborn & Fuentes in Stockholm. 145, 180, 197, 220

MAGAZINES; see *Design DK, Form, Form Function Finland, Kritisk Revy, Mobilia.*

ZERO;**360**

Acknowledgements

I would especially like to thank Pirkkoliisa O'Rourke of the Finnish Embassy in Bonn and Björn Springfeldt of the Swedish Embassy in Bonn for championing our project; and my thanks also go to Mårten Claesson, Eero Koivisto, and Ola Rune in Stockholm for their helpful tips; to Outi Raatikainen of the Design Forum Finland and to Stefan Ytterborn of CBI for their great help, to the gallery Ulrich Fiedler in Cologne, to Annegrete Usnarsky (Norwegian Embassy in Bonn), to Dr. Bernd Kretschmer (Danish Embassy in Bonn), and also to Elisabeth Knoll and Thomas Haulfe of Dumont Publishers, to Evelyne Duval and Debbie Berckerman of Booklink in London as well as to my mother Ingeborg Polster.

In addition the following have assisted in bringing this project to fruition: Paola Antonelli (Museum of Modern Art), Helge Aszmoneit (Rat für Formgebung, Design Council), Ulf Beckman and Anita Christiansen (Svensk Form), Jens Bernsen and Birgitta Capetillo (Dansk Design Centre), Uta Brandes, Cortina Butler, Birgit Cieplik and Gudrun Roweck, Antti Eklund, Joost Elffers, Michael Erlhoff, Wolfgang Galler (Orient Express Berlin), Marianne Güllöv (Fritz Hansen), Mrs. Hanisch-Raddatz and Wolfgang Raddatz, Kristofer Hansén, Ludwig Könemann, Catherina Lande (Norsk Form), Bodil Busk Laursen (Det Danske Kunstindustrimuseum), Erik Magnussen, Lars Mathiesen (Pelikan Design), Claudia Neumann, Antti and Vuokko Nurmesniemi, Ingegerd Råman, Liisa Reiterer, Jan van Rooij (Electrolux), Timo Salli, Dorrit Seest (Royal Scandinavia), Christian Springfeldt (Klara), Anne Stenros (Design Forum Finland), Ilkka Suppanen, Heike Tekampe, Ilkka Terho (Snowcrash), Mats Theselius, Tina Thomsen (Louis Poulsen), Arnold Thünker, Kaj Virtarinne (Foreign Ministry, Helsinki), Ann Wall (Svenskt Tenn), as well as Hans J. Wegner and his daughter.

A big thank you also to Donatella Cacciola, Christoph Johannsson, Julia Lenz, Ines Lusche, Alexandra Maus, and Ulrike Stiefelhagen for their indefatigable assistance.

This edition published in
Great Britain in 1999
by PAVILION BOOKS LIMITED
London House, Great Eastern Wharf
Parkgate Road, London SW11 4NQ

Concept and realization:
Howard Buch Produktion
editor: Bernd Polster
art director: Olaf Meyer

English translation

A CIP catalogue record for this book is available from the British Library.

ISBN 1 86205 307 3

Printed in Italy
10 9 8 7 6 5 4 3 2 1

This book can be ordered direct from the publisher. Please contact the Marketing Department.
But try your bookshop first.

Picture Credits

Unless specially noted otherwise, illustrations are reprinted with the kind permission of the designers and the companies.

Unless indicated otherwise, the copyright holders of the illustrations are the designers and companies. It was not possible in all cases to find the copyright holders of the illustrations. Justified claims will of course be honored in accordance with the usual agreements.

Markku Alatalo 100, 120 · **Pål Allen** 299 · **Archiv Danish Design Council, Kopenhagen** 15, 20, 32, 45, 48, 54, 56, 58, 63, 71, 77, 130, 131, 132, 134, 138, 140, 255, 256, 276, 279, 329 · **Archiv Design Forum Finnland, Helsinki** 51, 52, 66, 68, 72, 154, 177, 249, 329 · **Archiv Det Danske Industriemuseum** 129 · **Archiv Kunstindustrimuseum Kopenhagen** 56, 61 · **Archiv Nationalmuseum Stockholm** 18, 53 · **Archiv Norsk Form, Oslo** 27 · **Archiv Svensk Form, Stockholm** 14, 53, 55, 58, 59, 61, 64, 65, 67, 69, 73, 76, 154, 173, 275, 310, 320, 321, 322, 341, 343 · **Archiv Taideteollisuusmuseo Helsinki** 8, 81 **Curt Ekblom** 141, 233, 235, 337, 338 · **Patrick Engquist** 146, 147 · **Roberto Fortuna** 136, 137 · **Stefan Frank-Jenssen** 143 · **Kari Janzén** 338 · **Andreas Jung/ Galerie Ulrich Fiedler, Köln**: 12, 26, 99 · **Hans Hammarskiold** 135 · **Kennet Havgaard** 300 · **Berno Hjälmernd** 199 · **Kari Holopainen** 259 · **Åge Lund Jensen** 241 · **Kent Johansson** 280 · **Erik Karlsson** 139 · **Timo Kauppila** 216 · **Antti Kyldänpää** 213, 214, 215 · **Tuomas Martilla** 345, 346 · **Marco Melander** 114, 117 · **Lars G. Ohlsson** 343 · **Max Petrelius** 292, 293 · **Yukio Shimizu** 195, 243 · **Tommy Wiberg** 338